MEDIA AND AMERICAN COURTS

A Reference Handbook

Other Titles in ABC-CLIO's
CONTEMPORARY
WORLD ISSUES
Series

Books in the Contemporary World Issues series address vital issues in today's society such as genetic engineering, pollution, and biodiversity. Written by professional writers, scholars, and nonacademic experts, these books are authoritative, clearly written, up-to-date, and objective. They provide a good starting point for research by high school and college students, scholars, and general readers as well as by legislators, business people, activists, and others.

Each book, carefully organized and easy to use, contains an overview of the subject, a detailed chronology, biographical sketches, facts and data and/or documents and other primary-source material, a directory of organizations and agencies, annotated lists of print and nonprint resources, and an index.

Readers of books in the Contemporary World Issues series will find the information they need in order to have a better understanding of the social, political, environmental, and economic issues facing the world today.

MEDIA AND AMERICAN COURTS

A Reference Handbook

S. L. Alexander

CONTEMPORARY WORLD ISSUES

A B C CLIO

Santa Barbara, California
Denver, Colorado
Oxford, England

Library of Congress Cataloging-in-Publication Data
Alexander, S. L.
    Media and American courts : a reference handbook / S.L. Alexander.
        p.   cm. — (Contemporary world issues)
    Includes bibliographical references and index.
            ISBN 1-57607-979-1 (hardcover : alk. paper)
            ISBN 1-57607-980-5 (e-book)
    1. Free press and fair trial—United States.   2. Conduct of court proceedings—United States.   3. Newspaper court reporting—United States.   4. Mass media and criminal justice—United States.
5. Journalism, Legal—United States.   I. Title.   II. Series.

KF9223.5.A9154   2004
345.73'05—dc22

                                                            2004003210

08   07   06   05   04   10 9 8 7 6 5 4 3 2 1

This book is also available on the World Wide Web as an eBook.
Visit abc-clio.com for details.

ABC-CLIO, Inc.
130 Cremona Drive, P.O. Box 1911
Santa Barbara, California 93116–1911

This book is printed on acid-free paper ∞.
Manufactured in the United States of America.

Contents

Preface

Since the advent of Court TV in 1991, issues involving media and the courts have moved to the forefront of public interest. The widely publicized murder trial of O. J. Simpson, the legal problems of President Bill Clinton, the role of the U.S. Supreme Court in the election of George W. Bush, and coverage of the suspects in the 2001 World Trade Center incident are representative cases.

Media and American Courts begins with a historical perspective on media coverage of courts. Chapter 1 traces the development of free press/fair trial issues through an examination of twenty-seven representative cases tried in both state and federal courts. Certain themes emerge that are developed further in Chapter 2, which discusses current controversies, problems, and potential solutions. The chapter includes an examination of access to proceedings, evidence, and participants. It also explores how technological advances—from cameras in the courtroom to "virtual trials" netcast over the Internet—have introduced new areas of controversy. Chapter 2 concludes with an examination of potential solutions designed to balance free press/fair trial rights more effectively.

Chapter 3 presents a chronology of U.S. Supreme Court decisions and relevant events that highlight many of the issues and controversies introduced in earlier chapters. Key cases dealing with these controversies include the Sam Sheppard murder case (a prejudicial publicity case and the basis for *The Fugitive* television shows and movies); a Virginia murder case (which established the First Amendment right to courtroom access to criminal trials); and a Florida robbery case that established the states' rights to permit courtroom camera coverage (now allowed in all fifty states, some federal jurisdictions, and often available via the Internet).

Chapter 4 presents biographical sketches of many of the most significant people connected with the free press/fair trial conflict. Courtroom figures profiled include outspoken defense attorney and Harvard Law Professor Alan Dershowitz; renowned Manson family prosecutor and author Vince Bugliosi; and the presiding judge for the O. J. Simpson criminal trial, the Honorable Lance Ito. Broadcast journalists include Fred Graham (head of Court TV), Tim O'Brien (now a CNN legal correspondent), and Nina Totenberg (NPR Radio). Print journalists include Pulitzer-Prize winning Linda Greenhouse (*The New York Times*), Supreme Court correspondent Tony Mauro (American Lawyer), legal affairs correspondent Linda Deutsch (Associated Press), and author Dominick Dunne (celebrity cases for *Vanity Fair* and Court TV).

Chapter 5 begins with a description of research studies concerning media coverage of the courts. It includes descriptions of canons and codes of ethics produced by members of the media, the bar, and the judiciary. The chapter concludes with a discussion of guidelines for use of courtroom cameras, as well as state and federal plans for managing high-profile trials in the digital age.

Professional organizations for members of the media, associations for lawyers and judges, and court and government agencies are described in Chapter 6. Chapter 7 is an annotated list of selected print and nonprint resources, which is followed by an annotated list of legal citations. Finally, *Media and American Courts* includes a brief glossary of terms useful to anyone researching issues involving media coverage of the courts.

In sum, the handbook is an exciting new tool for students of political science, journalism, and law—as well as for teachers, scholars, and members of the general public interested in the fascinating topic of media coverage of the judicial process.

Acknowledgments

My appreciation to Dean Frank Scully and my colleagues at Loyola University, particularly members of the faculty sabbatical committee, communications assistants Lynda Favret and Phyllis Aleman, and the staffs of the main and law libraries; the staff of Latter Library; Alicia Merritt and Carla Roberts at ABC-CLIO; lawyers Cathy Glaser and Glenn Watts, PhD; Nicholas Richardson; and, as always, to my family: technical consultant Christopher Alexander, copyreader Alexandra Star, "Brother-Beans-The-Lawyer" Alexander, Richard, Charles, Angela—and especially Dee, our favorite media personality.

1

Free Press/Fair Trial: A Historical Overview

Should access to courtrooms and court documents be open to all or limited to trial participants? Is it appropriate to restrict the comments of witnesses, lawyers, and litigants—even to "gag" defendants in a criminal trial—in order to avoid prejudicial publicity? What about the propriety of allowing news cameras in courtrooms?

Although the new millennium has brought many exciting changes the age of digital communication begins, the basic issues involved with media coverage of American courts are as old as the republic itself. In 1791, as promised by federalists eager to see the Constitution ratified quickly, 10 amendments—the Bill of Rights—were added. No one could have foreseen the problems that continue more than 200 years later as courts attempt to balance the First Amendment rights of freedom of the press with the Sixth Amendment rights of defendants to a fair trial, the "free press/fair trial" conflict.

One of the first to note the conflict was Aaron Burr. Before his 1807 trial on charges of treason, Burr said the case should be dismissed because extensive news coverage meant jurors would be prejudiced against him. But in a decision still cited, the chief justice of the U.S., the Supreme Court's John Marshall, deemed it acceptable for jurors to have some advance knowledge of a case as long as they kept their minds open to a fair consideration of the testimony. And Burr was acquitted—found not guilty—by the jury, suggesting that jurors are able to keep an open mind despite some prior knowledge of the case (*U.S. v Burr*).

After Burr came the development in the 1830s of the "penny press" (newspapers designed to appeal to working people), followed in the 1890s by the growth of "yellow journalism" (a sensationalistic style popularized during the circulation wars between Hearst and Pulitzer newspapers). Both of these developments strengthened the tradition of court journalism.

One of the best-remembered cases involving extensive media coverage is the widely covered 1893 trial of Lizzie Borden, charged with murdering her parents in Fall River, Massachusetts. With a trial covered by 100 reporters, the case became the subject of numerous books, at least a dozen plays and broadcasts, an opera, and a ballet. Although the media coverage apparently did not prejudice the jury—like Burr, Borden was acquitted—the media coverage did have lasting effects on the public perception of the case. People today are more likely than not to think she was convicted, because they remember the refrain popularized by the press: "Lizzie Borden took an ax and gave her mother 40 whacks . . ."

This chapter provides a brief overview of select criminal and civil cases, heard in both federal and state courts, that tracks the development of free press/fair trial issues that remain unsettled today. This is just a sample of twenty-seven out of the hundreds that have received widespread media coverage since Lizzie Borden's day. In some of the cases, the actions of the reporters affected the course of the case; in two, the media themselves were litigants.

A look at the highlights of these cases shows the continuing role played by press coverage of the judicial process. These cases contributed to the development of the modern public perspective regarding the media and American courts.

Sob Sisters, Political Radicals, and the First "Trial of the Century"

The development of media coverage of trials in the early twentieth century clearly demonstrates both the occasional excesses of the media as well as the role of the press as a watchdog on the judicial system.

New York v Thaw: Playboys and Sob Sisters

Early in the twentieth century, several criminal cases received widespread, sensationalistic coverage in the press. One of these cases involved the "Girl in the Red Velvet Swing" (whose story was told in the 1955 movie of that name). In 1907, Pittsburgh millionaire Harry Thaw (the only son of a coal and railroad baron) was tried for the shooting death of Sanford White (a prominent architect of the Gilded Age) in New York City's Madison Square Garden, a building White designed (*New York v Thaw*). White had a lavishly decorated suite upstairs where he entertained on a red velvet swing showgirls such as Evelyn Nesbit, who later married Thaw. (The suggestion to "come up to see my etchings" reportedly originated with White's invitations.) Thaw's first trial began in January 1907 and ended in a mistrial in April, when after two days of deliberation, jurors could not agree whether he had acted in a jealous rage or whether he had been temporarily insane. Thaw, represented by five lawyers, blamed the shooting on his realization that it was White—a member of numerous sex clubs—who had "ruined" his wife. At Thaw's second trial in 1908, he was found not guilty by reason of insanity, "Dementia Americana." He escaped from a mental institute, was returned, freed again, and was in and out of trouble until his death in 1947. Thaw's story was the subject of three plays, a book, and a second film, the 1981 film *Ragtime* based on E. L. Doctorow's 1975 book.

According to *The New York Times*, the Thaw trial was "being reported to the ends of the civilized globe" from a special Western Union Telegraph office set up in the courthouse (Boyle 1997, 69). Four female reporters, including Winifred Black ("Annie Laurie") and Elizabeth Gilmore ("Dorothy Dix"), sat at their own special press table and were assigned to put a "female spin" on coverage. Their nickname "Sob Sisters" is still used today to describe reporters who use sentimental and sensationalistic techniques.

Georgia v Frank: "Little Mary Phagan Went to Work One Day . . ."

A second famous trial involved twenty-nine-year-old Leo Frank, convicted after a one-month trial in 1913 in Atlanta on charges that on Confederate Memorial Day he had murdered thirteen-year-old Mary Phagan, one of the employees in the pencil factory he managed (*Georgia v Frank*). Justice Oliver Wendell Holmes dissented from a U.S. Supreme Court decision affirming the conviction (*Frank v Mangum* at 345–349). Holmes's dissent was based primarily on his suspicion that jurors might have been led to convict Frank (who was Jewish) because they feared mob violence if he were acquitted. During the trial, crowds outside the courthouse had chanted, "Hang the Jew or we'll hang you" (Belth 1981, 64).

Holmes's dissent was prophetic, for although Georgia Governor John Slayton commuted Frank's death sentence to life in prison, a lynch mob broke into the prison and hanged Frank in 1915. (Today a small plaque commemorates the site.) On his deathbed in 1982, Alonzo Mann, who had worked in the National Pencil Company factory at the time of the murder, confessed that he had known that the African American night watchman Jim Conley had committed the murder, but Mann said he had been too frightened to testify. In 1986, Georgia issued a special posthumous pardon based on the state's failure to protect Frank.

The *Frank* case received wide publicity, starting with publications owned by Atlanta Populist politician Tom Watson. The murder and lynching were described in a popular ballad "Little Mary Phagan," which ended with the line "The Christian doors of heaven sent Leo Frank to hell" (Golden 1965, 359–360). With postcards of the lynch scene being sold throughout the South, the *Frank* case led to a resurgence of the Ku Klux Klan. The case also contributed to the development of the national Anti-Defamation League to fight anti-Semitism. Several books, plays, movies, and television shows were based on the Frank story, including the 1937 movie *They Won't Forget*; a 1987 NBC miniseries with Jack Lemmon playing Governor Slayton; and a 1998 New York show, *Leo Frank: The Musical*.

Massachusetts v Sacco and Vanzetti: "Misquotations, Misrepresentations, Suppressions, and Mutilations"

Ethnic prejudice also played a role in the case of Italian immigrants Nicola Sacco and Bartolomeo Vanzetti—one a worker in a shoe factory and the other a fish peddler. Sacco and Vanzetti were convicted of a 1920 payroll robbery-murder in Dedham, Massachusetts (*Massachusetts v Sacco and Another*). The two were radical anarchists, and their case became a cause célèbre for members of labor groups and Communist organizations who said the two were being railroaded due to their unpopular Socialist views and their opposition to war. During their seven-week-long trial, after their 1921 convictions, and again after their 23 August 1927 executions, there were demonstrations around the world. The controversy never died out completely, and in 1977 a special proclamation clearing Sacco and Vanzetti was issued by Massachusetts Governor Michael Dukakis.

During the trials, the *New York World* newspaper suspended the columns of Heywood Broun for protesting the prosecution of Sacco and Vanzetti. The *Boston Herald* newspaper carried on a pro-Sacco-and-Vanzetti campaign, and writers Upton Sinclair and Katherine Anne Porter wrote about the case. Future U.S. Supreme Court Justice Felix Frankfurter wrote a lengthy case analysis calling the judge's opinion a "farrago of misquotations, misrepresentations, suppressions and mutilations" (Frankfurter 1927, 104). Today's writers still disagree about whether either or both defendants deserved the guilty verdicts.

Illinois v Leopold and Loeb: Thrill Killers

A few years later in Chicago, "thrill killers" Nathan Leopold and Richard Loeb admitted they had randomly selected a fourteen-year-old boy, Bobby Franks, to kidnap and kill. Thus, their 1924 trial, where they were represented by renowned defense lawyer Clarence Darrow, was only to determine whether the sentence should be execution or life in prison (*Illinois v Leopold and Loeb*). After a famous hours-long closing argument by Darrow, the judge sentenced both to life. Loeb was killed in prison in 1936, and Leopold was paroled in 1958 with a condition that he have no media contact.

Indeed, the press itself had some effect on the course of events. Reporters for the *Chicago Daily News* came up with evidence that, despite his denials, Leopold had owned a typewriter similar to the one on which the ransom note had been typed. Publishing magnate William Randolph Hearst offered famed psychiatrist Sigmund Freud half a million dollars to examine the killers. (Freud said he was too ill to travel.) One newspaper ran a contest with the prize a "Date with Dickie" Loeb. Several books, plays, and movies were based on the case. In 1970, Leopold sued the authors of the 1959 fictionalized book and movie *Compulsion* for invasion of privacy, but he turned down a large settlement offer and then lost on grounds that as a convicted murderer he was not entitled to privacy and the case was a matter of public record (*Leopold v Levin*). Three other films were made of the story, including suspense master Alfred Hitchcock's 1948 *Rope*.

Scopes v Tennessee: Creationism and the Monkey Trial

The Scopes "Monkey Trial" of 1925 involved the controversial issue of whether schools could teach Charles Darwin's theory of evolution along with the Judeo-Christian biblical story of Creation. Twenty-four-year-old high-school teacher and football coach John Scopes volunteered to serve as a test case for the American Civil Liberties Union (ACLU), and he deliberately disobeyed a new Tennessee law outlawing the teaching of evolution. Clarence Darrow was the defense lawyer, up against three-time presidential candidate and Christian fundamentalist William Jennings Bryan, "the Great Commoner." The Republican, Methodist lay preacher judge refused to allow the introduction of any scientific experts in the eleven-day trial. In a highly unusual move, Darrow then called Bryan to the stand to defend the biblical version of creation. Darrow had actually asked for a conviction so he could appeal the case and obtain a ruling on the merits, and although after nine minutes of deliberation the jury obliged, the conviction was later overturned on a technicality (*Scopes v Tennessee*). The Tennessee law was thus never enforced, and in later cases in Arkansas and Louisiana, the U.S. Supreme Court held that laws banning the teaching of creationism were a violation of the First Amendment separation of church and state (*Epperson v Ark*, 1967; *Edwards v Aguillard*, 1985).

During the *Scopes* trial, hundreds of journalists crammed into the courtroom in Dayton. It was one of the first trials broadcast on the radio, Chicago's WGN-AM. In biting trial coverage, the renowned H. L. Mencken, working for *The Baltimore Sun*, described Bryan as a "sort of fundamentalist pope." Mencken's trial coverage is still being read today. By the end of the trial, journalists had filed an estimated 2 million words on the trial. The provocative nature of its subject matter resulted in the production of numerous books, plays, and movies such as the popular fictionalized play and movie *Inherit the Wind,* with Spencer Tracy as the Darrow-like lawyer in the film version.

New York v Snyder and Gray: The "Dumbbell Murder"

A 1927 New York murder case widely covered in the tabloid press was the two-week-long trial of Ruth Snyder (the "Bloody Blonde") and her lover, Judd Gray ("Lover Boy"), both convicted after less than two hours of jury deliberation on charges of murdering Snyder's husband (*New York v Snyder and Gray*). Albert Snyder was murdered in order for the lovers to obtain large sums of money from insurance policies, one with a double-indemnity clause. Famed writer Damon Runyon—one of more than 200 reporters covering the trial—called the case the "Dumbbell Murder" because the obviously guilty lovers, who each blamed the other for hitting the sleeping husband over the head with a window sash, were "so dumb" (Runyon 1927).

On execution day—January 12, 1928—a New York *Daily News* photographer at Sing Sing Prison used a hidden camera to snap Snyder's picture at the moment she was electrocuted. The full-page photo with its one-word headline ("Dead!") is still famous today as the only known execution photograph, due to the U.S. media's subsequent failed legal attempts to cover an execution with cameras. And the case inspired several feature films, including a classic film noir entitled *Double Indemnity* and two versions of *The Postman Always Rings Twice* (the 1946 classic and the 1981 rewrite), as well as a film entitled *Body Heat.*

The "Scottsboro Boys": Racism in the Judicial System

The trials of nine young African American men, charged with the rapes of two young Caucasian women on a train in Alabama, were held over the years 1931 through 1937. Referred to collectively as the "Scottsboro Boys," eight of the defendants were convicted and sentenced to death, and although all were imprisoned for different lengths of time, none of the death sentences was ever carried out. In the key case, *Powell v Alabama*, the U.S. Supreme Court in 1932 overturned the convictions on grounds that included failure of the defendants to have effective legal counsel. A second Supreme Court case in 1937, *Norris v Alabama*, overturned new convictions on grounds including the absence of any African American grand jury members—a denial of the defendants' due process rights. Both the U.S. Communist Party and the National Association for the Advancement of Colored People (NAACP) exploited the case, which received worldwide press coverage, to draw attention to issues of racism and civil rights in America's courtrooms. Writers Upton Sinclair and H. G. Wells were among those who wrote about the trials.

In 1976, NBC-TV produced a prize-winning docudrama entitled *Judge Horton and the Scottsboro Boys*. Unbeknownst to the writer or the producers, both alleged victims, Victoria Street-Price and Ruby Bates, were still alive, and they sued for libel (*Street v NBC*). At a 1977 trial, the court denied the claim on the basis that Street-Price (who had continued the case alone) remained a public figure, and the issue continued to be of public interest. The U.S. Supreme Court eventually agreed to hear an appeal, but Street-Price elected to settle out of court.

Little Gloria Vanderbilt:
The Mother, the Millionaire, and the Media

Another widely publicized case was the battle for custody of ten-year-old heiress Gloria Vanderbilt during the Great Depression in 1934. Gloria's widowed mother, Gloria Morgan (Mrs. Reginald) Vanderbilt, lived a wild life, spending much time abroad. The girl's aunt, Gertrude Vanderbilt Whitney, sued for permanent custody after little Gloria had been sent to her aunt's estate to recover from a tonsillectomy (*In the matter of Vanderbilt v Carew*). Whitney, considered the "richest woman in America," was worth $75 million. More than 100 reporters covered the seven-week-long hearings, but when testimony touched on such scandalous topics as hints of adult lesbianism, the judge closed the courtroom to the press and public.

The court awarded the aunt custody, with the mother allowed visitation on weekends. As one newspaper cleverly summed up the verdict: "Rock a bye baby, up on a writ/Monday through Friday, Mother's unfit/As the week ends, she rises in virtue/Saturdays, Sundays, Mother won't hurt you" (Goldsmith 1980, 543). The case would become the subject of books, movies, and later a television special. The decision was upheld on appeal, and Gloria Vanderbilt went on to write three autobiographical books and to head a successful fashion-design house.

Hauptmann and the First "Trial of the Century"

Although the *Vanderbilt* case and others in turn had been called the "Trial of the Century," the first case that really deserved the title was the 1935 trial of immigrant carpenter Bruno Richard Hauptmann for the kidnap and murder of Charles Lindbergh's baby. "Lucky Lindy" Lindbergh, at age 25, became one of the most famous men in the world after he flew in his plane the *Spirit of St. Louis* 3,500 miles across the Atlantic from New York City to Paris in 1927. Sixteen others had died in the attempt. Lindbergh collected a $25,000 prize and was given a ticker-tape parade upon his return. Lindbergh's twenty-month-old son was kidnapped from his home in Hopewell, New Jersey, in March 1932. Hauptmann was convicted at a 1935 trial (*Hauptmann v New Jersey*), sentenced to death, and executed in 1936. After this case, the "Lindbergh Law" was passed, making kidnapping a federal crime. (Lindbergh, who moved to England right after the trial, was later seen as a Nazi sympathizer. He died in 1974.)

Hauptmann's widow, Anna, continued to fight to clear her husband's name, and numerous books and documentaries supported her claim that Hauptmann had not received a fair trial. In 1983, she filed an unsuccessful civil rights suit against New Jersey officials and the Hearst Corporation, which she claimed had conspired to inflame the public against her German-born husband (*Hauptmann v Wilentz*). She also claimed Hearst's hiring of Hauptmann's defense attorney in exchange for exclusive rights to interviews had been a conflict of interest.

Coverage of the story, including the six-week-long 1935 trial, was described by newsman H. L. Mencken as the "biggest story since the Resurrection" (quoted in Ryan 1994–1995, 162). While the baby was still missing for 72 days in 1932, the press had generally cooperated with Lindbergh's requests regarding his attempts to pay ransom to recover the child, but a photographer later broke into the morgue, photographed the dead baby, and sold copies of the pictures for $5 each. The trial itself was the most widely publicized to date, with an estimated 700 newsmen, including 120 cameramen, covering the trial in Flemington, New Jersey. The courtroom was a circus, jammed with hundreds of spectators, while outside thousands of people milled around, and hawkers offered for sale tiny replicas of the wooden ladder used to take the baby out of his bedroom window. WOR-AM radio broadcasts were produced from the Union Hotel across the street from the courthouse, with commentary by prominent newsman Gabriel Heatter. During and after the trial, the jurors were offered stints in vaudeville shows.

Commentators agreed the trial was a disgrace. The director of the Federal Bureau of Investigation (FBI), J. Edgar Hoover, called it a "disgusting spectacle" but faulted the public and said, "The press is not to blame" ("Press Sympathetic" 1935, p. 1). However, at the time, much of the blame for the excesses associated with the trial was placed on the newsreel cameramen, who had agreed not to roll film except during recesses. The courtroom was so noisy the judge did not realize the newsreel cameras were rolling during the trial; only when he went to the movie theater at the end of the first week and saw the stories did he realize what had happened, and he threw the newsreel companies out of the courtroom for the rest of the trial. For the next fifty years—until revisionists examined the case with the benefit of hindsight—the *Lindbergh* case was cited as valid grounds for a ban on cameras in courtrooms. The story has been the subject of numerous books, documentaries, and fictionalized docudramas up to the present.

The Cold War, Turbulent Times, and the Second "Trial of the Century"

Although Russia was allied with the United States during World War II, postwar political developments led to the Cold War; consequently, during the Red Scare era, Americans who associated with the Soviet Union's Communist Party were suspected of disloyalty. U.S. Senator Joseph McCarthy, a Wisconsin Republican, made many charges of anti-Americanism before he was eventually discredited. The U.S. Senate censured him after the 1954 army McCarthy hearings, where Army Special Counsel Joseph Welch famously reacted to McCarthy's tactics by asking him: "At long last, have you no sense of decency, Sir?" Before that time, three simultaneous Cold War cases—each including intense press coverage of the investigations and legal proceedings—mingled as one in the public memory.

The "Hollywood 10" Case: The Red Scare Hits Hollywood

First, the "Hollywood 10" case involved hearings by the U.S. Congress House Committee for the Investigation of Un-American Activities (commonly called HUAC). The HUAC held a series of hearings; those in 1947 and 1951 examined the Hollywood film industry. In 1947, forty-one people were subpoenaed, and eventually ten refused to testify (U.S. Congress. House 1947). Following the indictments for contempt of Congress, the Committee for the First Amendment was organized in Hollywood, and stars including Humphrey Bogart, his wife, Lauren Bacall, Gene Kelly, and Spencer Tracy flew to Washington, D.C., to support the Hollywood 10. However, after all ten were convicted and served prison terms, they were blacklisted from jobs in Hollywood. The press, particularly the powerful Hearst and Scripps-Howard publications, supported HUAC.

The Case of Alger Hiss: The "Pumpkin Papers" Spy

At the same time, a senior editor at *Time* magazine, Whittaker Chambers, told the HUAC that both he and Alger Hiss, a former State Department official, had been Soviet agents. Hiss filed a $75,000 libel case against Chambers (*Hiss v Chambers*), in which Chambers produced evidence including material briefly hidden in a hollowed-out pumpkin, the "pumpkin papers." In 1950, after Hiss's first trial on charges of perjury for lying to the HUAC ended in a mistrial, a second trial ended in a conviction (*U.S. v Hiss*). Future President Richard Nixon, at the time a congressman, headed the subcommittee that investigated Hiss, and Nixon was ever afterward associated with the case. Chambers wrote a best-selling autobiography. In 1972, Hiss was successful in having his retirement benefits re-instated (*Hiss v Hampton*), and in 1975 he won re-instatement as a lawyer (*In the matter of Hiss*). And Hiss—who had served a prison sentence after his conviction—wrote two books and continued to deny his guilt until his death. In 1999, the American Historical Association was successful in obtaining release of most of the grand jury transcripts in the *Hiss* case (*In re American Historical Association*).

The Rosenbergs on Trial: Witch Hunt or Treason?

In 1951, charges of conspiracy to commit wartime espionage were filed against Julius and Ethel Rosenberg and their associates. Prosecutor Roy Cohn of New York was successful in showing they had passed atomic secrets to the Russians (*U.S. v Ethel and Julius Rosenberg*). The trial received worldwide coverage, with 3 million letters sent to the White House (including 2 different appeals from Pope Pius XII) pleading to save the Rosenbergs from execution. Nonetheless, the Rosenbergs were executed in 1953. Dozens of books were written about the case, many defending the Rosenbergs. Several written after 1990 with records newly released after the end of the Cold War suggested that the Rosenbergs had indeed passed some information, although perhaps not atomic secrets. Sam Roberts wrote a book about Ethel Rosenberg's brother, David Greenglass, who finally admitted he had perjured himself in implicating his sister. The Rosenbergs' son, Robert Meeropol, wrote his third book in 2003 in which he said the new evidence showed the possibility that his father had participated in illegal and covert acts.

Sam Sheppard and the Second "Trial of the Century"

In 1954, a case—which like Hauptmann's deserved to be described as the "Trial of the Century"—arose when Dr. Samuel Sheppard was charged with the July Fourth murder of his pregnant wife, Marilyn, at their home in Cleveland (*Sheppard v Maxwell, Warden*). Prosecutors never seriously considered anyone else as a suspect, although Sheppard had also been injured and continued to insist a "bushy-haired" intruder had committed the crime.

The first *Sheppard* trial remains a most egregious example of the failure of the U.S. judicial system to provide a fair trial for a murder suspect, and the media deservedly received some of the blame for the miscarriage of justice. Starting the day after the murder, the three Cleveland daily newspapers ran front-page coverage of the case, including editorials demanding Sheppard be arrested. Prosecutors held an inquest televised live from a school gym, where many irresponsible suggestions regarding Sheppard's guilt were made public to potential jurors. On the first day of jury selection, newsmen appeared on a live radio show debating "Which Newspaper Deserves the Most Credit for the Indictment of Dr. Sheppard?" (Neff 2001, 127). During the trial, the judge allowed reporters to sit in front of the bar that traditionally separates the public from trial participants.

Celebrity journalists who covered the trial included New York *Daily News* court reporter Theo Wilson and television and radio star Dorothy Kilgallen. Sheppard was convicted of second-degree murder and sentenced to life in prison. However, in 1961, defense attorney F. Lee Bailey began a series of appeals in Sheppard's case, based on the unfair trial. In 1966, the U.S. Supreme Court agreed with Bailey and overturned the conviction on grounds including the judge's failure to protect Sheppard from prejudicial publicity. A footnote in the Supreme Court case cited Dorothy Kilgallen's admission that during the trial the judge had taken her aside and told her Sheppard was "guilty as hell" (*Sheppard v Maxwell, Warden*, 384 U.S. 333, note 11 at 358).

A second trial was held in 1966, and this time Sheppard was acquitted. His attempt to resume his medical career was unsuccessful, as was an effort to become a professional wrestler. He sued several news organizations for libel for stories written during his 1954 trial (*Sheppard v Stevenson; Sheppard v Scripps*). Sheppard died in 1970, a few years after his release from prison.

Numerous books were written about the case, and a 1960s NBC television series, *The Fugitive,* which author Stephen King called "absolutely the best series done on American television" (Robertson 1993, xi), was thought to be based on the case (although the creator, likely hoping to avoid a libel suit, continuously denied it). The final episode in 1967, in which the "one-armed man" is discovered and Dr. Richard Kimble (actor David Janssen) is exonerated, was the highest-rated show ever until that time. A 1993 film also called *The Fugitive* (starring Harrison

Ford) and a 2000 CBS television series of the same name were admittedly based on the Sheppard case.

Sheppard's son Sam Reese Sheppard continued to fight to clear his father's name, although in 2000, he lost a ten-week-long trial, the longest civil case in the county's history, against Ohio officials for wrongful imprisonment of his father (*Estate of Sam Sheppard v Ohio*). During the civil case, the press lost a motion to open sealed records (*Ohio ex rel Cleveland Plain Dealer v Court of Common Pleas*), and a judge (who was a former prosecutor) filed a $15 million defamation lawsuit against *The New York Times* over its coverage of the trial (*Sweeney v New York Times*). In 2003, a federal court in Cleveland found that the *Times* had indeed mistakenly reported that the judge, who had been a prosecutor at the time of the 1966 Sheppard proceedings, had been involved in the *Sheppard* case and thus should have stepped down from considering the 2000 wrongful imprisonment case; in actuality, the judge had nothing to do with the earlier Sheppard case. However, the court held that since the newspaper had shown no "actual malice" and had corrected its error, the paper was not liable for damages.

In 2001, journalist James Neff, after successfully resisting government subpoenas for him to testify and turn over his notes, published a book based on ten years of research into the *Sheppard* case. Neff declared that "Dr. Sam Sheppard did not kill his wife" (Neff 2001, 382), and he implicated the Sheppards' window washer, Richard Eberling. Neff presented a great deal of evidence supporting this theory. In 2003, Bernard Conners published a book (*Tailspin: The Strange Case of Major Call*) in which he claimed that an AWOL air force major, James Call, could have killed Marilyn Sheppard. However, his evidence was not regarded as persuasive by most commentators.

New York Times v Sullivan: The Press as a Litigant

After the U.S. Supreme Court ruled in 1954 that racial segregation in public schools was unconstitutional, the civil rights movement became a dominant issue. The response of local and state governments to federal desegregation orders, as well as the activities of civil rights activists supporting nonviolent means to achieve change, were the focus of national news coverage throughout the 1950s and 1960s. Some who resisted change found they could discourage media coverage by filing libel suits against the press.

One such suit was filed in 1960 by a Montgomery, Alabama, public official who objected to a full-page *New York Times* advertisement that described civil rights activities in his city and called for support of further activities by Dr. Martin Luther King Jr. Montgomery City Commissioner L. B. Sullivan won his libel suit in a courtroom in which participants and spectators were separated by race. The verdict was upheld by the Alabama Supreme Court. However, in *New York Times v Sullivan,* in 1964, the U.S. Supreme Court overturned the decision and held on First Amendment grounds that a public official could not win a libel action unless he could prove "actual malice"—that the statements were made with knowledge of falsity or reckless disregard of the truth. The Court held that in order to encourage "robust debate" on matters of public concern, public officials should not be able to routinely prosecute the press in libel suits.

This decision was hailed as the most significant case to date involving the First Amendment rights of the press. Since that time, all fifty states have revised their libel laws to require that new national standards be met, and the number of libel cases has been reduced from dozens a year to five in 2002 ("Report Finds" 2003).

Louisiana v Shaw: JFK Assassination Conspiracy Theories

A major controversy developed after the 1963 assassination of President John F. Kennedy and the 1966 findings of the federal government's Warren Commission that assassin Lee Harvey Oswald—himself shot before he could be brought to trial—had likely acted on his own. Conspiracy theories, which abide to the present, were popular during the 1960s when New Orleans District Attorney Jim Garrison charged local businessman Clay Shaw with having participated in a conspiracy to murder JFK (*Louisiana v Shaw*). Garrison was a colorful figure, riding high after a U.S. Supreme Court victory in a criminal defamation case brought against him in 1960 by New Orleans judges whom he had accused of racketeering influences (*Garrison v Louisiana*). Garrison frequently battled with the press, accusing some journalists of being unduly influenced by the Central Intelligence Agency (CIA) and of lying.

The month-long *Shaw* trial in 1969, covered by journalists from around the world, concluded with a one-hour jury deliberation and an acquittal. Shaw was also victorious in a related case filed against Garrison, which forced Garrison to drop perjury charges against him (*Shaw v Garrison*). Despite his victories, however, Shaw died a broken man in 1974.

More than 100 books have been written about the JFK assassination, including a 1988 book (*On the Trial of the Assassins: My Investigation and Prosecution of the Murder of President Kennedy*) by Garrison about the *Shaw* trial. After Oliver Stone's 1991 movie *JFK* revived public interest in the case, Congress passed a special public-records law that led to the gathering of thousands of new documents pertaining to the assassination (*President John F. Kennedy Assassination Records Collection Act, 1992*). Until his death in 1992, Garrison (who played U.S. Chief Justice Earl Warren in *JFK*) continued to claim that Shaw had been part of a complicated conspiracy. Most authors have discredited Garrison for his prosecution of Shaw.

California v Manson: Helter Skelter

One of the longest trials in U.S. history was that of Charles Manson and other members of his "family" for the murders of actress Sharon Tate (pregnant wife of Hollywood director Roman Polanski) and three houseguests in 1969. The nine-month-long trial, which ran from June 1970 through March 1971 in Los Angeles, ended with convictions of all of the defendants (including one tried separately) (*California v Manson*). They all received death sentences, later commuted to life imprisonment when California halted all executions.

Intense publicity surrounded the case, based on its celebrity victims and the actions of chief prosecutor Vincent Bugliosi. Particularly bizarre were the antics of Manson, who had directed the murders as part of a scheme to lead eventually to a race war, which Manson described as "Helter Skelter." During the trial, President Richard Nixon told reporters he thought Manson was guilty, and the next day Manson jumped up in court and waved a newspaper headlined "Manson Guilty, Nixon Declares."

The appellate court upheld the convictions despite the defendants' claims they had not had a fair trial due to the extensive publicity, including violations of a "gag" order on trial participants. The court said the publicity was so extensive, it would have been useless either to delay the trial or to move it elsewhere.

Another memorable aspect of the press coverage of the Manson trial was the jailing of *Los Angeles Herald-Examiner* reporter William Farr for refusing to reveal his source for a story about one defendant's alleged admission that the family planned to murder other celebrities (*Farr v Superior Court,* 1971; *Farr v Pitchess,* 1975). Farr spent forty-six days in jail for contempt of court, a record at the time for a journalist so cited by a judge.

Several books and films resulted from the Manson case. Most notable was prosecutor Vince Bugliosi's 1974 book, *Helter Skelter: The True Story of the Manson Murders,* and the 1976 television movie, *Helter Skelter.* And litigation continues to the present: for example, in 2003, convicted murderer Susan Atkins, who had recanted her confession to participating in the murder, sued the governor of California and claimed that she had become a political prisoner due to his denial of parole for any convicted murderer.

New York Times v U.S.: The Pentagon Papers

A controversial issue in the 1960s and 1970s was the war in Vietnam. A copy of a military report, "History of the U.S. Decision-Making Process on Vietnam Policy"—popularly known as the "Pentagon Papers"—appeared on the desk of a *New York Times* reporter in 1971. (The source was later discovered to be Daniel Ellsberg, a Harvard PhD.) The newspaper studied the forty-seven-volume report on the events up to 1968, and after several months the *Times* began publication of a series based on the Pentagon Papers.

On June 14, 1971, President Richard Nixon, claiming national security was at stake, obtained a temporary *injunction,* an order halting further publication of the stories; and although a trial court upheld the newspaper's right to publish, the appellate court upheld the injunction against the *Times* and another newspaper, the *Washington Post,* that had begun to publish stories on the Pentagon Papers.

In one of the speediest actions ever taken by the U.S. Supreme Court, on June 30, 1971, the Court overturned the injunctions, and the newspapers were free to publish the Pentagon Papers (*New York Times v U.S.; U.S. v Washington Post*). The Court said that absent a showing of "immediate, irreparable harm," the government could not impose a prior restraint on the press. The *Times* and the *Post* resumed coverage, and the *Times* won the Pulitzer Prize for publishing the Pentagon Papers. Since then, the decision has been cited to show that even the government must have a compelling reason to override the First Amendment rights of freedom of the press.

Several books have been written about the Pentagon Papers. In the 2002 autobiography of Daniel Ellsberg, *Secrets: A Memoir of Vietnam and the Pentagon Papers,* the man who leaked the Papers finally tells all.

U.S. v Nixon: Watergate

After the Pentagon Papers case, the Nixon administration reacted by taking steps to avoid further leaks of information. The White House "plumbers" (assigned to stop the leaks) in 1972 broke into Ellsberg's psychiatrist's office in an attempt to discredit the man who had leaked the Pentagon Papers to the press. Then the plumbers broke into the Democratic National Headquarters, located in the Watergate Building in Washington, D.C.

Press coverage of Watergate was led primarily by the *Washington Post.* As a result of the allegations appearing in the media coverage, a special prosecutor was employed to investigate, and both a grand jury and a Senate committee were convened. It was discovered that President Nixon had audio-taped nearly four thousand conversations in the Oval Office. Dramatic events included the firing of the special prosecutor and revelations that one crucial tape had an eighteen-minute gap (later determined to be the result of deliberate erasure) and that two other tapes had disappeared.

In *In re subpoena of Nixon,* the President claimed executive privilege and argued that in the interest of national security, he should not have to turn over the Watergate tapes. The case was presided over by Judge John Sirica, who ordered Nixon in 1973 to turn over the tapes, a ruling upheld by the court of appeals later that year. Meanwhile, indictments were issued by the grand jury for Nixon associates John Mitchell, H. R. Haldeman, John Erlichman, and others for conspiracy to obstruct justice and for perjury. (Nixon was listed as an un-indicted co-conspirator.) All three men were convicted. In July of 1974, the U.S. Supreme

Court upheld Sirica's orders to turn over the tapes, and that same day the U.S. House Judiciary Committee began televised hearings. Impeachment orders were prepared, and in August 1974, Nixon resigned. (He was later pardoned by his vice president, Gerald Ford, who had become president.)

There was widespread national and international interest in the case, and the *Washington Post* won a much-deserved Pulitzer Prize for taking the lead in investigating Watergate. Dozens of Watergate books were written, and a 1976 movie, *All the President's Men,* based on the book by *Post* Watergate reporters Bob Woodward and Carl Bernstein, presented a dramatized version of the events. In March 2002, the National Archives made public the first batch of the Watergate tapes; at the same time work began on digital enhancement of Tape 342, the one with the famous eighteen-minute gap. In 2003, however, the archivist said he was giving up, at least for a time, the attempt to enhance Tape 342. Later that year, the University of Texas at Austin announced that the Watergate papers of Woodward and Bernstein would be housed there and made available to the public.

U.S. v Hearst: The Kidnapped Heiress and the Symbionese Liberation Army

A criminal case involving the kidnapping of heiress Patty Hearst, a nineteen-year-old art history major at the University of California, Berkeley, further dramatized the political turmoil of the times. In the 1970s, after violence between black inmates and white guards in California prisons, a small group of radicals calling themselves the Symbionese Liberation Army (SLA) was organized to support "The People" resisting the government. In 1973, the SLA killed a California school superintendent, and in February 1974, they kidnapped Patricia Hearst, wealthy granddaughter of newspaper publisher William Randolph Hearst. As ransom, the group demanded the Hearsts set up a food program for the poor, and the Hearsts complied, at a cost of $2 million. Then in April, the SLA—now including Patty Hearst, who called herself Tania, a self-described "urban guerrilla"—robbed a bank; a second bank robbery left one employee dead. A month later, Hearst and two others robbed a sporting-goods store, and police traced them to their hideout. The resulting shootout, in which six members of the SLA died, was broadcast live on national television and radio for several hours on May 16, 1974. But Hearst and two others had escaped.

Hearst was finally captured by the FBI in September 1975, and in 1976 she was tried on charges of armed robbery and use of a weapon to commit a felony. Her family hired F. Lee Bailey (who, it will be remembered, had successfully argued Dr. Sam Sheppard's appeal). Bailey claimed that Hearst had been brainwashed by her captors. The trial lasted 2 months, with 75 witnesses and 186 exhibits. She was convicted and sentenced to 7 years in prison (*U.S. v Hearst*).

The media blitz surrounding the kidnapping and particularly the SLA shootout was such that in 1978 Hearst moved to have her conviction set aside, or at least her sentence reduced, due in part to prejudicial pretrial publicity. Although the appellate court agreed that the *Hearst* case had been the subject of the "most extensive news coverage in recent history," the court rejected her argument because she had not asked for the trial to be moved and she had waited too long to complain (466 F Supp at 1073). The U.S. Supreme Court refused to consider the case.

After a campaign that Hearst later admitted was designed to use the media to change her public image, President Jimmy Carter reduced her sentence to the twenty-one months she had already served, and she was pardoned by President Bill Clinton on his last day in office in January 2001. Hearst, who has maintained that she was brainwashed by her captors and not responsible for her actions, renounced her comrades, including Kathleen Soliah, one of only a few SLA sympathizers who managed to escape detection until her 1999 arrest and 2001 plea agreement for a fourteen-year sentence. A 1975 bank robbery case against Soliah and three others also was settled with pleas and six-to-eight-year sentences in 2002.

Court TV, the Third "Trial of the Century," and the New Millennium

With the advent of Court TV in 1991, and the beginning of a three-year experiment with courtroom cameras in some federal courtrooms, public interest in courts was greatly increased.

Florida v Smith: Court TV and the Kennedys

In 1991, medical student William Kennedy Smith—a nephew of the late President John F. Kennedy—was charged with rape (*Florida v Smith*). The trial was televised on Court TV and became a media sensation. While visiting the Kennedy Palm Beach home, Smith and his uncle, Senator Ted Kennedy, had invited home two women they had met at a nightclub. Smith claimed one of the women had consensual sex with him, but she claimed it was rape.

The trial was broadcast live, gavel-to-gavel, on Court TV for ten days, with heavy coverage by CNN and the four major broadcast networks (ABC, CBS, NBC, and Fox). To protect the identity of the alleged victim, a technical device popularly called a "blue dot" masked the face of the accuser whenever she testified. One controversy arose when a witness admitted that before the trial she had accepted $40,000 from a tabloid television show; as a result she was not allowed to testify. Although Smith was acquitted after less than two hours of jury deliberation, his name is still associated with the case.

The Rodney King Beating Trials: The Los Angeles Police Department, the Media, and Mob Violence

Television also played a large part in the criminal trial of four white Los Angeles Police Department (LAPD) officers on charges of using excessive force and filing false reports (*California v Powell*, 1992). This occurred after their arrest of a fleeing black drunk-driving suspect named Rodney (Glen) King. Unknown to the LAPD officers, the beating of King during the arrest in March of 1991 had been captured on videotape by an amateur photographer, and the tape was shown repeatedly throughout 1992 and 1993 before their trial.

An appellate court directed the presiding judge to grant the officers' motion to move the trial to compensate for the prejudicial publicity (*Powell et al. v Superior Court of Los Angeles County*, 1991), and the trial was held in Simi Valley, California. The appellate court also disqualified the judge originally scheduled to hear the case on grounds that included his allowing the media to influence his handling of the case (*Briseno v Superior Court of Los Angeles County*, 1991).

Based on repeated pretrial viewings of the 82-second edited video of the beatings, the television-viewing audience for the trial, with 150 hours televised on Court TV, expected convictions. However, after a month-long trial and a week of jury deliberations, the all-white jury—with access to all of the evidence, including the unedited video—returned acquittals. When the verdict was announced on April 29, 1992, riots erupted throughout the south side of Los Angeles. The beating of a white man, Reginald Denny, by rioting black men, was broadcast live by news cameras on helicopters. Riots also spread to other cities, and on May 1, 1992, King appeared on a live broadcast to appeal for an end to the violence. In Los Angeles, more than 50 deaths and 2,000 injuries were blamed on the riots, as was as much as $800 million in property damage.

King later sued the four officers in federal court, charging them with violation of his civil rights (*U.S. v Koon and Powell*, 1993). Two of the officers, Stacey Koon and Laurence Powell, were convicted after a 1993 trial, and each was sentenced to 30 months in prison, a sentence which was upheld by the U.S. Supreme Court. In the end, King settled for nearly $3 million in cash and benefits from the city. In his subsequent book, *Presumed Guilty: The Tragedy of the Rodney King Affair*, convicted LAPD Sergeant Stacey Koon devoted an entire chapter to what he called the "media's responsibility" for the public reaction to the acquittals in the criminal case. Koon charged that television broadcasts of edited versions of the King beating that did not show King charging Powell had created a skewed public perception of the incident.

The criminal trial of two men charged with beating Denny and seven others during the rioting after the criminal acquittal of the police was also broadcast live on Court TV in late 1993 (*Gates et al. v Superior Court of Los Angeles County*). These men were convicted of lesser crimes than they were originally charged with and sentenced to time already served.

The Menendez Brothers Trials: Honor Thy Father and Mother

The first criminal trials of brothers Erik and Lyle Menendez, charged in the 1989 murders of their parents Jose and Kitty, were also televised live on Court TV to 12 million viewers (*California v*

Menendez, 1994). Jose Menendez was a wealthy executive of an entertainment corporation (his estate was valued at $14 million), and at first there was speculation that the murders were a mob hit. Lyle was a twenty-two-year-old tennis player under suspension from Princeton, and Erik was a nineteen-year-old Beverly Hills High School student who also played tennis. The brothers spent a great deal of money on cars, clothes, and girls in the six months after the murders.

However, Erik, who had been seeing a therapist after both boys had been involved earlier in neighborhood burglaries, reportedly confessed his guilt in the murders. After police obtained tapes of sessions with the therapist, they charged the boys with murder. The brothers admitted killing their parents but claimed it was in response to repeated sexual abuse. They sued unsuccessfully to block a Los Angeles television station from showing before the trial a docudrama based on their case (*Menendez v Fox*).

Their first trials were heard simultaneously by two separate juries. During those trials in 1993 and 1994, which ended in hung juries, defense attorney Leslie Abramson became something of a Court TV star. However, their second trials in 1995 and 1996 (for which camera coverage was denied) resulted in convictions and lifetime sentences without parole; they were sent to separate prisons.

The O. J. Simpson Trial: The Third "Trial of the Century"

In hindsight, the case most deserving to be called the "Trial of the (Twentieth) Century" was the 1995 murder trial of former-football-star-turned-actor O. J. Simpson. Simpson's ex-wife Nicole Brown Simpson and her friend Ron Goldman were murdered in June of 1994, and Simpson was scheduled to be arrested and charged a few days later. However, he appeared to be fleeing to avoid arrest, and the "Bronco chase" in which police and news helicopters followed him as he drove around the L.A. freeways was broadcast on live television (and cost the television networks an estimated $7 million in lost revenue).

After a successful motion by the media to allow cameras in the courtroom, the *Simpson* trial was broadcast gavel-to-gavel (*California v Simpson*, 1994). More than 2,000 media representatives, from the mainstream press to the tabloid infotainment shows, set up outside the courthouse what came to be called "Camp O. J." The *Simpson* case dominated print, broadcast, and the budding Internet media for more than a year. A record-breaking 150 million viewers watched the televised live verdict in October 1995. Although Simpson was acquitted, he was found liable in a civil suit subsequently filed by the victims' families, and he was ordered to pay them a total of $33.5 million; the decision was upheld in 2001 (*Rufo v Simpson*). (Cameras were banned at the civil trial, and the judge enforced a "gag" order on all trial participants.) Simpson later attempted to sue to block the 2000 showing of a CBS television miniseries based on the case, *American Tragedy*, with a screenplay by Norman Mailer.

More than 100 books have been written on the *Simpson* case. Racial aspects of the trial (Simpson is black, while both his victims were white), legal issues (anonymous, sequestered jurors; peremptory challenges), and the media (use of courtroom cameras) were all examined. (See Chapter 2 for an in-depth discussion of press issues associated with the case.) Into the new millennium, the *Simpson* case remained the quintessential example of media coverage of courts.

U.S. v McVeigh and Nichols: The Oklahoma City Bombing

There were other high-profile cases as the millennium approached. One was that of Timothy McVeigh, charged in the bombing of the federal building in Oklahoma City on 19 April 1995, when 168 people died, including 33 children and 8 federal law-enforcement officers. McVeigh claimed he had acted in response to federal raids in Ruby Ridge, Idaho, and Waco, Texas. In August 1995, McVeigh and Terry Nichols were charged on 11 counts, including conspiracy, use of explosives, and murder. Nichols's case was separated from McVeigh's.

Due to the public feelings in Oklahoma City and the pretrial publicity, the McVeigh trial was moved to Denver (918 F, Supp 1467, 1996). Although media requests to broadcast the proceedings had been denied (931 F. Supp 753, 756, 1996), after two acts of Congress the court allowed a first-ever closed-circuit television feed of the proceedings, so witnesses, victims, and families could watch from Oklahoma City. Many court records were sealed, and most of the sealing orders and a gag order on trial participants survived media challenges (931 F. Supp 753, 756, 1996; 964 F. Supp 313, 1997; 9 F.3d 806, 1997). McVeigh's motion to dismiss the case on grounds he could never obtain a fair trial due to prejudicial publicity was denied (955 F. Supp 1281, 1997). The jury convicted on all eleven counts after a nine-week trial in 1997, and the conviction and death sentence were upheld, despite appeals that included McVeigh's charge that pretrial publication on websites (including that of *The Dallas Morning News*) of reports of a confession had denied him a fair trial (153 F.3d 1166, 1998).

Nichols was later tried in the same courtroom under similar restrictions. He was convicted of conspiracy and of involuntary manslaughter in the deaths of the 8 officers, and his conviction was upheld (528 U.S. 934, 1999). In 1998, he was sentenced to life without parole and ordered to pay $14.5 million in restitution to victims. Starting in 2003, he was retried in Oklahoma state court on 160 counts of first-degree murder of the other victims of the bombing; this time a conviction could bring a death penalty. As in the federal case, in state court a gag order was issued, and most media requests for access were denied (*Oklahoma v Nichols*, 2000).

An Internet entertainment network sued to be allowed to netcast McVeigh's execution, and although the request was denied, the court did allow a closed-circuit broadcast of the execution, again limited to witnesses, victims, and families (*Entertain Net v Lappin*). More than 1,000 reporters covered the execution in June 2001, the first execution of a federal prisoner in nearly 30 years. It is estimated the government spent more than $80 million on the *McVeigh and Nichols* cases.

The Clinton Case:
The President, the Courts, and the Media

In 1998, the U.S. House of Representatives voted to impeach President William (Bill) Jefferson Clinton on two articles (or charges) of wrongdoing (U.S. Congress. House 1998), but in 1999, the U.S. Senate voted for an acquittal (U.S. Congress. Senate 1999). (CNN unsuccessfully petitioned the senators to televise the proceedings.) The complex case started with a sexual harassment suit, included the appointment of a Special Counsel to investigate the president's role in another case, and eventually culminated in the impeachment vote.

The former governor of Arkansas, Clinton was elected president in 1992, despite published rumors about an alleged adulterous affair with a woman named Gennifer Flowers. In 1994, former Arkansas state employee Paula Jones filed a $700,000 sexual harassment suit claiming that while he was governor, Clinton had made unwelcome sexual advances (*Jones v Clinton*). Although Clinton questioned whether a sitting president could be forced to testify in a civil suit, in May 1997, the U.S. Supreme Court ruled the *Jones* suit could go forward immediately (*Clinton v Jones*). After several lawsuits brought by the media, most of the *Jones* case records were eventually unsealed (138 F.3d 758 [1998]; 27 Med L Rptr 1156 [1998]).

There were also published rumors that both the president and his wife, Hillary Rodham Clinton, had been involved in shady financial transactions in Arkansas, and in 1994, Kenneth Starr was appointed the new U.S. Independent Counsel to investigate the "Whitewater" real-estate deal. Subsequent legal actions were brought against fourteen people, but no criminal charges were ever brought against the Clintons.

Meanwhile, from 1995 to 1997, the president was sexually involved with White House intern Monica Lewinsky. The *Jones* case, the Whitewater investigation, and the Lewinsky affair merged in December 1997 when Lewinsky's name appeared on the *Jones* case witness list. The Lewinsky affair was made public (although a gag order restricted Lewinsky's public comments), and Starr's duties were expanded to include investigating whether the president had interfered with Lewinsky's scheduled testimony in the *Jones* case.

From the tabloid coverage of the Flowers affair and of the *Jones* case, through the breaking of the Lewinsky story by gossip webcaster Matt Drudge, media coverage affected the story.

Once Starr began to investigate Lewinsky, the mainstream press found it difficult to treat with dignity the sordid particulars of the sex scandal, which—although not directly related to the investigation of Lewinsky's possible testimony in the *Jones* case—Starr's office pursued and leaked to the press. Outside the federal courthouse in Washington, D.C., the press camped out at "Monica Beach," reminiscent of the 1995 Camp O. J. in Los Angeles.

The Starr Report, with eleven recommendations of possible impeachable charges, as well as Clinton's grand jury testimony, was made public (*The Starr Report* on the Internet, the testimony on national television). In response, *Hustler* magazine publisher Larry Flynt offered $1 million to anyone offering details of "illicit sexual relations" with congressmen. This resulted in the resignation of House Speaker–designate Congressman Bob Livingston (a Louisiana Republican), who confessed to marital infidelities. There was speculation that Flynt's offer subdued many who had been clamoring for the president to resign. In January 1999, the Senate failed to uphold the December 1998 House impeachment of Clinton on two charges: perjury before the grand jury (for denying a sexual relationship with Lewinsky) and obstruction of justice (for possibly influencing Lewinsky's testimony in the *Jones* case—which had been settled in November 1998, shortly before the impeachment proceedings had begun) (*U.S. v Clinton*, U.S. Congress, 1999).

In April 1999, President Clinton was found in contempt of court and later ordered to pay a $90,000 fine. The day before he left office, he signed an agreement admitting he had given false testimony; he was fined another $25,000, and his law license was suspended. Lewinsky became something of a tabloid celebrity, in 2003 hosting a Fox TV reality show.

A score of authors wrote books on the *Clinton* case. Many authors outlined the orchestrated scandalmongering of conservative businessmen, politicians, and media personalities—actions designed to discredit Clinton throughout the 1990s. For instance, the "Arkansas Project," financed by Pittsburgh billionaire Richard Mellon Scaife, involved millions of dollars spent to manipulate media coverage. David Brock, author of a magazine article that resulted, later wrote an entire book repudiating his attacks on the Clintons. *The Starr Report* itself, which veered off track to detail the Lewinsky affair (mentioning "Whitewater" only twice while the word "sex" appeared at least 500 times), had cost more than $60 million by the time a final report was issued by Starr's successor in 2002 (Ray 2002).

As Joe Conason and Gene Lyons claimed in *The Hunting of the President*, media coverage of the *Clinton* case had "important journalists and news organizations succumbing to scandal fever, credulously and sometimes dishonestly promoting charges against the Clintons in heavily biased, error-filled dispatches, columns, best-selling books and TV news specials, and thus bestowing 'mainstream' prestige upon what was often little more than a poisonous mixture of half-truth and partisan malice" (Conason and Lyons 2000, xv). *Living History*, Hillary Clinton's highly successful 2003 book for which she received a reported $8 million advance, made much the same point.

U.S. v Microsoft:
The Appearance of Judicial Partiality

The media also played a crucial role in the case of *U.S. v Microsoft* (1999). Because the presiding judge had talked to journalists before handing down his final decision, when the appellate court partially overturned his holding, the judge was disqualified from hearing the retrial (253 F.3d 34 at 106–118).

In 1998, both the U.S. Justice Department and the attorneys general of twenty states filed antitrust suits charging Microsoft—the world's largest software company—with creating a monopoly in its operating system Windows, which runs more than 95 percent of the world's computers. The suits also charged Microsoft with illegally tying ("bundling") its web browser, Internet Explorer, with Windows software, to the detriment of browser competitors such as Netscape's Navigator.

The federal trial began in October 1998 and included the more-than-seventeen-hour videotaped testimony of Microsoft CEO Bill Gates. (The tapes were made public after successful media lawsuits [334 U.S. Ct Appl DC 165, 1999].) In November of 1999, the presiding judge, Thomas Penfield Jackson, released the first half of his decision, a Finding of Facts that suggested Microsoft was a monopoly (U.S. District, DC 98-1232-98-1233, 2000). Jackson then appointed appellate court judge Richard Posner to work out a settlement, but by April 2000 it was obvious no settlement would be reached. In June 2000, Jackson released his final decision, ordering Microsoft to break up into two separate companies. In February 2001, the appellate court allowed live audio broadcast of oral arguments over his decision.

In June 2001, the federal appellate court overturned Jackson's order to break up Microsoft, but the court upheld the finding that Microsoft was a monopoly and ordered a retrial (253 F.3d 34). The court took the unusual step of disqualifying Jackson from hearing the retrial, holding that the judge had behaved improperly by "giving secret interviews to select reporters" and by making offensive comments about Microsoft in public statements outside the courtroom, thus giving rise to an "appearance of partiality" (253 F.3d 34 at 106–118). The court admitted its decision was likely based on hearsay evidence, and no evidence of actual bias had been found, but it said Jackson had called into question the integrity of the judicial process. Among others, the court cited *New Yorker* writer Ken Auletta, who had conducted interviews with Jackson between the end of the trial in 1999 and his final decision in 2000. Some commentators speculated that the appellate court's displeasure with Jackson may have indirectly contributed to the decision to overturn his breakup order.

Before a new judge was selected for the retrial, Microsoft appealed to the U.S. Supreme Court in 2001. The Justice Department, now under a Republican administration, said it was dropping its pursuit of the Microsoft breakup and said it would also drop the separate browser-bundling charges. Nine states initially rejected a proposed settlement but accepted a later settlement offer in late 2002 (*New York v Microsoft*). In 2003, Microsoft settled a private lawsuit filed by AOL Time Warner regarding the tactics used in promoting the web browser Internet Explorer at the expense of AOL's Netscape. The settlement included an agreement that Microsoft would pay AOL $750 million as well other concessions. Other private lawsuits continued.

Bush v Gore: Thirty-Six Days

Another high-profile case in which the media played a significant role involved the challenge to the U.S. presidential election in 2000, which reached the U.S. Supreme Court as *Bush v Gore.* The candidates were President Clinton's vice president, Al Gore, and the son of former President George Bush, George W. Bush. The November 7 election was so close that on election night the Associated Press and the television networks, based on exit polls, first called Florida's vote and then the election for Gore, then moved Florida back to "undecided," and at 2:15 AM on November 8, called Bush the winner. Gore called Bush to concede but then retracted his concession, and by 4 AM on November 8, the networks had declared Florida "too close to call."

For the next thirty-six days, the presidential election, with recounts and court challenges, dominated the news. More than a dozen lawsuits were filed in Florida, and the Florida Supreme Court approved a statewide recount (*Palm Beach City Canvassing Board v Harris*, 2000). The U.S. Supreme Court first vacated that decision and sent it back to the Florida court to explain its reasoning (*Bush v Palm Beach City Canvassing Board*). In *Gore v Harris,* the Florida Supreme Court ordered that the recount be contin-ued. The High Court then halted the Florida Supreme Court's second decision to continue the recount (*Bush v Gore*, 531 U.S. 1046), and on 12 December 2000, the U.S. Supreme Court halted all counting of challenged votes on due-process grounds (*Bush v Gore*, 531 U.S. 98). Gore conceded the next day. In effect, the Supreme Court had chosen Bush the winner.

The intense coverage of *Bush v Gore* included a petition by the media to televise the arguments. Although the Florida Supreme Court hearings had been televised, the U.S. Supreme Court denied video coverage (*Siegel v LePore*). Urged by media organizations and supported by Senator Charles Grassley (an Iowa Republican) the U.S. Supreme Court did allow the proceed-ings to be audio-taped and then broadcast nationwide, setting a new precedent.

The U.S. Supreme Court vote in the elections case was 5 to 4, with the justices lined up in accord with the political parties with which they had been affiliated before being appointed to the Court: Republicans in the majority selected a Republican presi-dent. A huge outcry followed, with political, media, and legal commentators weighing in. Many pointed out apparent partisan motives of the five majority justices. (For instance, at least two wanted to retire with a Republican president in office to appoint their successors.)

News groups vowed to continue the count on their own, and eventually the *Miami Herald* published the final word on the count, predicting that Bush may have won even if the recount had been allowed to continue. The *Herald* found that only under the most restrictive method of counting might Gore have won in Florida. Many commentators concluded that the long-term effect of *Bush v Gore* would be to lead to electoral reform, to a law that the networks must not broadcast results before all polls were closed—and to decreased public confidence in the independence of the federal judiciary.

Conclusion

This brief look at high-profile court cases is by no means exhaus-tive. Numerous other cases have received extensive coverage, such as the trials of serial murderers Ted Bundy in Florida and

Wayne Williams in Atlanta; the attempted-murder trial of Claus Von Bulow; the libel case brought by the Reverend Jerry Falwell against publisher Larry Flynt; the murder trial of Joel Steinberg in New York; the obstruction-of-justice charges against Colonel Oliver North; the racketeering trial of John Gotti; the murder trial of Louise Woodward ("Nannygate") in Boston; the child-murder trial of Susan Smith in South Carolina; the cases against the Washington, D.C., snipers John Allen Muhammad and Lee Boyd Malvo; as well as the sexual assault charges against basketball player Kobe Bryant and the child molestation charges against pop singer Michael Jackson . . . the list goes on. However, the selected cases are representative, and they provide a historical perspective on the role of the media in coverage of the judicial process.

Several themes emerge. First, the public often sees the media as profit-driven and thus inclined to sensationalism. From the Sob Sisters of the *Thaw* trial to the hundreds of reporters camped out in front of courthouses in Camp O. J. and later at Monica Beach, the print, broadcast, and now cyberspace media have at times been guilty of egregious excesses. Further, the mergers of mainstream news outlets with giant, non-news conglomerates promise increased tabloidization of the news.

Second, the media themselves have at times become involved in the judicial process. Newspapers led campaigns protesting the convictions of Sacco and Vanzetti, and reporters contributed to evidence in the murder trial of Leopold and Loeb. Hearst paid for Hauptmann's lawyer in the *Lindbergh* kidnapping and murder case, and the papers themselves were litigants in *The New York Times* libel case and in the Pentagon Papers cases in New York and Washington, D.C. Prejudicial publicity brought Sam Sheppard a new trial, and the television-news broadcasts of LAPD officers beating Rodney King became the centerpiece of a trial that ended in deadly riots.

Third, the mainstream press, and to some extent the new media, continue the traditional governmental watchdog role in covering the judicial process. Due to heavy press coverage, a national dialogue developed during the political trials of Sacco and Vanzetti in the 1920s, and on the Hollywood 10, Alger Hiss, and the Rosenberg cases during the Cold War era. Racial inequities were dramatized by press coverage of the "Scottsboro Boys" case in Alabama. The public has been kept informed on political issues involving the U.S. presidency via media coverage of Watergate, the Clinton impeachment, and the election of George W. Bush.

Overall, despite occasional excesses, the media would be judged to have contributed positively to public appreciation and understanding of the judicial process. To better serve the public, at times the press has challenged the courts on issues such as gag orders, use of anonymous juries, access to documents and proceedings, and the use of courtroom cameras and other adaptations as the digital age begins. These controversies, problems, and potential solutions are the subject of Chapter 2.

References

Belth, Nathan. 1981. "The Violent Decade," in *A Promise to Keep: A Narrative of the American Encounter with Anti-Semitism*. New York: Shocken Books, 58–86.

Boyle, Janet. 1997. "The Case of Harry K. Thaw," in *The Press on Trial*, ed. Lloyd Chiasson. Westport, CT: Greenwood, 63–74 (citing *The New York Times*, 23 January 1907).

Conason, Joe, and Gene Lyons. 2000. *The Hunting of the President*. New York: St. Martin's Press.

Frankfurter, Felix. 1927. *The Case of Sacco and Vanzetti*. New York: Little, Brown.

Golden, Harry. 1965. *A Little Girl Is Dead*. Cleveland: World Publishing.

Goldsmith, Barbara. 1980. *Little Gloria, Happy at Last*. New York: Knopf.

Neff, James. 2001. *The Wrong Man*. New York: Random House, 2002.

President John F. Kennedy Assassination Records Collection Act. 1992. *U.S. Code Service*, vol. 44, sect. 2107.

"Press Sympathetic but Skeptical toward Control of Trial Ballyhoo." 1935. *Editor & Publisher*, 20 July, 1+ (quoting J. Edgar Hoover).

Ray, Robert. 2002. *Final Report of the Independent Counsel in re Madison Guaranty Savings and Loan Association*. 6 March and 20 March. Available at http://icreport.access.gpo.gov/final [2003].

"Report Finds Media Defendants Fared Well in 2002." 2003. Media Law Resource Center, via htttp://rcfp.org/news. Accessed 2003.

Robertson, Ed. 1993. *The Fugitive Recaptured*. Introduction by Stephen King. Los Angeles: Pomegranate Press.

Runyon, Damon. 1927. "Murder in the Worst Degree." International News Service, 19 April, 27 April, 28 April, 9 May.

Ryan, Bernard. 1994–1995. "Bruno Richard Hauptmann," in *American Trials of the 20th Century*, ed. Edward Knappman. Detroit, MI: Visible Ink, 162–168 (citing H. L. Mencken).

U.S. v Microsoft: Deposition of Bill Gates. Videotape. 1998. Washington, DC: Administrative Office of the U.S. Courts, 3 vols., 17 hours 21 min.

2

Controversies, Problems, and Solutions

The conflict between the First Amendment guarantee of a free press and the Sixth Amendment right to a fair trial has been apparent for 200 years. The chronological development of the issues, as illustrated primarily by pertinent U.S. Supreme Court cases, will be presented in Chapter 3.

Today's controversies, as revealed in recent cases, legislation, and commentary, may be divided into more than a dozen areas (Alexander 2003). After a brief discussion of the judicial process, current controversies regarding press coverage will be described, concluding with a discussion of the accomplishments of the press in covering courts—and some recommendations for improvement.

The Judicial Process

The judicial system in the United States is adversarial, with one side pitted against another in a process carried out in accord with *due process*—procedural safeguards designated by the U.S. Constitution. Both the federal and state governments support court systems, each divided into three levels: trial courts, where a case usually begins; intermediate or appellate courts, which may review the actions of the trial courts; and a high court, usually called a supreme court, which has the last word over all the courts in its jurisdiction. Every state designs its own court system. On the federal level, there are ninety-four trial courts, thirteen appellate courts, and, of course, the U.S. Supreme Court in Washington, D.C.

As a case travels through the justice system, the press shows varying degrees of interest. Most news media interest is in *criminal actions,* whereby the government prosecutes someone accused of breaking the laws of society. An estimated 95 percent of criminal cases never make it to trial, because about one-third are dropped by prosecutors and nearly two-thirds are settled without a trial.

Controversial Issues

The theoretical basis of a criminal trial is that a defendant is presumed innocent unless the government proves guilt beyond a reasonable doubt. The following discussion will describe controversies over news media coverage of the small minority of criminal and civil cases that make it to trial. The trial process is familiar to most people, since both fictional cases and true crimes are the popular subject of books, television shows, and movies. Coverage of the criminal justice system is the subject of as much as one-half of the local news in both print and broadcast media.

Grand Juries

In a criminal case involving a major crime (a *felony*), the judicial process generally begins with a statement of the charge (the *indictment*) issued after a grand jury meets and decides to prosecute. A *grand jury* is made up of twelve to twenty-three citizens called to work with the prosecutor (called the district attorney or state's attorney in a state case, the U.S. attorney in a federal case). The work of the grand jury is closed to the public in order to protect witnesses and those who are never charged with a crime. However, indictments are usually open, absent a compelling reason such as the need to arrest a suspect. After the arrest of anyone indicted, the indictment and other records are generally opened to the public.

Grand juries may also be convened to consider such general issues as corruption. The resulting grand jury report may or may not include indictments of individuals. In general, witnesses who have appeared before a grand jury are allowed to describe their own testimony after the grand jury has issued its report. However, there is some confusion over access to specific grand jury information, as demonstrated by the controversy over the grand juries considering cases involving President Clinton, Paula Jones, and Monica Lewinsky, described in Chapter 1.

Closed Proceedings

After someone is arrested by the police (as in most minor [*misdemeanor*] cases) or after indictment by a grand jury, he will face a preliminary hearing (in some cases called an *arraignment*) where he will officially be charged with the crime and allowed to plead guilty, not guilty, or no contest (a way of accepting the penalty without actually admitting guilt). If the suspect pleads Not Guilty, the judge will consider whether to allow the defendant to remain free after posting bail.

The typical criminal case involves several pretrial hearings, on such motions as those asking that the case be delayed or even dismissed. There are often hearings at which the defendant asks that certain evidence be excluded because of the unconstitutional manner by which it was obtained. Or the evidence may be so sensationalistic—such as a graphic photograph of a murder victim—that it may so prejudice the jurors that the defendant will not have a fair trial. Although these *suppression hearings* are frequently open to the media, they are particularly problematic since reporters may be revealing to the public information that will not be allowed at the trial.

If the journalist discovers in advance that a hearing will be closed, he may file a motion to have the hearing opened. One such case was the successful motion of the press to obtain access to the 2000 murder arraignment of Michael Skakel, Robert F. Kennedy's nephew. Skakel eventually was convicted of having murdered his fifteen-year-old neighbor, Martha Moxley, in Greenwich, Connecticut, when he was a teenager (*Connecticut v Skakel*, 2000). The press was unsuccessful in obtaining access to a 2002 Baltimore hearing involving seventeen-year-old John Lee Malvo, one of two suspected snipers in a case that resulted in thirteen deaths in five states and Washington, D.C. (*In re Washington Post Motion to Open Juvenile Detention Hearing*). However, a hearing in the *Malvo* case in Virginia in 2003 was opened to the public and the press (*In re Commonwealth of Virginia v Malvo [and Muhammed]*).

The issue of access to administrative court-like deportation hearings involving those suspected of terrorist ties remains unsettled. One federal appellate court heard an appeal led by the *Detroit Free Press* for access to the proceedings involving Rabih Haddad, one of several "special interest" detainees held after the events of September 11, 2001. Saying "Democracies die behind closed doors," the court held in 2002 in the Michigan case that such hearings should be open (*Detroit Free Press v Ashcroft*). However, a few months later, a different federal appellate court came to the opposite conclusion in a New Jersey case involving deportation proceedings of special interest detainees Ahmed Raza and Malek Zeidan. The appellate court held in the second case that "[W]e are unable to conclude that openness plays a positive role in special interest deportation hearings at a time when our nation is faced with threats of such profound and unknown dimension" (*North Jersey Media Group v Ashcroft 308 F.3d 198*). The U.S. Supreme Court in 2003 refused to consider the appeal of the New Jersey newspapers, leaving conflicting decisions pending in different jurisdictions (2003 U.S. LEXIS 4082).

If a judge orders a hearing closed when the court is already in session, journalists are trained to stand and ask the judge to halt the proceeding until they can contact lawyers for their news organizations to come to court and argue that the reporters should be allowed to stay in the courtroom. Many reporters carry cards printed with the exact words to read in court.

Sealed Records

In criminal cases, most records are presumed open, including arrest warrants and *returns* (records of action taken under warrants) and police blotters, which chronologically list police actions taken. Similarly, the court *docket,* a chronological record of court activity, is available with some exceptions, such as juvenile records. The Federal Juvenile Decency Act creates a presumption that most juvenile court records in federal courts remain closed unless a child is being prosecuted as an adult. Many states have similar laws.

The news media may attempt to obtain access to closed records by filing motions before or during a trial, although these motions are often unsuccessful. For instance, in 2000, during the federal corruption trial of four-time former Louisiana Governor

Edwin Edwards, almost all 1,500 records filed in the case remained sealed until after the trial (*U.S. v Edwards*), as did most records that year in the trial of David Alan Westerfield for the kidnapping and murder of 7-year-old Danielle Van Dam (*In re Copley Press [California v Westerfield]*). Many records remained sealed in cases involving priests charged with sexual abuse, such as the *Rosado* case (*Rosado v Bridgeport Roman Catholic Diocesan Corp*) or in a case involving a grand jury hearing charges of sexual abuse by priests in Los Angeles (*Los Angeles Times v Supr Ct, 2003*). And in 2003 the media failed to obtain access to sealed records in the case of NBA star Kobe Bryant who was charged with sexual assault (*Colorado v Bryant*).

However, in the case of seventeen-year-old sniper suspect John Lee Malvo, although his 2002 preliminary hearing in Baltimore was closed, in 2003, a magistrate granted the *Washington Post*'s motion and allowed access to the Malvo hearing transcript and to his other juvenile records (*In re Washington Post Motion to Open Juvenile Detention Hearing*).

Similarly, a coalition of media organizations including Dow Jones fought to open corporate documents in the case of Enron, the defendant in a class-action securities fraud case. After a judge in 2002 denied Enron's request for a blanket order sealing all 19 million documents involved, the corporation filed a second request to prevent access to documents that included those pertaining to personnel information, past legal matters, sales of assets, and "competitively sensitive" information. In 2003, the judge rejected Enron's request, saying the categories were too broad, and she ordered the company to keep a log of documents and to separate nonconfidential documents on a continuous basis (*In re Enron Corp Securities Litigation [Newby v Enron]*). The media will not obtain automatic access, but the litigants may disclose nonconfidential documents if they so choose. Furthermore, the media may challenge the categorization of a document as confidential.

Laws passed after the terrorist attacks on September 11, 2001, such as the USA Patriot Act of 2001, made it more difficult for journalists to obtain records regarding surveillance information. The Homeland Security Act, passed in 2002, criminalized leaks of information and gave immunity from prosecution to businesses that shared information with the government. The American Civil Liberties Union (ACLU) and other groups resisted the Patriot Act and laws such as the Domestic Security Enhancement Act (nicknamed the "Patriot Act II") proposed in 2003.

The press has had some success in obtaining documents but only after court fights. For instance, after motions for access, the government eventually released the transcripts of closed hearings in the Michigan deportation case of Rabih Haddad, a special interest detainee after the events of September 11, 2001 (*Detroit Free Press v Ashcroft*). And after a motion by a coalition of news groups, a state judge in New Jersey agreed to release the transcripts of a hearing in the case of Mohammed El-Atriss, who admitted he sold fake documents to two of the September 11th hijackers (*In re New Jersey v Mohammed El-Atriss*). In 2002, a federal judge in Colorado denied access to a hearing involving James Ujaama, accused of supporting the Taliban with computer equipment and plans to set up a terrorist training camp in Oregon. Ujaama pleaded guilty and agreed to serve as a witness in another terrorist case.

In 2003, media groups (including the major television networks and newspapers) filed a lawsuit to obtain access to court records in the criminal case of accused terrorist Zacarias Moussaoui. French-Moroccan Moussaoui was the only U.S. defendant charged in a civilian criminal court as a conspirator in connection with the September 11, 2001, terrorist attacks. He represented himself, with the assistance of standby lawyers. The federal appellate court held that unclassified documents attached to the *Moussaoui* case's appendices should be released on a document-by-document basis, provided the First Amendment presumption outweighed the need for secrecy (*In re U.S. v Moussaoui*). In a similar case, the Center for National Security Studies filed a Freedom of Information (FoI) complaint to obtain information about detainees. Although a federal district court in 2002 said the government should release some of the information, an appellate court in 2003 reversed the lower court and said the information could remain sealed (*Center for National Security Studies et al. v U.S. Department of Justice*).

Evidence

Rules on access to evidence are not universal, and often such rules are not clearly defined by the courts. Generally, the public has access to evidence that has been filed with the clerk, but courts are divided on whether there is a right to copy exhibits and taped evidence used in trials.

In the O. J. Simpson criminal case, journalists successfully used the California Public Records Act to obtain copies of the tapes of 911 calls Nicole Simpson had made during earlier domestic disturbances. (The tapes were released just in time for the local five o'clock television newscasts and received wide coverage, which led to defense charges that the prosecution was attempting to manipulate public opinion before a jury had been selected.) Later, Judge Lance Ito denied the news media permission to copy at least three of the most gruesome photographs of the murder victims; he speculated that they would use the photos in an inappropriate and sensationalistic manner (*California v Simpson*).

As discussed in Chapter 1, the press was also unsuccessful in attempts to obtain access to sealed documents in the *McVeigh* case (*U.S. v McVeigh and Nichols*, 119 F.3d 806). But some documents were eventually unsealed in the sexual harassment case related to the Clinton impeachment (*Jones v Clinton*), and there are other recent examples of successful media access.

For instance, a Pennsylvania court supported post-trial access to a videotaped confession of a convicted murderer (*Commonwealth of Pennsylvania v Gallman*). And in a trial involving charges of police misconduct, a New Jersey court ordered the police department to release to *The Daily Journal* in Vineland the 911 audiotapes used as evidence (*In re Daily Journal v Police*).

However, in a noted case involving the death of race-car driver Dale Earnhardt, the courts upheld a decision denying public access to the autopsy photos (*Earnhardt v Volusia County Office of Medical Examiner*). Florida legislators then passed a retroactive law requiring confidentiality of all photographic, audio, and video records of autopsies. The law, although challenged, has become a model for several other states.

For example, in a 2003 California case that received wide publicity, Scott Peterson was charged with the murder of his pregnant wife, Laci, and their unborn son. During the pretrial proceedings, the court granted some media motions to open records such as death certificates stating the cause of death but kept search warrants and autopsy records closed, at least until a later hearing (*California v Peterson*, 2003).

Electronic Records

More and more court records are available online. The National Center for State Courts (NCSC) has set up an online information clearinghouse at http://www.ncsc.online.org with links to state court and federal court websites as well as to court records available to the public. The NCSC and the State Justice Institute (SJI) in 2002 issued guidelines for policy development regarding electronic access, with a report including recommendations for state legislatures to follow in attempting to balance privacy and access concerns (NCSC/SJI 2002). A coalition of media groups issued a report critical of some aspects of the guidelines and calling for a presumption of openness (Reporters Committee 2002).

The federal courts have set up an online service, PACER (Public Access to Court Electronic Records), at http://www.pacer.psc.uscourts.gov As of this writing, PACER currently allows up to ten dollars' worth of free access per year to selected records and charges seven cents a page thereafter. The Judicial Conference of the United States—the governing body on federal courts—has voted to extend online access to certain federal criminal files, such as those involving the suspects in the September 11, 2001, terrorist incidents. The conference also conducted an experiment with online access to criminal records in one appellate court and in ten trial courts. The conference later voted to continue the experiment, while keeping certain information such as home address sealed.

The U.S. Supreme Court also has a website at http://www.supremecourtus.gov Included are dockets, transcripts of oral arguments and briefs, opinions, and media advisories in high-profile cases.

Several private services also provide online public access to case records, including Lexis One and West Doc; law schools at Cornell, Emory, Northwestern, and Stanford universities; and Online Legal Services.

Civil Cases

In a *civil action,* instead of the state's prosecuting a defendant for breaking a law, a plaintiff—usually a private citizen—sues another person or a corporation to resolve some conflict. The goal of a plaintiff is to be compensated for the alleged wrong, usually by payment of money by the defendant (or *respondent*). As with criminal cases, about 90 to 95 percent of civil cases never make it to trial but are settled beforehand.

Many participants in civil court desire privacy, and civil court judges often grant requests for sealed records, particularly denying access to *depositions*—sworn testimony taken outside of court prior to trial during the investigative process known as *discovery.* Sometimes the press is successful in winning access to depositions, such as those given by Microsoft's Bill Gates (*U.S. v Microsoft*, 334 U.S. Ct. Appl., D.C. 165), discussed in Chapter 1. This is especially significant in major class-action lawsuits, in which plaintiffs' lawyers file suits on behalf of large groups or classes of people who are affected by the defendant's actions. For instance, in the 1994 *Domestic Air Transportation Antitrust Litigation,* an airline-rate case, more than 4 million people were owed money due to the airlines' misconduct. The judge unsealed the records regarding airline payments to the plaintiffs. In a 2001 case involving tire manufacturer Bridgestone/Firestone, after the *Chicago Tribune* filed motions, the trial court unsealed some records and was ordered by the appellate court to consider unsealing others (*Chicago Tribune v Bridgestone/Firestone*). In 2002 and 2003, sealed records in cases of sexual abuse of children by Catholic priests became the subject of proposals for rules banning secret settlements.

In a 1999 suit filed by an NBC television affiliate, the California Supreme Court ruled that court records in a contract dispute between actor Clint Eastwood and his former companion Sondra Locke should be opened. The court held that access demonstrates that justice is meted out fairly, allows citizens to keep watch for abuse, and enhances truth finding (*NBC [KNBC-TV] v Superior Court of Los Angeles County*). California then passed rules prohibiting sealed records in civil cases without good reason, and similar legislation is pending in other states.

There is a growing trend, referred to generically as *alternative dispute resolution*, toward settling civil disputes out of court. Or a case may begin in a civil court and be moved to a nonjudicial forum. In *arbitration*, both sides usually are bound by the decision of an appointed referee. In *mediation*, a mediator counsels both sides in an attempt to help the parties reach a compromise. Such settlements are generally closed to the public unless one of the parties is a public body or unless the parties submitted the settlement to a court for public approval.

In 2002, the American Bar Association (ABA) approved the Uniform Mediation Act, which may be adopted on a state-by-state basis. The act would allow each state to decide what information would be kept sealed from the public, but it recognizes that some states require revealing information if public safety is at stake.

Plea Bargains

At any point before a trial, a criminal defendant may agree to accept a *plea bargain*. Generally the process is conducted in private, with lawyers for both sides working out the agreement. The state is often willing to reduce the charges in order to persuade the defendant to plead guilty, thus avoiding a lengthy, costly trial that the state might lose if the defendant were acquitted. The defendant is often willing to accept a lower penalty for a lesser crime in order to avoid the risk of a conviction on the original charges. After agreement is reached, the participants schedule a hearing in open court for the judge to approve the deal.

The public may not even learn of the plea bargain until it is presented in court. In some cases, the results of the plea bargain, although approved in open court, are then sealed. Since anywhere from one-half to two-thirds of criminal cases end in a plea bargain, there is much controversy over whether journalists should be allowed to observe the process in order to share with the public the reasons why the state chooses not to proceed to trial in the majority of criminal cases.

Prejudicial Publicity

In order to maintain the likelihood of impartial jurors, the presiding judge in a high-profile case may take certain steps to avoid possible effects of prejudicial publicity caused by news media coverage. For instance, before the trial the judge may move the case to a different *venue* (location) where fewer people have firsthand knowledge of the case, as the federal court did in moving the Oklahoma City bombing cases to Denver (*U.S. v McVeigh and Nichols*, 918 F. Supp. 1467), and as the courts ordered in the trials of Lee Boyd Malvo and John Allen Muhammed, in the Washington, D.C., area sniper case (*In re Commonwealth of Virginia v Malvo [and Muhammed]*). Or a judge may *continue* (delay) a trial until some of the intense publicity has died down. In some cases, the *venire* (jury pool, or the group of people from which the jury is selected) may be brought in from outside the place where the events occurred.

Once jury selection begins, the judge must see that care is taken to eliminate any biased jurors. This is accomplished by carefully questioning prospective jurors during the *voir dire* (jury selection) process. Anyone who says he would be unable to forget about what he has learned about the case from the news coverage should be excused from serving for that reason ("for cause"). Each side also has a limited number of *peremptory challenges*, by which a potential juror may be excused for no reason, as long as it is not related to the person's race or gender.

Additionally, a decision may be made to *sequester* (isolate) the jurors during a trial in order to avoid exposure to prejudicial publicity, as was done with the jurors in the O. J. Simpson case. And the judge will frequently *admonish* (warn) the jurors not to follow coverage of the case in newspapers, magazines, broadcast outlets, or on the Internet.

It has become clear from such cases as the murder trial of O. J. Simpson and the McVeigh and Nichols trials in the Oklahoma City bombings that it is very difficult to avoid prejudicial publicity. Due to modern communications—twenty-four-hour broadcast news stations, not to mention the Internet and World Wide Web—concerns are heightened regarding the ability of defendants in high-profile cases to obtain a fair trial with impartial jurors.

Gag Orders

At any point in a court case, a judge may issue a *"gag"* order (restraining order) on trial participants, including the lawyers, witnesses, and even the defendants in the case. A gag order forbids a trial participant from speaking to anyone outside the court about the details of the case. As with access cases, journalists may challenge such orders by filing motions asking that the orders be rescinded. Such motions were filed in a 2000 Arkansas case involving a juvenile (*Arkansas Democrat-Gazette v Zimmerman*) and in a 2002 Georgia case involving the operator of a crematorium who was arrested in connection with the finding of 300 unburied corpses (*Georgia v Marsh*). In both cases, the press was successful in modifying the gag orders.

However, more often the press is unsuccessful in attempting to have gag orders lifted. For instance, as mentioned in Chapter 1, the news media failed to have gag orders lifted in either the *Simpson* civil trial (*Rufo v Simpson*) or in the *McVeigh* case (*U.S. v*

McVeigh and Nichols, 931 F. Supp. 753; 964 F. Supp. 313). In the *Clinton* case, witness Monica Lewinsky was bound by a gag order under terms of an immunity agreement with prosecutor Kenneth Starr. Despite motions by the *Houston Chronicle,* gag orders were also upheld in the 2001 Texas murder trial of Andrea Yates, convicted of drowning her five children (*In re Houston Chronicle*).

One of the most extreme examples was the gag order on trial participants including the defendant, former Louisiana Governor Edwin Edwards, in the federal corruption case mentioned earlier (*U.S. v Edwards*). A gag order was also upheld in another federal case involving Edwards and Louisiana Insurance Commissioner Jim Brown, despite the fact that the objection to the gag came from the codefendant Jim Brown rather than the media (*U.S. v Brown*). In 2003, the media were unsuccessful in fighting a gag order in the case of sniper suspects Lee Boyd Malvo and John Muhammed (*In re Commonwealth of Virginia v Malvo [and Muhammed]*), as well as in the case of Scott Peterson, accused of murdering his wife, Laci (*California v Peterson,* 2003).

Judges

All judges must follow codes of ethics that require them to maintain neutrality (see Chapter 5). Federal judges are appointed via a political process that itself is often the subject of great public scrutiny. Access to information on federal judges is controversial, as evidenced by the uproar in 2000 when APBNews.com, the (now defunct) crime and court news website, sued to be allowed to publish federal judges' financial records (*APBNews.com v Committee on Financial Disclosure*).

Sitting judges have been criticized for even talking to journalists. Judge Lance Ito, who presided over the *Simpson* criminal case discussed in Chapter 1, was criticized for participating in a five-part television interview prior to the trial, as well as for granting requests of other judges, writers, and celebrity reporters to sit in on portions of the case and to visit with him in his chambers. A superior court judge in California was censured in 1998 on grounds that included talking with journalists about some unique sentences he had imposed (*Broadman v Commission on Judicial Performance*). And as mentioned in Chapter 1, the presiding judge in the Microsoft antitrust case was banned by the appellate court in 2001 from hearing the retrial on the grounds that he had presented an appearance of partiality by talking to reporters before issuing his final decision (*U.S. v Microsoft*, 253 F.3d 34 at 106–118).

As many as 90 percent of state judges are elected. In 2002, in a case involving the Republican Party of Minnesota the U.S. Supreme Court held that a rule prohibiting judges running for office from publicly announcing their views on controversial issues was unconstitutional (*Republican Party of Minnesota v White*). The speculation was that now judges may be subjected to more extensive press coverage since they may be more open when running for office and may answer more media questions (see Chapter 3).

Contempt Citations

A trial judge has great power to find someone in contempt of court, punishable by a fine and even a jail sentence. In the *Simpson* criminal case, several reporters were *subpoenaed* (ordered to appear in court under threat of contempt) in attempts to discover the source of leaked information. Judge Lance Ito also threatened several others with contempt, removed two reporters from the courtroom for whispering too loudly during proceedings, and reprimanded a reporter for chewing gum in a distracting manner. During the trial, he controlled a hidden security camera used to catch courtroom miscreants.

A widely publicized contempt conviction involved Vanessa Leggett, an author writing about a Texas murder case in 2001. Leggett refused to reveal her sources, and the judge who had subpoenaed her jailed her for a record 168 days. The U.S. Supreme Court refused to hear her appeal (*Leggett v U.S., In re Grand Jury Subpoenas*). In 2002, another writer was threatened with a subpoena to find the source of leaked information in the case of the American Taliban fighter John Walker Lindh (*U.S. v Lindh*), but the issue became moot when Lindh pled guilty.

Judges also have found in contempt reporters covering civil cases. One judge cited two reporters for publishing information about a civil case settlement involving Conoco Oil after a court clerk mistakenly gave one of them records meant to be sealed (*Ashcraft v Conoco*).

Lawyers

Lawyers, like judges, are officers of the court, sworn to uphold the rights of all. As with judges, lawyers are bound by their own canons and codes of conduct (see Chapter 5). For instance, although they may discuss a case in general, they are limited in discussing the specifics of a case.

Lawyers have challenged the rules limiting their speech. In a 1991 U.S. Supreme Court case from Nevada (*Gentile v State Bar of Nevada*), the Court said that such rules must be specific or they might violate the lawyer's First Amendment rights (see Chapter 3).

There is a growing trend among lawyers to apply "spin control" in cases in which they represent high-profile defendants. Dozens of lawyers, such as O. J. Simpson defense attorney Robert Shapiro, have written articles describing how to manipulate the press. Shapiro advises lawyers to pick out the "precise words you want aired. . . . Repeat them continuously and they will be repeated by the media. After a while, the repetition almost becomes a fact. That is your ultimate goal" (Shapiro 1994, 29).

The field of litigation public relations (PR) has recently become a new specialty for professional PR practitioners. Some law firms employ full-time "spin doctors" to deal with the news media coverage of clients' high-profile cases. This controversial practice is (understandably) not widely publicized.

Anonymous Juries

Juror secrecy is an issue of growing concern. It will be remembered that the judge in the Oklahoma City bombing case had a wall built that partially obscured the jurors from public view. Also in federal court, a case involving Louisiana politician Carl Cleveland and others included anonymous jurors, with bans on juror interviews in effect continuing even after the verdicts (*In re U.S. v Cleveland*). In New Jersey in 2002, reporters were charged with contempt of court for violating orders not to contact jurors after a mistrial in the case of a rabbi accused of murdering his wife; the contempt was upheld by the state supreme court, and the U.S. Supreme Court in 2003 refused to hear the appeal (*In re Philadelphia Newspapers v New Jersey and Fred Neulander*).

However, in a 1998 case involving the Arizona trial of former U.S. Senator John Symington, a federal appellate court held that the judge who had closed hearings held during jury deliberations had been wrong to do so (*Phoenix News v U.S. District Court*). In 2001, the Kentucky Supreme Court in a case involving

Cape Publications held that a judge had improperly banned access to jurors in a murder case (*Cape Publications v Braden*).

In 2002, the Missouri Supreme Court first ruled that jurors' names should be presumed sealed from the public. The action came after a prisoner who had served sixteen years of a life sentence was released because the jury had not known witnesses against her had made deals with prosecutors, and representatives of the *Montel Williams* talk show had attempted to obtain the names of the jurors in the case. However, media representatives met with the Missouri Supreme Court justices, and the meeting eventually led instead to the presumption of access to jurors' names.

In Ohio, the *Akron Beacon Journal* fought to obtain access to juror lists and questionnaires during a murder trial. The Ohio Supreme Court held in 2002 that the material was not public record, but that the First Amendment required a presumed right of access. Certain information, including Social Security and driver's license numbers, may be excluded from revelation (*In re Beacon Journal Publishing Company v Bond*).

In 2002, PBS-TV's *Frontline,* which had taped juror deliberations in two other states, was granted permission to tape deliberations in a Texas murder case for a documentary on the death penalty, but an appellate court ruled in 2003 that taping of jurors was forbidden under Texas law (*[Texas v Poe] in re Texas v Harrison*). Meanwhile, in 2003, the Colorado courts followed those in Arizona and granted ABC-TV permission to include jury deliberations in its coverage of criminal trials for its program *State v.* The programs will air only after verdicts in the cases covered.

The U.S. Supreme Court

A new term of the U.S. Supreme Court begins each year on the first Monday of October and runs through early July. When the Court "sits" to hear opinions on Mondays through Wednesdays, the public and press are allowed to observe from 10 AM to 3 PM each day. Each argument lasts about an hour, thirty minutes per side. Opinions are generally released on Tuesday and Wednesday mornings and on the third Monday of each sitting. In May and June, the Court sits only to announce orders and opinions. Copies of the opinions are available from the Public Information Office about thirty minutes after they are announced.

As of 2003, fewer than a dozen reporters regularly covered the proceedings of the U.S. Supreme Court, including those from several large newspapers as well as the wire services Associated Press (AP) and Reuters. None of the major television networks had a full-time reporter on the U.S. Supreme Court beat, nor did the major national newsweeklies. There was room for about three dozen members of the press corps in the Supreme Court courtroom, with access controlled by the Court's Public Information Office. The inadequacy of press coverage of the Supreme Court has been the subject of some academic research (see Chapter 5).

Courtroom Cameras

The controversy regarding courtroom cameras has been around for nearly seventy years. As of 2003, all fifty states permit some type of camera coverage, whether on an experimental or permanent basis. Most states allow coverage of both trial and appellate courts; a few allow coverage of appellate courts or of trial courts only. In 2000, Court TV sued for access to the controversial trial of four police officers charged with the murder of an unarmed African immigrant, and although a New York trial judge struck the ban (*In re Court TV [New York v Boss]*), a higher court upheld the constitutionality of the ban on camera use (*Court TV v New York*).

In 1996, the Judicial Conference of the United States voted to let each of the thirteen circuits decide whether to allow cameras in federal appellate courts; only the circuits headquartered in New York and California have voted to do so. About a dozen judges in the ninety-four federal trial courts have permitted camera coverage of some isolated cases in recent years.

The U.S. Supreme Court does not allow photographic or broadcast coverage of proceedings, with few exceptions such as the delayed audio taping of two hearings in the 2000 *Bush-Gore* election case (mentioned in Chapter 1). A third instance of granting of access occurred in April 2003, when the Court released a tape of the two-hour proceedings in a Michigan affirmative-action case right after the arguments (*Grutter v Bollinger; Gratz v Bollinger*). And in late 2003, the Court also allowed audiotaping of arguments in the campaign finance reform case (*McConnell v Federal Elections Commission*). However, audio tapes of Court arguments are usually not available from the National Archives until months after a court session ends. And there is only one known still photograph of the Court in session, taken secretly in 1935.

An incident that many observers consider emblematic of the High Court's aversion to broadcast coverage occurred in 2003. Justice Antonin Scalia was awarded the City Club of Cleveland's Citadel of Free Speech Award honoring his support of First Amendment issues. However, in an ironic move, the justice made a condition of his acceptance speech the banning of broadcasts of the award proceedings.

Congress has been considering passing the "Sunshine in the Courtroom Act," which would allow coverage of all federal courts at the discretion of the presiding judge. Bills were introduced from 1997 to 2003. Traditional objections to courtroom cameras include their presumed impact on the process of the trial, possible violation of the privacy of witnesses, and the added administrative burden on the court. However, the great majority of studies fail to support speculation that cameras interfere with the judicial process (see Chapter 5).

Court TV today reaches more than 70 million viewers, and since signing on in 1991, it has covered more than 700 cases of the estimated 2 million in the United States each year. As discussed in Chapter 1, these include high-profile trials covered gavel-to-gavel such as the rape trial of William Kennedy Smith, the police brutality trial involving Rodney King, the first murder trials of the Menendez brothers, and the criminal trial of O. J. Simpson.

Although camera coverage of the *McVeigh* bombing cases in 1997 and 1998 was denied, it will be remembered that the court did allow the first-ever closed-circuit broadcast feeds of the trials so that witnesses, victims, and families from Oklahoma City could watch the trial, which had been moved to Denver. As also discussed in Chapter 1, portions of President Clinton's videotaped grand jury testimony were released to broadcasters, and the impeachment hearings themselves were broadcast live; similarly, oral arguments in the appeal in the Microsoft antitrust case were also broadcast. However, motions for camera coverage were denied in the 2003 Washington, D.C., sniper case (*In re Commonwealth of Virginia v Malvo [and Muhammed]*).

In the 2002 case of Zacarias Moussaoui, the first person charged in the September 11, 2001, terrorist attacks, the judge denied the request of Court TV to allow broadcast coverage (*In re U.S. v Moussaoui*, 205 FRD 183). The Terrorist Victims Courtroom Access Act allowed a limited closed-circuit broadcast of the trial, similar to that provided to the families of the victims in the *McVeigh* case.

Virtual Courtrooms

Florida began televising oral arguments live by satellite and over the Internet on an experimental basis beginning in 1997. In 1999, a Florida attempted-murder trial, *Florida v Eagan,* became the first trial netcast in full by a court system live over the Internet. Other jurisdictions have followed suit, such as an Ohio court starting in 1999, the South Dakota Supreme Court proceedings beginning in 2002, and a Nevada courtroom as of 2003.

In 1999, a study for the NCSC predicted that the *"virtual trial,"* a trial taking place all-electronically, was still in the future. Nonetheless, the commentator added that trials with significant portions portrayed electronically were already possible (Lederer 1999). Videoconferencing and online calendaring, video depositions, video witness testimony, and online trial transcripts are already found in courtrooms throughout the country.

It will be remembered that *The Starr Report,* which recommended the impeachment of President Bill Clinton (discussed in Chapter 1), was immediately available on the Internet. One of the grounds for appeal of the conviction in the *McVeigh* case was the publication of reports of McVeigh's confession on Internet websites including that of *The Dallas Morning News.*

At the corruption trial of former Louisiana Governor Edwin Edwards in 2000 (*U.S. v Edwards*), the virtual trial was on its way to becoming a reality. Docket information was posted online on the court's website; the judge, defendants, lawyers, jurors, and members of the press wore headsets allowing them to listen to the extensive audio-taped evidence; the judge could turn on "white noise" to allow only himself, defendants, and lawyers to hear information; and, finally, everyone in the courtroom could view documentary evidence on eight computer terminals shared by jurors and two shared by the public and the press.

Conclusion

Most of the mainstream coverage of the courts is highly regarded. Several reporters have won the Pulitzer Prize, the highest possible award for print journalists, for their outstanding coverage. These include Linda Greenhouse, the U.S. Supreme Court correspondent for *The New York Times;* her predecessor, Anthony Lewis, who retired from journalism in 2001; and Thomas French of the *St. Petersburg Times,* who won for a book-length feature on a murder case. Their work, along with that of such other award-winning journalists as Linda Deutsch, AP correspondent; Fred Graham, current head of Court TV; Tony Mauro, currently with American Lawyer; Tim O'Brien, currently with CNN; and Nina Totenberg, legal affairs correspondent for National Public Radio (NPR), will be discussed more fully in Chapter 4.

Many others such as the following have produced award-winning courtroom coverage for print, broadcast, and the Internet, and several have written book-length works:

- Magazine writer Jonathan Harr won the National Book Award for the best-seller *A Civil Action,* the true story of a courtroom showdown between two giant corporations accused of dumping toxic waste that caused twelve deaths, including those of eight children. The book also was adapted as a feature film starring John Travolta, and a student case-study book has been published.
- Edward Humes, Pulitzer Prize–winning journalist, is the author of *Mississippi Mud,* the story of the Dixie Mafia's corruption of city government in Biloxi, Mississippi, with crimes extending to the murders of Judge Vincent Sherry and his mayoral candidate–wife Margaret—and the involvement of Judge Sherry's law partner.
- Another Pulitzer winner, James Stewart of *The Wall Street Journal*, has written several book-length investigations, such as *Blind Eye*, the story of how a handsome young medical doctor who became a serial murderer of his patients avoided detection by the medical establishment.
- Award-winning *New York Times* writer Kurt Eichenwald in 2000 published *The Informant*, a fascinating story of the FBI and U.S. Justice Department investigations of the international criminal conspiracy involving Archer Daniel Midlands.
- Former *The Times-Picayune* (New Orleans) and current *Miami Herald* reporter Tyler Bridges wrote a book in 2001, *Bad Bet on the Bayou*, which tells the story of four-time Louisiana Governor Edwin Edwards's thirty years of

trials and tribulations, including the riverboat-casino licensing case, which was his Waterloo.

- Maurice Possely, award-winning legal reporter for the *Chicago Tribune,* is the co-author of *Everybody Pays,* a 2001 in-depth look at a murder case and the effects in human terms of the corrupt justice system in Chicago.

These writers and others, such as John Berendt, author of *Midnight in the Garden of Good and Evil,* a "nonfiction novel" about a Savannah murder case (the book was on the best-seller list for nearly four years and the movie was a commercial success), have written so many best-sellers that "true crime" books now occupy a separate section in most bookstores.

Courtroom journalists have written stories that reveal numerous abuses in the criminal justice system, including police misconduct and bribes to fix murder cases, discrimination in setting bail, prosecutorial misconduct, incompetent defense lawyers, disparities in sentencing, and mistreatment of prisoners. Coverage of the civil-court system has exposed growing evidence of perjury by plaintiffs, defendants, witnesses, and even lawyers. News stories have focused on such systematic problems as the trend toward not publishing opinions in official reporters (thus avoiding public scrutiny), as well as the growing acceptance of motions "*to vacate*," by which parties settle out of court, and miscreant corporations force sealed records and even insist on the wiping of the opinion off the books as conditions of settlement.

The work of journalists has led to instances where after investigative stories were published, wrongly convicted criminal defendants have been freed. One of the pioneers in this type of journalism was the *Miami Herald's* Gene Miller. Miller was awarded the Pulitzer Prize for his stories that resulted in the release of Florida death-row inmates Freddie Pitts and Willie Lee in 1975. Numerous journalists have written similar stories with similar results.

Michael Mello, the lawyer for a man who was wrongfully convicted of murder, credits the *Miami Herald's* eleventh-hour stories inspired by Miller for saving his client from execution in 1995. Since 1996, Northwestern University journalism students and their professor David Protess have seen their efforts investigating old murder cases bring results: 4 men who had spent 18 years in prison were released in 1996; a man who had spent 17 years on Death Row was freed in 1999. In 2001, Illinois Governor George Ryan halted all executions pending a study of capital cases, and in 2003, citing the work of the Northwestern University students and the *Chicago Tribune,* he commuted the sentences of 167 prisoners on death row.

Steve Weinberg, a veteran investigative journalist active in the Investigative Reporters and Editors organization (IRE), joined Neil Gordon, a researcher with the public watchdog organization the Center for Public Integrity (http://www.public integrity.org), on a project investigating prosecutorial misconduct leading to wrongful convictions at the federal, state, and local levels.

On the other hand, as seen in Chapter 1, media coverage of the criminal justice system is often the deserving subject of charges of sensationalism. Some practices, particularly the excesses of the sensationalistic "tabloid" media, have had an impact on the judicial process. For instance, *"checkbook journalism"*—payment by media organizations to potential witnesses to tell their stories prior to testifying in court—had an impact in California cases. It led to the canceling of appearances of several witnesses (such as a cutlery-store owner and a Brentwood neighbor) in the O. J. Simpson criminal trial. As a result of paid appearances on tabloid television shows, witnesses' appearances were also canceled in the murder trials of Eric and Lyle Menendez.

After the *Simpson* case, California—seemingly the center of such sensationalized coverage—attempted to solve the aforementioned problem when legislators passed laws making it a crime for prospective witnesses to accept money from the media or for jurors to sell their stories less than ninety days after the end of the trials on which they had served. However, both laws were successfully challenged on constitutional grounds and such practices continue.

The current trend in ownership of media companies is for traditional news organizations to be taken over by giant conglomerates that have themselves often been the subject of charges of wrongdoing. Corporation accountants with an eye toward maintaining huge profits in order to keep stockholders and Wall Street advisors happy are replacing professional journalists as decision makers at even the most respectable news organizations. Thus, the trend toward tabloidization of news, and the accompanying sensationalistic coverage, is spreading from supermarket tabloids such as *Globe* and television programs such as *Entertainment Tonight* to more established news organizations.

The authors of a book-length study *Tabloid Justice* (Fox and Van Sickel 2001) conducted a national poll and concluded that the tabloidization of trial coverage has misled the public about how the criminal justice system works, has contributed to a loss of public interest in more significant issues, and in some ways may have contributed to diminishing public confidence in the criminal justice system.

Lawyer Lincoln Caplan described what he called "The Failure (and Promise) of Legal Journalism" even at traditional news outlets. He said that courtroom journalism stresses personalities of court participants over ideas, narrowly focuses on proceedings, and often is presented sports style, complete with play-by-play. Caplan suggests that journalists need to provide a frame of reference for their coverage, particularly when providing live coverage of courts (Caplan 1996).

Judges and lawyers have begun taking steps to encourage improvements in coverage of courts. The NCSC has published two editions of a widely available reference book for judges, *Managing Notorious Trials* (Murphy 1998; see Chapter 5). The manual serves as a valuable resource for judges presiding over high-profile trials and includes specific suggestions for dealing with the press, rules concerning electronic media coverage, and other tips on balancing rights guaranteed under the Constitution.

Numerous courts around the states sponsor bench/media forums where judges and journalists can work on improving relations between the courts and the news media. On the federal level, the National Judicial College joined the University of Nevada in creating the Reynolds Center for Courts and the Media in Reno, where two national bench/press/bar conferences have already been held.

As U.S. Supreme Court Justice Stephen Breyer told the Inter-American Press Association in 2002, even those on the High Court have to learn to get along with the press: "We need the press because it is the press that sometimes in saying things we don't like at all will convince the public . . . that in fact this is an honest institution" (Breyer 2002).

The ABA has been extremely active in working to enhance press coverage of courts, including producing publications designed to help journalists understand the judicial process (see

Chapter 5) and sponsoring numerous bench/press/bar conferences such as the "Law School for Journalists" forums being held around the country. ABA-accredited law schools are beginning to recognize the need to educate lawyers about the rights and responsibilities involved in press coverage of their work. For instance, since 1999, Vanderbilt Law School has been offering a course entitled "Litigation and Journalism: Client Representation and Ethical Conduct in High Visibility Cases."

Regardless of attempts by the legal profession and judges, the bottom line is that members of the journalism profession need to strive to improve their court coverage. A First Amendment Center study concluded: "The Constitution's promise of a fair trial cannot be left entirely to the courts to fulfill, since courts at every level have shown themselves vulnerable to prejudice, pressure and (occasionally) corruption. As part of its First Amendment duty, the press is responsible for keeping a watchful eye regularly trained on court performance—a duty it is not currently fulfilling" (Westfeldt and Wicker 1998).

Journalism schools recognize the need to better educate aspiring journalists, with the inauguration of courses such as "Covering the Courts," offered by the University of Massachusetts at Amherst. Organizations such as the Society of Professional Journalists (SPJ) and the Radio-Television News Directors Association (RTNDA) have developed codes of ethics requiring adherence to principles of balanced coverage (see Chapter 5). And several organizations such as the Reporters Committee for Freedom of the Press (RCFP) produce a steady stream of materials to aid the courtroom journalist (see Chapter 6).

The work of some of the specific judges, lawyers, and journalists who have contributed to the effort to balance rights and responsibilities in covering the courts will be discussed in Chapter 4. But first, the chronological development of those free press/fair trial ideals will be discussed in the next chapter.

References

Alexander, S. L. 1999. *Covering the Courts: A Handbook for Journalists.* Lanham, MD: University Press of America (rev. 2003 Rowman and Littlefield).

Breyer, Stephen. 2002. Cited by Associated Press. 21 June.

Caplan, Lincoln. 1996. "The Failure (and Promise) of Legal Journalism," in *Postmortem,* ed. Jeffrey Abramson. New York: Basic Books, 199–207.

Fox, Richard, and Robert Van Sickel. 2001. *Tabloid Justice: Criminal Justice in an Age of Media Frenzy.* Boulder, CO: Lynne Rienner Publishers.

Lederer, Fredric. 1999. *The Road to the Virtual Courtroom?* Williamsburg, VA: State Justice Institute/William and Mary Law School.

Murphy, Timothy. 1998. *Managing Notorious Trials.* Williamsburg, VA: National Center for State Courts.

NCSC/SJI (National Center for State Courts/State Justice Institute). 2002. *Developing* CCJ/COSCA Guidelines *for Public Access to Court Records: A National Project to Assist State Courts.* Available at http://www.courtaccess.org/modelpolicy. Accessed 2003.

Reporters Committee for Freedom of the Press. 2002. *Electronic Access to Court Records.* Fall. Available at http://www.rcfp.org. Accessed 2002.

Shapiro, Robert. 1994. "Secrets of a Celebrity Lawyer," *Columbia Journalism Review,* September–October: 25–29.

Westfeldt, Wallace, and Tom Wicker. 1998. *Indictment: The News Media and the Criminal Justice System.* Nashville, TN: First Amendment Center.

3

Chronology

The development of the free press/fair trial conflict is best illustrated by tracing the treatment of the matter through decisions of the U.S. Supreme Court. A brief glance at the inspiration for the conflict more than 200 years ago will be followed by a description of related events of the twentieth century into the new millennium, including major Supreme Court cases. Other significant events include advancements in the use of courtroom cameras and the latest technology as the digital age begins.

The Bill of Rights:
The Free Press/Fair Trial Conflict Begins

1791   The free press/fair trial conflict was born when the first ten amendments, called the Bill of Rights, were added to the U.S. Constitution. Designed to limit the power of the federal government and to retain for individuals and state governments all rights not explicitly granted to the federal government, the Bill of Rights included the First Amendment, which guarantees individual liberties in the areas of religion, expression, assembly, and grievances. According to the language of the First Amendment: "Congress shall make no law respecting an establishment of religion, or prohibiting the free exercise thereof; or abridging the freedom of speech, or of the press, or the right of the people peaceably to assemble, and to petition the Government for a redress of grievances."

At the same time (and given the same weight, for the order of the amendments was insignificant, and the first actually started out as the third), the Sixth Amendment was dedicated to assuring that anyone accused of a crime would not suffer bewildering secrecy as in the British legal system but would be assured a fair—and very public—trial. According to the language of the Sixth Amendment: "In all criminal prosecutions, the accused shall enjoy the right to a speedy and public trial, by an impartial jury of the State and district wherein the crime shall have been committed; which district shall have been previously ascertained by law, and to be informed of the nature and cause of the accusation; to be confronted with the witnesses against him; to have compulsory process for obtaining witnesses in his favor, and to have the assistance of counsel for his defense.'

No one could foresee at the time the conflict between the First Amendment guarantee of a free press and the Sixth Amendment right to a fair trial with an impartial jury. Although there were occasional references to the problem—such as Aaron Burr's 1807 complaint that press coverage of his trial was interfering with his right to an impartial jury, as well as a handful of other cases—the conflict did not reach the status of an important issue until well into the twentieth century.

The Twentieth Century

1931   *Near v Minnesota.* In a 5 to 4 decision, the U.S. Supreme Court held in this landmark case that a Minnesota statute that prohibited publication of a certain sensationalistic newspaper, which ran stories critical of government officeholders, was unconstitutional because it imposed a *prior restraint* on criticism of public officials, a violation of the First Amendment's ban against abridging freedom of the press. Via a complex reasoning process referred to as *incorporation*, the Court also said that the Fourteenth Amendment due process clause meant that the First Amendment ban against the federal government's interference with a free press ("*Congress* shall make no law. . .") also applied to other levels of government, such as the state statute in this case. Since this case, the protection from interference by the federal government coupled with individual liberties provided by the Bill of Rights also extends to protection from interference by other levels of government. The history of free press/fair trial cases includes conflicts between the press and not only the federal courts, but also state and municipal courts as well.

1937   Canon 35. After the sensationalistic coverage of the New Jersey trial of Bruno Hauptmann for the kidnap and murder of the Lindbergh baby (discussed in Chapter 1), the American Bar Association (ABA) voted in a blanket ban on courtroom cameras, which appeared in the *ABA Reports* as "Canon 35." According to Canon 35:

Proceedings in court should be conducted with fitting dignity and decorum. The taking of photographs in the courtroom during sessions of the court or recesses between sessions, and the broadcasting of such proceedings are calculated to detract from the essential dignity of the proceedings, degrade the court, and create misconceptions with respect thereto in the minds of the public and should not be permitted. (American Bar Association 1937, 1134–1135)

1941   *Bridges v California.* In the first noted contempt-of-court case, the U.S. Supreme Court held that neither private citizens nor the press could be held in contempt of court merely for publicly criticizing judges' actions. Two cases were heard together. In the first, a labor official had been found in contempt for comments he wrote in a telegram. These comments, in which he called a judge's decision in a labor action "outrageous" and threatened a strike if the decision were enforced, were reported in a newspaper. In the second, the *Los Angeles Times* editorialized that a judge should choose prison sentences rather than probation for labor-union members convicted of assault. The contempt citations were based on charges of attempting to intimidate the judge to decide a certain way. The Court voted 5 to 4 that judges could not hold journalists in con-

1941,   tempt for publishing such comments unless, as Justice
cont.   Black said, speaking for the Court, there was an "ex-
        tremely high" likelihood of their causing some "ex-
        tremely serious" evil (at 262).

1946   *Pennekamp v Florida.* This was a contempt case similar to
        Bridges v California, this time regarding two newspaper
        editorials and a cartoon criticizing a judge's actions as
        too favorable to criminals and gambling interests. Al-
        though there were minor inaccuracies in the *Miami Her-
        ald* editorials written by John Pennekamp, the Court
        voted 7 to 0 that the comments did not interfere with the
        judicial process. Speaking for the Court, Justice Reed
        said that the "danger under this record to fair judicial
        administration has not the clearness and immediacy
        necessary to close the door to permissible public com-
        ment" (at 350).

        Rule 53, *Federal Rules of Criminal Procedure.* This rule pro-
        vided for a flat ban on the use of cameras (and radio
        broadcasting equipment) in courtrooms in federal courts.
        According to the rule, "the taking of photographs in the
        courtroom during the progress of judicial proceedings or
        radio broadcasting of judicial proceedings from the
        courtroom shall not be permitted by the court."

1947   *Craig v Harney.* The U.S. Supreme Court found that a con-
        tempt citation against a newspaper for editorials that
        criticized a judge was unconstitutional. Speaking for the
        Court, which voted 7 to 2, Justice Reed said the Court
        found no "imminent and serious threat to the ability of
        the court" and overturned the contempt citation (at 378).
        Part of the *Craig v Harney* holding referring to the right of
        the press to cover courts is widely quoted in free
        press/fair trial discussions: "[A] trial is a public event.
        What transpires in the courtroom is public property. . . .
        Those who see and hear what transpired can report it
        with impunity" (at 374).

1952   The ABA revised Canon 35 to add a ban on television
        cameras to the ban on film and broadcast (radio) cover-
        age of trials.

1959   *Marshall v U.S.* The first of five U.S. Supreme Court deci-
       sions that overturned criminal convictions on grounds of
       prejudicial publicity, this case involved the conviction in
       federal court in Colorado of Howard Marshall, charged
       with dispensing prescription drugs without a license. Al-
       though the prosecutor's request to enter into evidence
       two prior convictions for the same crime had been de-
       nied, local newspapers had reported the earlier convic-
       tions. One story claimed Marshall had prescribed drugs
       for singer Hank Williams, who had died in 1953. At least
       seven of the jurors admitted they had read the articles, al-
       though they told the judge they would not let this knowl-
       edge affect their decisions. According to the 8 to 1 deci-
       sion issued *per curiam* (without any explanation of the
       reasoning in the case), the harm that resulted when prej-
       udicial information denied admission into evidence was
       brought before jurors through newspapers meant that a
       new trial was necessary. The Court noted that it was not
       basing the decision on constitutional grounds, but rather
       on its supervisory power over federal courts.

1960   *Irvin v Dowd.* The High Court voted unanimously to
       overturn the murder conviction of Leslie Irvin, described
       as "Mad Dog Irvin" in the intense publicity surrounding
       the case, including reports of his confession to this and
       other murders and polls showing public support for a
       conviction. Dowd was granted a change of venue, but
       only to the next county, and his request to move the trial
       farther away was denied. Ninety percent of the potential
       jurors said they had some degree of belief that Dowd was
       guilty. The Court said the publicity contributed to a "pat-
       tern of deep and bitter prejudice" among the jurors (at
       728). Justice Frankfurter wrote a particularly scathing
       concurrence in which he described the case as a "miscar-
       riage of justice due to anticipatory trial by newspapers
       instead of trial in court before a jury" (at 730). He implied
       that the First Amendment might not be interpreted as al-
       ways protecting the press in such cases: "The Court has
       not yet decided that, while convictions must be reversed
       and miscarriages of justice result because the minds of ju-
       rors or potential jurors are poisoned, the poisoner is con-
       stitutionally protected in plying his trade" (at 761).

1962   *Wood v Georgia.* During an election campaign, incumbent
        sheriff James Wood, while running for re-election, criti-
        cized a judge regarding that judge's instructions to a
        grand jury investigating allegations that candidates were
        paying bribes to African American voters to ensure "Ne-
        gro bloc voting." The court found the sheriff in contempt
        for his criticism, and the Georgia Appeals Court upheld
        the contempt. The Georgia Supreme Court refused to
        hear the case. By a 7 to 2 vote, the U.S. Supreme Court
        overturned the contempt on grounds the comments did
        not create a "clear and present danger" to the administra-
        tion of justice. According to the Court, "Particularly in
        matters of local political corruption and investigations, is
        it important that the freedom of communication be kept
        open" (at 390).

1963   *Rideau v Louisiana.* In another prejudicial-publicity case,
        the Court voted to overturn the conviction of Wilbert
        Rideau, a murderer whose interview with the sheriff—in
        which he confessed to a bank robbery and the subse-
        quent kidnapping of three bank employees, one of whom
        was murdered—had been televised three times in the
        Louisiana parish where the trial was to be held. The 7 to 2
        decision, written by Justice Stewart, held that the trial
        court should have granted Rideau's request for a change
        of venue on due process grounds in order to avoid a jury
        pool of people who had seen the television interview. Ac-
        cording to Stewart: "For anyone who has ever watched
        television, the conclusion cannot be avoided that this
        spectacle, to the tens of thousands of people who saw
        and heard it, in a very sense *was* Rideau's trial—at which
        he pleaded guilty to murder. Any subsequent proceed-
        ings in a community so pervasively exposed to such a
        spectacle could be but a hollow formality" (at 726). A sec-
        ond trial resulted in a second conviction and death sen-
        tence, which was also overturned when a federal judge
        found that potential jurors opposed to the death penalty
        had been excluded. A third conviction resulted in a third
        death sentence, which was commuted to life in 1973
        when the U.S. Supreme Court declared the capital pun-
        ishment laws of the time to be unconstitutional. Finally,
        in 2001 the U.S. Supreme Court let stand a lower court

decision overturning Rideau's third conviction on the grounds that blacks had been excluded from the grand jury that had indicted him. Rideau was immediately re-indicted, and as of 2004, a fourth trial was scheduled. Meanwhile, Wilbert Rideau has become a nationally known prison journalist and has been described widely as the "most rehabilitated prisoner in America."

1965   *Estes v Texas.* The High Court voted 5 to 4 to overturn the swindling conviction of Billie Sol Estes based on denial of due process. During the first trial, a two-day pretrial hearing had been carried live on television and radio, and although live broadcasting was forbidden during the trial itself, silent cameras operated intermittently, and excerpts were shown on the news each night. (In a rare instance, photos—showing the broadcast equipment in the courthouse—were included as an appendix to the Supreme Court decision.) Justice Clark, writing for a *plurality* (representing only four of the five justices voting in the majority), said that television coverage might improperly influence jurors, impair the testimony of witnesses, distract judges, and burden defendants. He said that the mere presence of cameras violated Estes's Sixth Amendment rights. However, Justice Potter Stewart dissented, saying: "The idea of imposing upon any medium of communication the burden of justifying its presence is contrary to where I had always thought the presumption must lie in the area of First Amendment freedoms" (at 615). (Estes was eventually retried and again convicted.)

1966   *Sheppard v Maxwell, Warden.* Discussed at length in Chapter 1, this landmark case dealt with pretrial publicity surrounding the murder trial of Dr. Sam Sheppard, convicted in 1954 of killing his wife. It will be remembered that a three-day inquest had been televised live and that during the trial a debate on the case had also been broadcast live. Also, a prisoner's claim that she had borne Sheppard's child was widely publicized. The U.S. Supreme Court held 8 to 1 in this landmark case that due process had been denied, and the conviction was overturned. However, speaking for the Court, Justice Clark said that the responsibility for the unfair trial was that of

1966, the judge, not the press: "A responsible press has always
cont. been regarded as the handmaiden of effective judicial administration, especially in the criminal field." The press also "guards against the miscarriage of justice by subjecting the police, prosecutors, and judicial processes to extensive public scrutiny and criticism" (at 350). The trial judge could have taken steps to lessen the impact of pretrial publicity, including controlling the behavior of the press inside the courtroom, insulating the witnesses, and controlling the release of information by trial participants.

1972 Canon 3(A) 7. After *Estes* and *Sheppard,* the ABA strengthened its position against courtroom cameras. In the revised Code of Professional Responsibility, Canon 35 became Canon 3(A) 7, generally permitting cameras for educational purposes only and allowing news cameras in courtrooms at the discretion of each state's high court. According to Canon 3(A) 7:

> A judge should prohibit broadcasting, televising, recording or photographing in courtrooms and areas immediately adjacent thereto during sessions of court, or recesses between sessions, except that under rules prescribed by supervising appellate court or other appropriate authority, a judge may authorize broadcasting, televising, recording, and photographing of judicial proceedings in the courtrooms and areas immediately adjacent thereto consistent with the right of the parties to a fair trial and subject to express conditions, limitations, and guidelines which allow such coverage in a manner that will be unobtrusive, will not distract the trial participants, and will not otherwise interfere with the administration of justice. (American Bar Association 1984, *Standards,* 3rd ed. 1997, 53)

Branzburg v Hayes. Three different cases were heard together by the U.S. Supreme Court in this landmark case in which subpoenaed reporters refused to testify in criminal cases. In a Kentucky case, *The Courier-Journal* (Louisville) reporter Paul Branzburg wrote stories describing drug activity and was subpoenaed and ordered to reveal confidential information to grand juries. Massachusetts television reporter Ike Pappas and *New York Times* reporter Earl Caldwell in San Francisco wrote about the Black Panthers and were also subpoenaed by grand juries. The reporters were all found in contempt of court. The U.S. Supreme Court voted 5 to 4, with the decision written by Justice White, that the First Amendment does not protect journalists who witness criminal activity from having to testify before grand juries. Justice White said news gathering is not without some First Amendment protections, but that legislators, not the courts, should decide whether journalists need a privilege protecting them from having to testify. Justice Stewart's dissent included a three-part test to be applied when courts are deciding whether to force journalists to testify: (1) the court must show cause to believe the journalist has relevant information; (2) it must demonstrate that the information cannot be obtained by alternative means; and (3) it must demonstrate a compelling need for the information. This test has been incorporated into most of the shield laws in the states that have passed such laws to protect the rights of journalists subpoenaed to testify. (A subsequent case involved CNN's coverage of deposed Panamanian leader Manuel Noriega, who was standing trial for drug trafficking in the United States. The U.S. Supreme Court in *In re U.S. v Noriega* [1990] refused to hear a case in which the lower court upheld a contempt citation after CNN refused to turn over tapes—made illegally by some unknown party—of Noriega talking to his lawyers in prison).

1972–
1973
In re U.S. v Dickinson. In a case the appellate court called a "civil libertarians' nightmare," the First Amendment right of the press to publish information was pitted against the Sixth Amendment right of the accused to a fair trial. A black civil rights worker in Baton Rouge, Louisiana, was charged with conspiracy to murder the mayor, but state officials were accused of trumping up the murder case solely because of the defendant's civil rights activities. At a hearing in the case, the presiding judge announced that no details of the hearing could be

1972–
1973,
cont.

reported, an order disobeyed by reporters including Larry Dickinson. The U.S. Fifth Circuit Court of Appeals held that the judge's order had been invalid (*In re U.S. v Dickinson*, 465 F.2d 496). However, the court also held that despite the eventual finding of unconstitutionality of the order, journalists must follow orders of the court when they are given. The U.S. Supreme Court refused to hear the case (*In re U.S. v Dickinson*, 414 U.S. 979), which stands in conflict with the 1986 *In re Providence Journal* case discussed later in this chapter.

1975

Cox Broadcasting v Cohn. With an 8 to 1 vote, the U.S. Supreme Court said, in a landmark decision by Justice White, that the government could not punish someone for accurate publication of information obtained from open court records available in connection with a public prosecution. The case involved the violation of a Georgia statute forbidding the publicizing of the name of a rape victim, but the journalist had obtained the name of the victim—who had been raped and murdered—from open court records. The Court did not strike the statute as unconstitutional, and more narrow laws forbidding the public identification of rape victims remain on the books in Georgia and several other states.

Murphy v Florida. Miami's Jack ("Murph the Surf") Murphy was the subject of extensive publicity when he was convicted of stealing the Star of India sapphire from a New York museum in 1964. He was later convicted in a murder case, but before that, he was convicted of robbery. Murphy contended that the robbery conviction should be overturned because his request for a change of venue had been denied and because jurors had been exposed to extensive publicity about his other crimes. The Court, however, voted 8 to 1 to affirm the robbery conviction. Justice Marshall, writing for the majority, said that none of the jurors in the robbery case showed any evidence of prejudice, and anyone who did so had been dismissed during jury selection. Also, Marshall said the news articles had been written seven months before the trial, and there was no evidence the factual stories interfered with Murphy's due process rights. Murphy remained imprisoned until 1986 after he had served seventeen years in prison.

1976   *Nebraska Press Association v Stuart.* Speaking for a unanimous U.S. Supreme Court, Chief Justice Warren Burger held in this landmark case that the trial judge who imposed a gag order against the media in the trial of a farmhand charged with the brutal murders of all six members of a neighboring family should have considered alternative means of protecting the defendant's rights, such as a change of venue or a continuance, rather than restraints on the press. According to Burger, "Pretrial publicity—even pervasive, adverse publicity—does not invariably lead to an unfair trial" (at 554). He concluded that "Prior restraints on speech and publication are the most serious and the least tolerable infringement on First Amendment rights" (at 559). The Court suggested that before a gag order on the press could be implemented, the trial judge should apply the clear and present danger standard as part of the "*Nebraska Press* Test," asking: (1) what is the nature and extent of pretrial coverage; (2) whether other measures could better mitigate prejudicial publicity; and (3) whether the gag order would be effective in reducing the likelihood of interference with the judicial process. A portion of Justice Brennan's concurrence is often quoted when defending the right of the press to have full freedom in coverage of the criminal justice system:

> Secrecy of judicial action can only breed ignorance and distrust of courts and suspicion concerning the competence and impartiality of judges; free and robust reporting, criticism, and debate can contribute to public understanding of the rule of law and to comprehension of the functioning of the entire criminal justice system, as well as improve the quality of that system by subjecting it to the cleansing effects of exposure and public accountability. (at 587)

1977   *Oklahoma Publishing v District Court.* A newspaper published the name and photograph of an eleven-year-old boy charged with second-degree murder, which violated a state law ordering all juvenile hearings closed unless

1977,   specifically ordered open by the court. In a unanimous
cont.   per curiam opinion, the U.S. Supreme Court overturned
the order on the grounds that the identity of the juvenile
had not been obtained unlawfully. According to the
Court, the pretrial order violated the First and Fourteenth Amendments because the state statute represented a prior restraint against publication of truthful information obtained during criminal proceedings.

1978   *Landmark Communication v Virginia. The Virginian Pilot*
printed a story about the activities of the state Judicial
Review Commission, which was investigating a judge on
a misconduct complaint. The state court found that the
paper had violated a state statute that made it a crime for
anyone to divulge the commission's activities. The Virginia Supreme Court upheld the newspaper's conviction.
On a 7 to 0 vote, the U.S. Supreme Court overturned the
lower court. The Court held that the statute violated the
First Amendment and that any risk to the orderly administration of justice could be eliminated through internal
procedures to protect the confidentiality of commission
proceedings.

Nixon v Warner Communications. As discussed in Chapter
1, the U.S. Supreme Court held in the Watergate case,
U.S. v Nixon, that the president had to comply with orders to turn over audiotapes of conversations made in
the Oval Office. The investigation of actions taken by the
president's associates, including breaking into the Democratic National Headquarters located in the Watergate
Building, eventually led to the preparation of impeachment orders and the resignation of President Nixon in
1974. During a related criminal trial of 7 of the president's associates on charges of obstruction of justice, 22
hours of the tapes were played in court and entered into
evidence. The U.S. Supreme Court voted 5 to 4 to uphold
the denial of public access to the tapes. In this case, there
was an alternative plan to release the tapes to the public,
the Presidential Recordings and Materials Preservation
Act. (It will be remembered that the first batch of tapes,
covering 500 hours of the testimony, was released by the
National Archives in 2002.)

1979   *Smith v Daily Mail.* The *Charleston Daily Mail* and *The Charleston Gazette* newspapers published stories identifying a fourteen-year-old boy and describing his arrest in connection with the shooting of a fifteen-year-old classmate. The stories violated a state law that made it a crime for a newspaper to publish, without the written approval of a juvenile court, the name of a minor charged in juvenile court. The West Virginia Supreme Court held that the law was unconstitutional, and the U.S. Supreme Court, voting 8 to 0, agreed. First, the Court noted that the statute punished only newspapers, not broadcasters. Then, as in the Oklahoma and Virginia cases, the Court said that the state interest in protecting the anonymity of the juvenile offender to further his rehabilitation could not justify the statute, which violated the First Amendment.

Gannett v de Pasquale. The defense asked the judge to close a pretrial hearing requesting suppression of evidence in a Rochester, New York, murder case, and when the prosecutor agreed, the judge complied. The next day, a reporter for local Gannett newspapers protested the closure, but the judge refused to vacate his order or to provide a transcript of the hearing. The New York appellate court vacated the judge's order, but the New York high court upheld the closure, and the U.S. Supreme Court, in a 5 to 4 vote, affirmed the decision. The dissenters said, "The Sixth Amendment, in establishing the public's right of access to a criminal trial and pretrial proceeding, also fixes the rights of the press in this regard" (at 446). The public response to this decision was overwhelmingly negative, and a year later, *Richmond News v Virginia,* a landmark case, supported public access to criminal trials. (Later decisions supported public access to pretrial hearings).

1980   *Richmond News v Virginia.* The U.S. Supreme Court, voting 7 to 1 in this landmark case, held that the closure of a murder trial should not have been allowed. Chief Justice Burger, speaking for the court, described the history of open trials and said, "People in an open society do not demand infallibility from their institutions, but it is difficult for them to accept what they are prohibited from ob-

1980, cont.
serving" (at 572). He concluded, "Plainly it would be difficult to single out any aspect of government of higher concern and importance to the people than the manner in which criminal trials are conducted" (at 575). Justice Brennan emphasized the importance of access: "Open trials assure the public that procedural rights are respected, and that justice is afforded equally. Closed trials breed suspicion of prejudice and arbitrariness, which in turn spawns disrespect for the law" (at 595).

1981
Chandler v Florida. After the 1965 *Estes* case (which was not an absolute ban on the use of courtroom cameras), many states banned courtroom cameras, but some began to experiment with camera usage as technology changed. During the Florida experiment, two Miami Beach policemen appealed their burglary convictions on the grounds that the use of news cameras (for three minutes of their trial) had violated their constitutional rights. The Florida appellate court upheld the convictions, and the state supreme court refused to hear the case. Chief Justice Warren Burger delivered the 8 to 0 opinion of the U.S. Supreme Court, concluding that although "dangers lurk in this, as in most experiments," unless television coverage under all conditions were to be prohibited by the Constitution, "the states must be free to experiment" (at 582). (As discussed in Chapter 2, as of 2003, all fifty states allowed some form of camera coverage, and some federal courts also allowed some camera usage.)

1982
Globe Newspaper v Superior Court. The press sought to cover the trial of a tennis pro charged with raping three high-school girls. The judge closed the trial because of a Massachusetts law closing trials involving sex crimes when the victims are under age eighteen, as in this case. The Supreme Judicial Court of Massachusetts upheld the constitutionality of the statute (the defendant was acquitted). In a 6 to 3 vote, the U.S. Supreme Court reversed the decision to close the trial. Justice Brennan wrote that the statute violated the First Amendment and could not be justified despite the interest in protecting victims. Ac-

cording to the Court, mandatory closure cannot be justified in all such cases, although a rule ordering closure on a case-by-case basis would be acceptable.

1984 *Waller v Georgia.* The defendants asked for closure of a pretrial suppression hearing on charges including violation of the Georgia racketeering laws. All the defendants were acquitted on the racketeering charges, but two were convicted on gambling charges, and they appealed their convictions on grounds including the closing of the hearings. The Georgia Supreme Court affirmed the opinion of the lower-court judge. The U.S. Supreme Court reversed and *remanded* (ordered a new trial). According to the Court, the right to a public trial under the Sixth Amendment included suppression hearings. Standards for closing a trial included the showing of likely prejudice of open proceedings, limiting of closure, consideration of reasonable alternatives, and findings on the record that closure is necessary. (In *El Vocero v Puerto Rico*, in a per curiam decision the High Court held in 1993 that trial rules regarding open hearings in Puerto Rico must conform to those on the mainland United States.)

Seattle Times v Rhinehart. A religious group called the Aquarian Foundation sued the *Seattle Times* and the *Walla Walla Union-Bulletin* for libel and invasion of privacy but refused to reveal certain information until the court ordered them to do so. The court denied the newspaper, which was itself a *litigant* (party) in the case, the right to use the information for anything except the lawsuit. The Washington Supreme Court upheld the decision, and the U.S. Supreme Court agreed. The opinion, delivered by Justice Powell, said that since the order was limited to the context of pretrial discovery and did not forbid publication of information gathered from other sources, it did not violate the First Amendment. (Since the *Seattle Times* decision was so narrowly tailored to fit the facts in this specific case, it is not considered the last word on access to records in civil trials.)

1984, *Patton v Yount.* High-school math teacher Jon Yount con-
cont. fessed that a day earlier he had murdered one of his students; he claimed temporary insanity but was convicted
of first-degree murder and sentenced to life. The Pennsylvania Supreme Court held that because Yount had not
been properly read his rights, his trial was unfair and his
conviction was overturned. After he was denied a change
of venue, he was again convicted. The Third Circuit
Court of Appeals agreed with Yount that he had not had
a fair trial due to prejudicial publicity stemming from the
media coverage of the second trial. However, in 1984, by
a 6 to 3 vote, the U.S. Supreme Court disagreed and upheld the conviction. Justice Powell wrote that since the
second trial was held four years after the first, prejudicial
publicity had been greatly diminished: "That time
soothes and erases is a perfectly natural phenomenon, familiar to all" (at 1033).

Press Enterprise v Riverside Superior Court I. During jury
selection in a rape and murder case, the defense was
granted a request to close the court. After the defendant
was convicted and sentenced to death, the press filed repeated motions for access to the jury-selection transcripts, but the judge refused, and the California
Supreme Court upheld his decision. The U.S. Supreme
Court, in a unanimous decision written by Chief Justice
Burger, voted to vacate the judge's decision. The Court
said that under the First Amendment, defendants wish-
ing to close jury selection must show that openness of
pretrial activity would cause the substantial probability
of danger to a fair trial. (Since this decision, courts rarely
attempt to exclude the press and public from jury selection, although appellate courts have occasionally upheld
the practice.)

1986 *Press Enterprise v Riverside Superior Court II.* Referred to as
Press Enterprise II, this case also involved the exclusion of
the public and press from pretrial proceedings; rather
than closed jury selection, this case dealt with closed pretrial hearings. In a 7 to 2 decision by Chief Justice Burger,
the Court held that the public's qualified First Amendment right to criminal proceedings applies to prelimi-

nary hearings, and that the proceedings cannot be closed unless specific, on-the-record findings are made demonstrating that closure is essential. The standard for closure is the substantial probability that access would deprive the defendant of a fair trial. Moreover, the Court noted that since many cases end without a trial, often a preliminary hearing presents the only opportunity for the public to observe proceedings.

In re Providence Journal. This decision conflicts with the holding in *In re U.S. v Dickinson,* discussed previously in this chapter. In *In re Providence Journal,* the Providence, Rhode Island, *Journal* had continuously sought information about organized crime figure Ray Patriarca. After finally obtaining Federal Bureau of Investigation (FBI) information after Patriarca's death, the paper prepared stories on the subject. However, Patriarca's son filed a complaint against the FBI alleging that the release of the information violated his privacy, and the court hearing the case ordered the *Journal* not to publish the information. When the paper published the information anyway, it was found in contempt of court. The U.S. First Circuit Court of Appeals found that the order against publication had been "transparently invalid" (*In re Providence Journal* 820 F.2d 1342 at 1344) and then that a publisher seeking to challenge an order must make a "good faith effort" to appeal the order—but that having done so, the paper may not be held in contempt (*In re Providence Journal* 820 F.2d 1354 at 1355). The U.S. Supreme Court refused to hear the case, which left two conflicting appellate court cases.

1989   *Florida Star v BJF.* A weekly newspaper printed a brief description of the robbery and rape of a woman at a bus stop. The paper accurately described the crime with information obtained from the police report. The victim claimed she suffered from the publication of her name and that the newspaper had violated a Florida law banning the publicizing of a rape victim's name. An appellate court upheld the award of damages to the plaintiff, and the Florida Supreme Court refused to hear the case. By a vote of 6 to 3, the U.S. Supreme Court reversed the deci-

1989,
cont.

sion. Justice Marshall stressed the unique facts of the case and said that punishing the newspaper violated the First Amendment. First, the law applied only to "instruments of mass communication," but in this case it was the police who had released the victim's name (at 532). The law remains, but it must apply to all, not just to the press.

1990

The Judicial Conference of the United States began a four-year experiment with cameras in federal civil courts.

Butterworth v Smith. A Florida reporter was subpoenaed to serve as a grand jury witness and then wanted to write about his own testimony. However, a Florida law forbade a participant in a grand jury from ever revealing his own testimony. The trial court upheld the law, but the Eleventh Circuit Court of Appeals reversed. In a unanimous decision, the U.S. Supreme Court agreed that the law punished speech in violation of the First Amendment. The Court suggested that if the law were upheld, critics of the government could be silenced simply by calling them to be grand jury witnesses. The Court also pointed out that neither the federal government nor the majority of states had similar laws.

1991

Courtroom Television Network. Court TV began broadcasting, at a cost of more than $60 million and headed until 1997 by Steven Brill. Since that time, Court TV has covered more than 700 trials.

Mu'Min v Virginia. A Virginia prisoner, serving time for the first-degree murder of a cab driver, was convicted of the murder of a store clerk, an act that he committed while he was out of prison on work detail. Dawud Majid Mu'Min claimed his second conviction should be overturned because during jury selection in that trial, the judge had not allowed him to question potential jurors individually regarding forty-seven news articles written about him. He felt the articles merited a change of venue. On a 6 to 3 vote, the Supreme Court affirmed his conviction. In a decision written by Justice Rehnquist, the Court held that as long as the judge had questioned jurors in general about their ability to put aside any information based on pretrial publicity and to decide a case solely on the evidence in the courtroom, there was no cause for overturning the conviction despite extensive publicity.

Gentile v State Bar of Nevada. The U.S. Supreme Court held in this landmark case—in which a lawyer had held a press conference right after his client was indicted—that the First Amendment may protect a lawyer's speech, but such protection is not absolute. The lawyer, responding to what he said was prejudicial publicity by the prosecution, said it was likely a police detective, not his client, who was guilty of theft. The High Court said that some limitations on lawyers' speech may be constitutional, since lawyers are officers of the court, and lawyers' speech is subject to more restrictions than that of other individuals. However, the specific rules in question here were too vague. In general, lawyers in a pending case are allowed to describe the general nature of the criminal charges and the defense, to present any information available as a public record, to describe the scheduling of stages of a trial, to request help in obtaining evidence, to give out information necessary to warn the public of any possible danger, and to give out directory information (names, addresses, facts about the arrest).

1995   *Florida Bar v Went for It.* In a second case involving lawyers' speech, lower courts said the Florida Bar Association restrictions on "ambulance chasing" that required lawyers to wait at least thirty days before sending letters of solicitation to victims of accidents and catastrophes violated the First Amendment. The U.S. Supreme Court, on a 5 to 4 vote, overturned the lower courts and upheld the rules. The opinion by Justice O'Connor said that commercial speech does not have the same degree of protection as other speech, and that the state has an interest in protecting personal-injury victims and in protecting the reputations of Florida lawyers. Subsequently, several other states have passed similar rules restricting lawyers' speech.

1996   The Judicial Conference of the United States expanded its rules governing court cameras. The Judicial Conference

1996, voted to allow each of the thirteen appeals courts to de-
cont. cide whether to allow cameras in federal appeals courts
in its jurisdiction. Only the Second Circuit (centered in
New York) and the Ninth Circuit (centered in California)
voted to allow cameras in at a judge's discretion. Additionally, more than a dozen of the ninety-four federal
trial courts have allowed cameras in some isolated cases.

1997 Congress first considered the "Sunshine in the Courtroom Act," a proposal to allow camera coverage of all
federal court proceedings at the discretion of the presiding judge. The legislation became part of the Judicial Reform Act of 1998 and was introduced in subsequent sessions.

1999 An attempted-murder trial in Florida, *Florida v Eagan*, became the first trial netcast in full by a court system live
over the Internet.

The New Millennium

2000 *In re New York v Boss*. Court TV sued the state of New
York, challenging the constitutionality of a blanket ban
on courtroom cameras.

2002 *Republican Party of Minnesota v White*. In the most recent
High Court case dealing with coverage of courts, the U.S.
Supreme Court on a 5 to 4 vote overturned lower courts
and held that restrictions limiting judicial candidates
from speaking out on controversial issues when they are
campaigning violated the First Amendment. However,
other restrictions, such as a ban on campaign promises
by judicial candidates, were not affected by the decision.

2004 The free press/fair trial controversies continue. Current
issues likely to involve court challenges include increased use of anonymous jurors, access to electronic
records, and concerns associated with the trend toward
the virtual courtroom and the netcasting of trials in the
digital age.

4

Biographical Sketches

This chapter presents biographical sketches of representatives of both the media and the courts. By no means is the list exhaustive, but the journalists, judges, and lawyers included here have all had a great impact on the free press/fair trial issues discussed.

F. Lee Bailey (1933–)

Once rated the most admired lawyer in the country, F. Lee Bailey was the first media celebrity lawyer. Bailey has been involved in numerous high-profile cases, including the Sam Sheppard, Patty Hearst, and O. J. Simpson cases (discussed at length in Chapter 1), but he has faced his own legal problems along the way.

Born in 1933 in Waltham, Massachusetts, Bailey attended Harvard University for two years, starting when he was seventeen. He dropped out and joined the navy, then transferred to the marines, where he served four years and developed a lifelong love of flying (at one time owning a helicopter factory). Bailey graduated from the University of Boston School of Law in 1960 with the highest grade-point average in the history of the school. While still in school, he ran an investigative agency, and he later studied lie detectors at the Keeler Polygraph Institute in Chicago.

Meanwhile, Bailey had married and divorced the first of his four wives, with whom he had three sons. He gained fame with his representation of Dr. Sam Sheppard, both in the successful appeal of the murder conviction and in the acquittal in the retrial (see Chapter 1). Other noted clients included the Boston Strangler (Albert DeSalvo, who confessed to thirteen murders); Captain Ernest Medina (who was court-martialed for his involvement in the Mai Lai massacre in Vietnam); and Patty Hearst (see Chapter 1), who blamed his (rare) loss of her armed-robbery case on his interest in writing a book about the case rather than competently representing her.

For all his famed success defending clients in criminal courts, Bailey had his own legal problems. He was censored by the Massachusetts Bar in 1970 for talking too much to the media. In 1971, New Jersey suspended for a year his license to practice law in the state after he suggested prosecutors had bribed witnesses in a murder case. In Florida, he was indicted and tried for conspiracy and mail fraud in a case against Glenn Turner and his company Kosmetics for the Kommunities of Tomorrow (KOSCOT) (*Florida v Glenn Turner et al.,* 1972). The government claimed Turner's company did not really sell a product as much as it sold the right to sell the product, an illegal pyramid-sales scheme. Alan Dershowitz was one of Bailey's numerous lawyers in the year-long case, which ended in a mistrial when the jury deadlocked (*Florida v Glenn Turner et al.,* 1972); the government never retried the case. Bailey claimed he had been charged with mail fraud only because of what he had written about the Plymouth mail robbery case in his best-selling early autobiography, *The Defense Never Rests.*

In 1982, Bailey was defended on a drunk-driving charge by Robert Shapiro, who made him godfather of his child and later hired Bailey to join the O. J. Simpson criminal defense "Dream Team." During the 1995 *Simpson* trial, Bailey was most noted for his cross-examination of racist cop Mark Fuhrman, during which he forced Fuhrman to admit his use of the "N" word. However, Shapiro decried Bailey's joining their fellow defense lawyer Johnnie Cochran in "playing the race card," and due to disagreements over the case, Shapiro vowed never to speak to Bailey again.

Subsequently, Shapiro was a key witness in a case the government brought against Bailey, who spent forty-three days in jail for contempt of court in 1996 (*U.S. v Bailey,* 1999). The government said Bailey had illegally obtained millions of dollars in stocks and money that his client, drug smuggler Claude Duboc, had promised to turn over to the government as part of a plea bargain. (Shapiro had been part of the original Duboc defense team and sided with the government and testified against Bailey in the case.) Bailey claimed the funds were his legal fee and sued the federal government (*Bailey v U.S.,* 2002), but the court found there had been no implied contract to that effect, and he was ordered to give up $16 million worth of stock and his yacht.

Bailey was also ordered to pay $5 million in a second, similar case involving television pitchman William McCorkle, who was convicted of fraud in 1998 (*U.S. v McCorkle*). As a result of these government cases, Bailey was disbarred in Florida and Massachusetts in 2001 (*The Florida Bar v F. Lee Bailey; In re F. Lee Bailey*), and he lost his privilege to argue before the U.S. Supreme Court in 2002. In upholding his disbarment in 2003, the Supreme Judicial Court of Massachusetts said that Bailey's successful career did not mitigate the damage he had done: "Our standards of ethical conduct apply to all attorneys, whether they are well known for their victories in high profile cases or whether they practice law in quiet obscurity" (*In re F. Lee Bailey*).

However, for many years Bailey was one of the most highly regarded criminal lawyers in the country. He cowrote a dozen books in the Criminal Law Library series still found in law schools across the country, and in addition to the 1971 best-seller *The Defense Never Rests,* he wrote a second autobiography, *For the Defense*, in 1975. The first edition of *To Be a Trial Lawyer* was published in 1985. The popular book is must reading for anyone who plans to attend law school or for those who want to understand how a trial lawyer really thinks.

Bailey's 1978 novel *Secrets* tells of a Boston lawyer indicted for first-degree murder of a former client. It is interesting for its allusions to Bailey's own cases (such as the *Sheppard* case) and also for its take on relations between lawyers and the press: a prosecutor manipulates the press; a newspaper editor has an out-of-state reporter second-guess his own reporters; the editor then sends one of his reporters to pressure a judge and another to pass on information that damages the defense.

Bailey, the first real media celebrity lawyer in the country, hosted his own show on ABC-TV as early as 1967. He has hosted several other television shows, made countless appearances, and given more than a thousand lectures, generally on topics including demands for prosecutorial reform. In 2002, Bailey first announced he would earn an MBA at IMPAC University in Florida, and then it was announced that Bailey had been appointed chairman of IMPAC Control System, a Connecticut company that advises clients on improving management productivity. As of 2004, Bailey reportedly had moved back to Massachusetts, where he was working as a consultant.

Steven Brill (1950–)

In 1991, Steven Brill founded Court TV, one the most significant events in the development of the issue of free press/fair trial.

Born in 1950 in New York City, Brill earned his undergraduate and law degrees at Yale University. He wrote for several magazines (*New York, Esquire,* and *Harper's*) and authored a best-selling book, *The Teamsters.* In 1979, Brill founded an iconoclastic magazine, *The American Lawyer,* four-time winner of the National Magazine Award. The magazine took a fresh look at the legal profession, including investigative stories and criticism of lapses in ethics. In 1989, he and the staff published a collection of in-depth articles, *Trial by Jury.* Meanwhile, Brill bought several local legal newspapers.

Courtroom TV (as it was originally called) cost $60 million to start up. Brill's initial partners included NBC, Warner, Liberty Media, and Cablevision. Court TV today reaches more than 70 million viewers and has covered more than 700 trials.

In 1997, Brill sold American Lawyer Media and Court TV to Time Warner, and in 1998, he founded *Brill's Content,* a monthly magazine that he called the Independent Voice of the Information Age. The "Reader's Welcome" said the magazine was based on a "new idea—that consumers of news and information in this Information Age should know how what they watch, read, or log on to is produced, and how much they can rely on" (Brill 1998, 7). The first issue, with a lengthy examination of "Pressgate"—how the press was what Brill called the "enabler" of Kenneth Starr's abuse of power in the *Clinton* case (see Chapter 1)—was widely read. The second issue included Starr's six-page response as well as Brill's apology for having failed to disclose his own donation to Clinton's re-election campaign.

In 2000, Brill started an Internet business and headed a media holding company. After *Brill's Content* folded, Brill began to appear as a news analyst on NBC-TV and taught a journalism seminar at Yale University. Starting in December of 2001, he began a regular column in *Newsweek,* "Homefronts," a follow-up to the terrorist attacks of September 11, 2001.

After: How America Confronted the September 12 Era was Brill's 700-page book on the aftermath of the attacks. A day-by-day account of the year following the attacks, based on 347 interviews, the book wove together the stories of representative Americans—from the U.S. attorney general, to the head of the new Department of Homeland Security, to the executives of the Red Cross, to the American Civil Liberties Union (ACLU), to insurance executives and lawyers, to the widow and children of one victim, and to a cobbler whose business was nearly destroyed. Brill concluded that his work showed the resilience of a system built on a "generosity of spirit in a time of crisis," and that the battles "more often than not produced a messy, drawn-out, but good result" (Brill 2003, 619).

Vincent Bugliosi (1934–)

The prosecutor of ritual murderer Charles Manson and his Family (see Chapter 1), Vince Bugliosi cowrote a book about his successful prosecution in the high-profile case. *Helter-Skelter* was one of the best-selling true crime books ever.

Born in 1934 in Hibbing, Minnesota, Bugliosi served as a captain in the army and later was elected president of his 1964 class at the University of California, Los Angeles (UCLA), Law School. For the next eight years, he was an assistant district attorney in Los Angeles, where he won 105 of 106 felony jury trials, including 21 murder cases. In 1972, he entered private practice.

Helter-Skelter was adapted into a successful television miniseries, as were two other books based on Bugliosi's high-profile cases, *Til Death Us Do Part* and *And the Sea Will Tell.* While continuing work as a defense lawyer, Bugliosi wrote several other books, including two co-authored true-crime novels and his self-described magnum opus, *The Phoenix Solution: Getting Serious about Winning America's Drug War.* In 1984, he served as the prosecutor for a BBC-TV (scriptless) mock trial, *On Trial,* which required him to work for hundreds of hours over a period of six months in preparation. The twenty-one-hour docudrama, with a federal judge and a real Dallas jury, voted to "convict" President John F. Kennedy's assassin, Lee Harvey Oswald.

Bugliosi has continued to write books on media-spotlighted cases, including many discussed in Chapter 1: the prosecution of O. J. Simpson (who he says in his best-seller *Outrage* was allowed to "get away with murder"); *Jones v Clinton* (which he says the Supreme Court justices should have delayed hearing since it involved a sitting president—he called their decision to proceed "egregiously wrong"); and *Bush v Gore,* in which he accuses the majority justices of "borderline treason" for their decision. According to Bugliosi, Justices Clarence Thomas and Antonin Scalia should have recused (excused) themselves from hearing the election case due to conflicts of interest—and Gore's lawyer, David Boies, was not effective. Most significantly, he says, the fact that the Court limited the decision to the 2000 case is evidence the justices knew they were wrong.

Bugliosi has made numerous appearances on television news and talk shows. The television series *The DA,* starring Robert Conrad, was supposedly modeled on his career. He still lives in Los Angeles, where he is reportedly working on a two-volume book on the J.F.K. assassination.

Marcia Clark (1953–)

The key female lawyer in the courtroom during the O. J. Simpson criminal trial, prosecutor Marcia Clark joined the ranks of celebrities known by a single name, "Marcia."

Clark was born Marcia Rachel Kleks in 1953 in Berkeley, California, the daughter of an Israeli-born chemist who worked for the U.S. Food and Drug Administration, and a New York–born mother. Orthodox Jews, the family—including her younger brother, who became an engineer—moved around from New York, to Maryland, Michigan, and California.

Clark married Gabriel Horowitz, a professional backgammon player, in 1976. Divorced in 1980, she married Gordon Clark, a computer programmer with whom she had two sons. She had earned a BA in political science in 1974 at UCLA and a law degree in 1979 at Southwestern University Law School in Los Angeles.

After two years in private practice, Clark joined the office of L.A. District Attorney Gil Garcetti in 1981. She spent four years in the Special Trials Unit, where she won all but one of twenty-one murder cases, including the successful prosecution of the murderer of actress Rebecca Shaeffer. From 1993 through 1995, she gave up trial work for a supervisory job, but just before the Simpson murders, she returned to the Special Trials Unit and was assigned as a prosecutor.

As the first lawyer on the Simpson murder scene, Clark became the immediate center of unrelenting media attention concerning everything she did and said, from her hairstyle to her skirt length. She also became the subject of much comment when her need to arrange for care for her children (she had divorced their father in 1994) arose one evening during the trial.

Both *Ms.* and *Esquire* magazines later named her the 1995 Woman of the Year.

After Simpson's acquittal, Clark left the district attorney's office and reportedly received a $4 million advance, one of the largest in nonfiction history to that date, for her cowritten autobiography, published in 1997. In *Without a Doubt,* Clark says of the Simpson murder case: "No other criminal case in history has generated such massive publicity" (3), and "No matter what happened in court, the sheer amplitude of media coverage would distort these proceedings like never before" (97). She says the prosecutors had made a pact that no one would speak to the press until after the trial.

Regarding the *Simpson* case, Clark also said, "We lost because American justice is distorted by race. We lost because American justice is corrupted by celebrity" (482). Although the district attorney's office had a policy not to object to courtroom cameras, Clark says she learned that the cameras can miseducate the public: "The cameras in the Simpson courtroom not only encouraged lawyers to preen for the lens and prolong the life of every goddamned motion to increase their time on the air, it reduced the criminal trial to the status of a sporting event" (485–486).

In recent years, Clark has become a media personality, hosting a radio show, attempting to syndicate a television program, *Lady Law,* and appearing on numerous news and talk shows on NBC/CNBC/MSNBC and Fox, including a 1998 special, *Lie Detector,* in which figures associated with crimes were interviewed after taking lie detector tests. In 2002, Clark began a stint as a legal expert for *Entertainment Tonight*'s coverage of various trials, including those of actor Robert Blake, charged with killing his wife, and Scott Peterson, charged with killing his wife, Laci, and their unborn son.

Johnnie Cochran (1937–)

One of the best-known defense lawyers in the world, Johnnie Cochran led the O. J. Simpson "Dream Team" to victory in what was likely the most highly publicized trial in U.S. history (see Chapter 1).

Born in 1937, in Shreveport, Louisiana, Cochran says he knew since age eleven that he wanted to be a lawyer. In his high-school years, Cochran moved to California, where he once worked as a paperboy for the *Los Angeles Herald Examiner.* He earned a degree at UCLA while working part-time at the post office and also with his father in an insurance office. In 1962, he graduated from Loyola Marymount Law School in Los Angeles. After graduation, Cochran served as one of the first black attorneys in the L.A. City Attorney's Office and later as one of the first Black attorneys in the L.A. District Attorney's Office.

In 1982, Cochran returned to private practice, where he has defended numerous victims of police abuse. One such victim was Abner Louima, sodomized by the police while he was in jail; the case was settled in 1997 with an $8 million payment awarded to Louima. Another high-profile case involved Elmer "Geronimo" Pratt, a Vietnam veteran and leader of the Black Panthers. With Cochran's help, Pratt had his 1972 murder conviction overturned in 1997 (and received a $4 million damage settlement from the government). Cochran's clients have also included Aretha Franklin, Stevie Wonder, Michael Jackson, Reginald Denny (who was beaten in the Los Angeles riots following the *King* case; see Chapter 1), and Wilbert Rideau, whose murder conviction was originally overturned due to prejudicial publicity (see Chapter 3). He also defended rapper Snoop Doggy Dogg on a 1995 murder charge and Sean "Puffy" Combs on a weapons charge in a case involving a nightclub shooting.

Cochran generally supports the use of cameras in courts, although he is critical of the sensationalistic aspects of coverage of the *Simpson* case. He said, "The O. J. Simpson trial ought to provide the American media with an opportunity for some searching discussion of where the line between the serious press and the tabloid media—both print and electronic—ought to be drawn. In our case it blurred, to the detriment of everyone involved" (Cochran 1996, 376).

Several participants in the *Simpson* case were critical of Cochran's handling of the case, including (as would be expected) prosecutors Marcia Clark and Christopher Darden, but also Cochran's cocounsel Robert Shapiro, who decried Cochran's playing of the "race card." Cochran has also been accused of stealing cases from other lawyers. In a 2000 libel suit against a columnist who said Cochran would say or do just about anything to win, Cochran was unsuccessful on the grounds that the column was protected opinion.

Since the Simpson trial, Cochran has cowritten two autobiographical books, *Journey to Justice* (1996) and *A Lawyer's Life* (2002). In *Journey to Justice*, he denied charges by his first wife that he was abusive, although he admitted that while married he had a child with his white mistress, Patricia Cochran, who later filed a palimony suit against him.

Cochran's speaking skills are widely admired. Fans (and comics) remember his urging the jury to acquit Simpson when gloves entered into evidence seemed too small for Simpson's hands: "If the gloves don't fit, you must acquit." (And in the *Combs* case: "If it doesn't make sense, you should find for the defense.") He is a popular speaker and stresses to young lawyers and aspiring lawyers the secret of his success: "Preparation, preparation, preparation!"

Cochran had a show on Court TV for 2 years, and he also has won several awards, including recognition by The *National Law Journal* as one of the 100 most influential lawyers in the United States. He points out that in addition to the celebrity clients such as O. J. Simpson, he has also represented many "NoJ's" such as the family of a college student who was murdered in his jail cell. He also founded a domestic violence center.

Since the Combs case, Cochran has concentrated on civil rights and personal-injury cases rather than criminal defense. He represented civil rights icon Rosa Parks (whose refusal to move to the back of the bus sparked civil rights activities) in an appeal of a decision allowing a rap group in Atlanta to use her name as a song title. He was involved in a 2003 racial and sexual discrimination suit against Microsoft as well as a huge class-action suit calling for reparations to descendants of slaves due to exploitation and oppression of their ancestors during slavery. He has also threatened to sue the National Football League over the lack of African American coaches. Cochran currently heads a law firm with offices in eight cities including New York City, where he moved with his second wife and their two daughters in 1997.

Christopher Darden (1956–)

In the Simpson criminal trial, Christopher Darden was in a unique position as a black coprosecutor of a black celebrity, a difficult situation that has come to be known as the "Darden Dilemma"—the subject of an entire book (*The Darden Dilemma: 12 Black Writers on Justice, Race, and Conflicting Loyalties,* 1997) by twelve prominent black writers.

Born in 1956 in California, Darden, one of eight children, earned a degree at California State University at San Jose and his law degree at California's Hastings Law School in 1980. He worked in the L.A. District Attorney's Office in special investigations, where he tried twenty-one murder cases before working with Marcia Clark to prosecute O. J. Simpson. He was against allowing cameras in the trial and later said that the cameras had adversely affected all the lawyers in the Simpson case, including himself.

After the trial, Darden cowrote a book in which he said that some "black prosecutors have a name for the pressure they feel from those in the community who criticize them for standing up and convicting black criminals . . . the 'Darden Dilemma'" (383). Some commentators suggest blacks should refuse to work as prosecutors since the criminal justice system is racist. Darden insists this is an inappropriate response: "We cannot defeat their racism with our own; we cannot defeat bigotry by cheating justice" (Darden 1996, 382–383).

In recent years, Darden has set up his own law firm, taught at two law schools, and made television appearances as a commentator on trials. He also worked briefly as a television actor, for example, playing a police detective investigating a murder in ABC's 1998 *Crimes of Passion: One Hot Summer*. He also played a bit part as a preacher in an episode of *Touched by an Angel*. He has won several awards, including Humanitarian of the Year from a California women's shelter.

Darden has also co-authored four courtroom thrillers. In *The Trials of Nikki Hill* (1999) a fictional African American L.A. prosecutor, Nikki Hill, works on a case involving the murder of a popular white talk show host whom she discovers was blackmailing celebrities; in *L.A. Justice* (2002) she prosecutes a wealthy man's son on charges of murdering his girlfriend. *The Last Defense* (2002) and *Lawless* (2004) feature a promising young lawyer in private practice.

Lyle Denniston (1931–)

The author of the definitive textbook on covering the courts, Lyle Denniston was considered the "Dean of the Supreme Court Press."

Born in 1931 in Nebraska City, Denniston worked on his high-school paper and yearbook as well as for the *Nebraska City News-Press* before attending college. In 1955, he worked part-time on the *Lincoln Journal*, and, after graduating Phi Beta Kappa from the University of Nebraska, he earned an MA from Georgetown

University. He became a copyeditor for *The Wall Street Journal* and then worked on legal newsletters for Prentice Hall.

Denniston started covering the U.S. Supreme Court in 1963 for the *Washington Star,* where he worked until 1981. He continued the beat in 1981 when he moved to *The Baltimore Sun,* where he wrote about the *Clinton* case and the 2000 election case (both discussed in Chapter 1).

The Reporter and the Law: Techniques of Covering the Courts was published in 1980 and revised in 1992. The bible for print journalists, the book describes the structure of the court system, explains the work of lawyers and judges, and deals with all stages of the judicial process in criminal and civil courts as well as in special tribunals.

In 2001, Denniston began part-time work on the *Boston Globe.* He has served as an adjunct professor at Georgetown, Johns Hopkins, American, and Penn State universities. He has also worked as a legal commentator for C-SPAN and for various radio and television outlets. In a 1998 law review article, Denniston suggested that the current "paparazzi style" of reporting (sensationalistic coverage, incivility of reporters) might influence First Amendment jurisprudence, causing Supreme Court justices to become wary of the press and more skeptical of claims of First Amendment protection. In fact, Denniston suggests the experience of Justice Clarence Thomas in his nomination proceedings, and an awareness of the behavior of the press in the Simpson and Clinton cases, contribute to the justices' unwillingness to allow cameras in the Supreme Court (Denniston 1998).

Denniston is a frequent speaker and panelist on press and Supreme Court issues. He has won numerous awards, including an honorary PhD and the 2001 American Judicature Society Toni House Journalism Award. He is working on a text on constitutional history.

Alan Dershowitz (1938–)

The man who has been called the top lawyer of last resort for criminal trial appeals, Harvard law professor Alan Dershowitz is a prolific writer and a media personality.

Dershowitz was born in Brooklyn in 1938 and raised in the Orthodox Jewish faith, and he frequently writes on religious themes, including the changing forms of anti-Semitism. He graduated from Yeshiva High School and magna cum laude from

Brooklyn College in 1959 and again in 1962 from Yale University Law School, where he was first in his class and editor of the *Yale Law Journal*. He clerked for the chief judge of the Washington, D.C., U.S. Circuit Court of Appeals, David Bazelon, and then for U.S. Supreme Court Justice Arthur Goldberg. In 1964, Dershowitz was hired by Harvard University Law School, where he became the youngest full professor in 1967 and the Felix Frankfurter Professor of Law in 1993. He has taught courses in criminal law, civil liberties, human rights, and legal ethics.

Dershowitz specializes in criminal case appeals: his clients have included F. Lee Bailey, Claus von Bulow, Leona Helmsley, Michael Miliken, Mike Tyson, various death-row inmates, O. J. Simpson (see Chapter 1) and Louisiana Governor Edwin Edwards (see Chapter 2). He has been awarded an honorary MA and several honorary PhDs.

Dershowitz has written numerous books, including one about the *von Bulow* case and another about Simpson; several collections of syndicated columns; and two courtroom thrillers. *Reversal of Fortune* (1990; about von Bulow) and *The Advocate's Devil* (1994, fiction) were made into movies: the first starred Jeremy Irons, who won the Oscar for Best Actor. Dershowitz also wrote the introductions to a series of book reprints, the "Notable Trials Library," including many on cases discussed in Chapter 1 (Thaw, Frank, Sacco and Vanzetti, Leopold and Loeb, Scopes, Hauptmann, and the "Scottsboro Boys").

Dershowitz approves of courtroom cameras. Regarding the Simpson case, he wrote, "The circus took place outside the courtroom and would not have been affected by exclusion of the camera from the courtroom" (Dershowitz 1996, 203). However, he is critical of the press for not questioning the actions of judges: "The press performs a crucial function in monitoring and exposing all three branches of our government. . . . We need more, rather than less, reporting about criminal cases" (129).

Dershowitz generally supports press coverage of the courts, claiming that "freedom of the press rarely interferes with the right of a defendant to obtain a fair trial. . . . It is reasonable to wonder whether . . . alleged concern for the rights of the defendant to a fair trial is not sometimes invoked as an excuse for restricting the press" (Dershowitz 1992, 172–173). In 2000, he took a sabbatical from teaching and worked as a host of daytime trial coverage for Court TV.

Dershowitz has been profiled by major magazines including *Life, Esquire,* and *New York Magazine.* His writing has appeared in law journals as well as the popular press. Sometimes his opinions have caused controversy. For example, his opinion that a system of elected judges leads to corruption (lawyers cannot buy judges but via campaign contributions they can "rent them") caused some comment in the legal community. His suggestion that the original murder conviction of the British nanny (see Zobel, later in this chapter) in Boston was not surprising since many on the jury were Irish Catholics led to complaints of bigotry from the Catholic Action League. His claim that the success of Arab terrorists would not be possible without a lack of opposition by members of the European Community, the Vatican, and the United Nations led to complaints from various groups including Muslim groups in France. His suggestion after the attacks on September 11, 2001, that torture might be necessary as a response to terrorism was scorned by some critics. In 2003 Dershowitz published his twentieth book, *The Case for Israel.*

Linda Deutsch (1943–)

"America's premier trial reporter," Linda Deutsch has covered the trials of Sirhan Sirhan, Angela Davis, Daniel Ellsberg (these three cases are discussed in Chapter 1), Charles Manson, Patty Hearst, William Kennedy Smith, the police officers charged in the King case, the Menendez brothers, and O. J. Simpson.

Born in 1943 in New Jersey, Deutsch was president of the local Elvis Presley Fan Club and started the *Elvis Times* newspaper before she earned a degree in English at Monmouth College. She worked on the *Perth Amboy News* (New Jersey) and the *Asbury Park Press* (New Jersey) before moving to *The Sun* (San Bernardino). She has been working for the Associated Press for more than twenty years and was named one of a handful of special correspondents in 1992.

Deutsch's best friend and mentor, Theo Wilson, covered trials for the *Daily News* (New York) and wrote an autobiographical book, *Headline Justice,* about her colorful doings. When Wilson died in a limousine taking her to the *Tom Snyder Show,* her first scheduled stop on the *Headline Justice* book tour, Deutsch—who had written the foreword to the book—took over and has been promoting Wilson's book ever since. Deutsch cowrote a book on the *Simpson* case, *Verdict: The Chronicle of the O. J. Simpson Trial* (1995). Her coverage of the criminal trial was nominated for a Pulitzer Prize. She was featured in the *Associated Press Reporting Handbook* published in 2001. She has won several awards including the University of Missouri Honor Medal, the Monmouth Alumnus of the Year, and the Society of Professional Journalists' (SPJ) First Amendment Award.

In 1998, Deutsch was the subject of an SPJ fundraising roast at which Simpson lawyer Johnnie Cochran declared: "If the story was fair, Linda Deutsch was there." Since then she has continued her courtroom coverage of such cases as Michael Jackson's bankruptcy case, a dog-mauling murder trial, the shoplifting trial of Winona Ryder, the civil lawsuit against rock musician Tommy Lee over the drowning of a young child at his son's birthday party, and the murder case of actor Robert Blake, charged with killing his wife.

Dominick Dunne (1925–2003)

When it comes to the trials of Hollywood celebrities and international socialites, there is no match for the work of Dominick Dunne, book author and special correspondent for *Vanity Fair.*

Born in Hartford, Connecticut, in 1925, Dunne was one of six children (his younger brother John Gregory Dunne was a writer married to writer Joan Didion). Dunne earned a BA from Williams College in Williamstown, Massachusetts, in 1949 and later a Bronze Star for service in the army. He then worked in early television, including serving as stage manager for the *Howdy-Doody Show,* before moving to Hollywood, where he worked as a screenwriter, studio executive, film producer (*The Panic in Needle Park*), and television producer (*Adventures in Paradise*).

Dunne married Ellen (Lenny) Griffin, with whom he had two sons (the older is actor Griffin Dunne) and a daughter. Dunne fell on hard times, and after bouts with depression, alcohol, and cocaine (written about in his memoir *The Way We Lived Then)* and an arrest for marijuana possession, he left Hollywood in 1979. When his actress daughter, Dominique, was murdered in Los Angeles in 1982, Dunne wrote about the trial and conviction of John Sweeney for the crime. He says he was horrified at the proceedings: Sweeney was sentenced to only two and one half years in prison, and Dunne credits the outcome with inspiring his interest in crime victims' rights.

Dunne then wrote a series of books, most about famous cases disguised as fiction, including *The Two Mrs. Grenvilles* (based on the 1955 murder of William Woodward by his wife, Ann); *People Like Us; An Inconvenient Woman* (inspired by the murder of Vicki Morgan, mistress to President Ronald Reagan's confidant Alfred Bloomingdale); and *A Season in Purgatory* (based on the murder of Martha Moxley by Kennedy cousin Michael Skakel). The last work led in turn to a nonfiction book on the case by *Simpson* cop Mark Fuhrman and the re-opening of the case, which led to Skakel's murder conviction in 2002. All four of Dunne's novels were made into network television miniseries.

Judge Lance Ito granted Dunne a permanent seat at the O. J. Simpson case, about which Dunne wrote monthly articles for *Vanity Fair* as well as a book, *Another City, Not My Own: A Novel in the Form of a Memoir.* He has also published three collections of magazine articles.

Dunne has recently been faced with some legal problems of his own. In 2002, former Congressman Gary Condit sued him for slander and asked for $11 million in damages for implying Condit had knowledge of the kidnapping and murder of his intern Chandra Levy. In 2003, Robert F. Kennedy Jr. wrote a letter to *Vanity Fair* as well as a lengthy article in the *Atlantic Monthly* in which he blamed media coverage—Dunne's "decade-long fixation"—for the conviction of an "innocent man," his cousin Michael Skakel. Dunne refuted many of Kennedy's charges in *Vanity Fair.*

In 2002, Court TV began the program *Dominick Dunne's Power, Privilege, Justice,* in which Dunne takes an in-depth look at—what else?—court cases involving celebrities. He lives in Connecticut and is working on another novel, to be called *A Solo Act.*

Thomas French (1958–)

Thomas French's fine coverage of a Florida murder case, based on years of work, earned him the Pulitzer Prize for feature writing in 1998.

French was born in 1958 in Columbus, Ohio. After earning a degree at Indiana University in 1980, he went to work on the *St. Petersburg Times,* where he has worked ever since. French has covered police news and courts and has worked as a general-assignment reporter. He now specializes in feature writing, particularly book-length narratives published one chapter at a time on successive days. "Babyland," was about unwed teenage mothers. "A Cry in the Night" took an in-depth look at the murder of an everyday young woman and the investigation leading eventually to the conviction of the friendly fireman who lived across the street. ("A Cry in the Night" was later published in book form as *Unanswered Cries: A True Story of Friends, Neighbors and Murder in a Small Town*.)

"Angels and Demons," which told the stories of the police and courtroom follow-ups to the murders of a mother and two daughters visiting Florida from the Midwest, won several awards, including one from the SPJ, another from the American Society of Newspaper Editors, and then the Pulitzer Prize.

French has been a frequent speaker at workshops and seminars on writing. He has continued working on in-depth features, including another award-winning series published as a book, *South of Heaven: Welcome to High School at the End of the Twentieth Century*, for which he spent a year at Largo High. The 2000 series "Judgment Day: The Valessa Robinson Case" described the criminal case of a young woman on trial for the murder of her mother; "Reverberations Still Felt from Afar" dealt with response to the terrorist attacks of September 11, 2001. Published in 2003, "13: Life at the Edge of Everything" was a six-part series following a group of Tampa seventh graders. French, who has two sons, has also written about life in preschool and first grade.

Fred Graham (1931–)

Chief anchor and managing editor of Court TV, Fred Graham has seen all sides of courtrooms, from work as a government lawyer to work as a correspondent for *The New York Times* and CBS TV News.

Born in 1931, Graham lived in Texarkana before his father's work as a Presbyterian minister took the family to Nashville, Tennessee. After earning a degree at Yale University, he served in the marines and then earned a degree at Vanderbilt University Law School, where he worked on the law review and would one day be named Distinguished Alumnus. He was awarded a Fulbright Scholarship to Oxford University, where he received a Diploma in Law in 1960.

During law school, Graham worked on *The Tennessean* (Nashville) and then entered private practice before working as counsel to the Judiciary Committee, chaired by Senator Estes Kefauver, and as an assistant to Secretary of Labor Willard Wirtz. In 1965, he succeeded Anthony Lewis as the law correspondent for *The New York Times.* He was the first lawyer to hold the job.

Graham became the first legal correspondent for CBS News, where he obtained a copy of and broadcast excerpts from the arguments in the Pentagon Papers case (see Chapter 1). He has won American Bar Association (ABA) Silver Gavel Awards, Emmys, and a Peabody Award (the last for coverage of the Watergate case, also discussed in Chapter 1). He has written extensively for law reviews, professional journals, and the popular press.

In 1987, Graham returned to Nashville for a short stint as a local television anchor for the ABC affiliate. His 1990 autobiography (*Happy Talk: Confessions of a TV Newsman*) focused on the deterioration of local television news. In 1991, when Court TV signed on, Graham was the first employee hired, as the chief anchor and soon managing editor. He hosts a daily trial-analysis program, *Open Court,* and participates in various other programs. The cases he has covered include the confirmation hearings of Justice Clarence Thomas as well as the William Kennedy Smith, Rodney King, and O. J. Simpson cases discussed in Chapter 1. He was a founding member of the Reporters Committee for Freedom of the Press (see Chapter 6). He currently divides his time between New York and Washington, D.C., while continuing to head Court TV.

Linda Greenhouse (1947–)

Winner of the 1998 Pulitzer Prize for coverage on the Supreme Court beat, *New York Times* reporter Linda Greenhouse is one of the most influential courtroom reporters in the country.

Born in 1947 in New York City, Greenhouse was raised in Hamden, Connecticut. She graduated magna cum laude and Phi Beta Kappa from Radcliffe College with a degree in government. In 1978, she was awarded a Ford Foundation Fellowship and earned a Master of Studies in Law from Yale University Law School.

In 1968, Greenhouse started at *The New York Times* as clerk to columnist James (Scotty) Reston and progressed through the ranks: general assignment reporter, Westchester County correspondent, night rewriter, and state capital bureau chief. Since 1978, she has been the U.S. Supreme Court correspondent. She writes a question-and-answer column on legal issues (access to the column is available online). Since 1980, she has published numerous articles in law reviews, has been a regular guest on PBS's *Washington Week in Review,* and frequently has been invited to speak at law conferences.

Greenhouse has speculated that the Supreme Court's reluctance to allow news cameras in the High Court may be because the justices like their privacy. She says they do not want to be recognized outside of the court, but television turns everyone into a celebrity.

In addition to the Pulitzer Prize, Greenhouse has been awarded several honorary LLD (Doctor of Laws) and DHL (Doctor of Humane Letters) degrees. Her awards also include the New York Bar Association's John Peter Zenger Special Award. In 2002, she and Anthony Lewis were the first nonlawyers to win the American Law Institute's Henry J. Friendly Medal. She is married with one daughter and lives in Bethesda, Maryland.

William L. Howard (1948–)

As the judge in the 1995 high-profile case of Susan Smith, who drove her car with her two sons into a lake where they drowned, Judge William Howard won wide admiration.

Judge Howard was born in 1948 in Ann Arbor, Michigan, and graduated from Dickinson College, where he served in the Army ROTC. He earned his law degree at the University of South Carolina in 1973. He entered private practice with a former Federal Bureau of Investigation (FBI) agent in Charleston, where one of their clients was the Ford Motor Credit Corporation. Judge Howard worked as a prosecutor and city attorney in Mount Pleasant, South Carolina, and became a judge in 1988, defeating the incumbent, a rarity. He was voted the top judge in the state by the 1,600-member South Carolina Bar Association in 1994.

For the *Smith* trial, Judge Howard issued a gag order, including restricting the doctor's competency report that had been commissioned to determine whether Smith was capable of understanding the consequences of her actions in the drownings. After *The Columbia State*'s (South Carolina) Twila Decker wrote about the report despite his orders not to, the judge found her in contempt. However, after the trial (and Smith's thirty-years-to-life sentence), the judge and the reporter appeared together on several panel discussions of the case.

Judge Howard allowed cameras in pretrial hearings but denied their use at the Smith trial on grounds they might affect witness behavior, saying, "The witnesses, until now, have been private people who live in a small town and ask nothing more than to be able to live their lives . . . in peace and quiet. I also have to consider the possibility of community hostility for witnesses" (Truit 1995).

In 1996, Judge Howard, who had served as an acting judge in the appellate court, returned to the court of appeals. He continues to be widely praised for having maintained a tight rein over the Susan Smith trial. He sat a jury in less than a week and kept court going for lengthy sessions with few breaks. He is married with grown children.

Lance Ito (1950–)

Judge Lance Ito is perhaps the most well known trial judge in the country—a poll (Fox and Van Sickel 2001, 2) showed 6 times more people recognized his name than that of the chief justice of the United States. Judge Ito presided over the 1994 to 1995 criminal trial of O. J. Simpson, the case that launched 100 books (see Chapter 1).

Judge Ito was born in 1950 in Los Angeles. His parents, both teachers, had met at an internment camp in Wyoming during World War II. Judge Ito was an active Boy Scout and was president of John Marshall High School (which presented him with the Distinguished Alumnus Award in 1996).

After graduating cum laude from UCLA in 1972, Judge Ito earned a law degree from Boalt Law School at the University of California, Berkeley. He spent two years in private practice and then worked in the L.A. District Attorney's Office. He was appointed to the bench in 1989. One of his famous cases involved Charles Keating, a key player in the savings and loan scandal: at the time of sentencing, Mother Teresa, who had received more than a million dollars from Keating, wrote Judge Ito on Keating's behalf.

Judge Ito and the media faced many conflicts during the Simpson trial, including concerns over a possible gag order and his threats to find reporters in contempt of court for various infractions. He allowed cameras into the trial but threatened to remove them when a substitute cameraman accidentally panned to show an alternate juror, and again during closing when the camera showed Simpson writing on a legal pad (see Chapters 1 and 2). Judge Ito's wife, Margaret York, the highest-ranking woman in the Los Angeles Police Department (currently deputy chief), was a prosecution witness in the case.

Many commentators criticized the judge's handling of the *Simpson* case. Prosecutor Marcia Clark said he was overly sensitive to his press notices. Her colleague Christopher Darden called him "Judge Ego" and said he favored the defense and was too impressed with visiting celebrities. Vincent Bugliosi, former prosecutor turned defense attorney and author, called the judge an egomaniac who played a tape of the "Dancing Itos" parody from the Jay Leno show for visitors and was partly to blame for Simpson's having "got away with murder." *Saturday Night Live* segments featuring an Ito impersonator were a big hit.

However, other commentators have expressed sympathy for the difficult burden of presiding over the "Trial of the Century." Judge Ito receives scores of invitations to speak, most of which he turns down. In 2002, the judge, perhaps weary of the endless fall-out from the Simpson trial, requested a move to the less chaotic juvenile court, where most proceedings are held in private with only participants and parents allowed.

Thomas Penfield Jackson (1937–)

Judge Thomas Penfield Jackson will likely be remembered as the judge who presided over the landmark antitrust case *U.S. v Microsoft* and saw his sentence overturned because of a claimed impropriety in his dealing with press coverage of the case (as discussed in Chapter 1).

Judge Jackson was born in 1937 in Washington, D.C., and he earned degrees at Dartmouth University and—after a stint in the navy—Harvard University Law School. From 1964 to 1982, Judge Jackson was in private practice with his father's law firm in Washington, D.C. He was active in Republican politics (including working with Richard Nixon's infamous Committee to Re-Elect the President during the Watergate years). He was head of the Washington, D.C., Bar Association when President Ronald Reagan appointed him to the bench in 1982. However, the judge's conservatism was moderated by his family background, including both grandfathers' working in civil-service jobs and expressing admiration for President Franklin D. Roosevelt.

Judge Jackson presided over the 1987 perjury trial of former presidential aide Michael Deaver, which included a fight with the press when he was ordered to make public juror questionnaires, as well as the 1990 perjury and drug trial of the mayor of Washington, D.C., Marion Barry. Outside the courtroom in Barry's case, the judge described the government's strong case and expressed concern about pro-acquittal jurors; inside, he sentenced Barry, acquitted on most charges, to the maximum six months. In 1994, he ordered U.S. Senator Robert Packwood, accused of sexual misconduct, to turn over his diaries to the investigating committee, and in 1998, he ordered Iran to pay damages to hostages such as Terry Anderson. At one time, he was criticized for presiding over lengthy trials with frequent recesses, although he was praised for his efficient handling of the *Microsoft* case.

In the *Microsoft* case, as discussed in Chapter 1, the appellate court upheld Judge Jackson's decision finding the company violated antitrust laws but threw out his sentence because he had allowed journalists to interview him in the time between the conclusion of testimony and when the court-ordered mediation fell through and he issued his decision. According to Judge Jackson, the interviews (in which he compared Microsoft's action to those of gangland killers) were embargoed until after the conclusion of the case, and he felt he needed to correct some public distortions of the facts by some of the parties involved.

The judge, described by *The New York Times* as a "judge from central casting . . . big, white-haired, avuncular," said he found the intense media coverage of the *Microsoft* case "pretty good." He added that a "significant shortcoming was the amount of attention that was paid to me—things that I did or facial expressions that I was perceived to have" (Collins 2000).

Judge Jackson, who had been editor of his high-school newspaper, said he once briefly considered a career in journalism but decided on law instead: "It was my impression that journalists wrote about a lot of things that fell on deaf ears, and they didn't produce results. Lawyers were able to go into court and produce a result that would have concrete consequences" (Hamilton 2000).

Anthony Lewis (1927–)

Two-time Pulitzer Prize winner Anthony Lewis is one of the best-known legal reporters in the country.

Born in 1927 in New York City, Lewis graduated from Horace Mann School and then earned a degree at Harvard University in 1948, where he was a Nieman Fellow during the 1956–1957 academic year. Lewis worked in *The New York Times* Sunday Department for four years and then returned to the paper after a brief stint at the *Washington Daily News*. He was Supreme Court correspondent from 1957 to 1964, covering the Warren Court and the civil rights movement, and then London correspondent for eight years. After returning to the United States in 1973, he continued work as a columnist until his retirement in 2001. He has also been a lecturer at Harvard University Law School and the James Madison visiting professor at Columbia University for fifteen years.

Lewis has written and/or edited several books, including one on the famous *New York Times v Sullivan* libel case (see Chapter 1) and *Gideon's Trumpet*, about the Supreme Court case that led to the requirement that all defendants accused of serious crimes are entitled to a lawyer. The Gideon book became a highly praised television movie starring Henry Fonda in 1979.

Lewis has won several awards including a Pulitzer for national reporting in 1955 (while still on the *Washington Daily News)* for a series on the federal loyalty-security program. In this series, he focused on a navy employee who had been unfairly fired as a security risk; after the stories, the man was rehired. His second Pulitzer was awarded in 1963 for beat reporting, covering the Supreme Court, including cases on reapportionment.

Lewis has said the 2000 *Bush-Gore* case (see Chapter 1) was unconvincing, and the decision of the majority justices was out of line with their earlier decisions. After the terrorist act of September 11, 2001, he expressed concern with the trend toward government secrecy.

Lewis has traveled widely, in the Middle East, Europe, Asia, and South Africa. He has received honorary degrees from more than half a dozen colleges and universities. In 2002, he taught a First Amendment course at Harvard University. A Fellow of the American Academy of Arts and Sciences, he and Linda Greenhouse became the first two nonlawyers to win the American Law Institute's Henry J. Friendly Medal.

Tony Mauro (1950–)

Tony Mauro has been covering courts for virtually his entire career.

Born in 1950 in New York City, Mauro earned a degree in political science at Rutgers University and an MA at Columbia University Journalism School. He worked on local newspapers before covering the Supreme Court for Gannett for two decades, including *USA Today* (a Gannett publication) from its inception. Since 1999, he has covered the High Court for the *Legal Times* and other publications of American Lawyer Media, and he also is legal correspondent for the First Amendment Center.

Mauro says that the Court's "cult of secrecy" was apparent in its response to the release of Justice Thurgood Marshall's papers soon after he died and to the release of tapes of their oral arguments, as well as the Court's resistance to camera coverage of their proceedings (Mauro 1995).

Mauro was one of ten contributors to the ABA Silver Gavel Award–winning *A Year in the Life of the Supreme Court,* in which he described in depth the cult of secrecy. He is also the author of *Illustrated Great Decisions of the Supreme Court.* The book includes the Clinton, *New York Times,* "Pentagon Papers," and "Scottsboro Boys" cases discussed in Chapter 1 and the Branzburg, Near, Richmond, and Chandler cases discussed in Chapter 3.

Mauro is an active member of professional organizations such as the Reporters Committee for Freedom of the Press (RCFP) and the SPJ. He also serves on the prestigious Advisory Board of the Reynolds Center for the Courts and the Media of the National Judicial College. He has been a guest on numerous television programs on CNN, Court TV, CNBC, and also on NPR. His awards include a 1998 certificate of merit from the ABA for his in-depth reporting on law clerks at the Supreme Court. In 2001, *Washingtonian Magazine* named him one of the fifty top journalists in Washington.

Tim O'Brien (1943–)

Tim O'Brien—who was the longtime legal correspondent for ABC News—along with Fred Graham at CBS and Carl Stern at NBC, was one of the first network news reporters covering the legal beat who had earned a law degree.

Born in 1943 in New York City, O'Brien earned a degree at Michigan State University while working at the local paper and radio and television stations. He earned an MA in political science at the University of Maryland. O'Brien also worked in local television news at stations in Detroit and in Washington, D.C., and at two stations in New Orleans, the second while working on a law degree at Loyola University. He then became the legal correspondent at ABC TV News, where he worked from 1977 until 1999. At ABC, he covered the Supreme Court, the Justice Department, and the FBI. His Court reporting led to some controversy when he reported stories based on leaked information involving decisions before they were officially announced by the Court.

O'Brien has won New Orleans Press Club, Associated Press, Emmy, and ABA awards. Since leaving ABC, he has taught law and since 2001 has worked at CNN in Washington, D.C.

Kelli Sager (1960–)

One of the most widely known media lawyers, Kelli Sager has represented various media organizations, including those seeking access to the O. J. Simpson criminal and civil trials.

Sager was born in 1960 in Ohio and, after attending the University of Southern California, she earned a journalism and political science degree cum laude from West Georgia College and a law degree from the University of Utah, where she was editor of the law review.

Sager is a partner in Davis, Wright, and Tremain in Los Angeles. Her clients have included *The New York Times*, the *Los Angeles Times*, and Court TV. She represented various media coalitions during the Simpson cases (see Chapter 1), as well as the David Westerfield kidnapping, Winona Ryder shoplifting, and Scott/Laci Peterson murder cases mentioned in Chapter 2. She chaired the ABA Forum on Communications Law and coedited the ABA *Communications Lawyer* in the 1990s. She has also worked as an adjunct professor of law and has published several law-review articles.

Among the awards Sager has won are the ACLU First Amendment Award, Distinguished Alumna in Residence at Utah, and the SPJ's Freedom of Information Award. In 2001, the *National Law Journal* named her one of the top fifty women litigators. She also serves on the prestigious Advisory Board of the Reynolds Center for the Courts and the Media of the National Judicial College.

Carl Stern (1937–)

Carl Stern became the first lawyer to serve as a network television legal correspondent when he was hired by NBC TV News in 1967.

Born in 1937 in New York City, Stern earned degrees at Columbia University in 1958 and 1959 and his law degree at Cleveland State University in 1966.

While working at NBC, Stern covered the Justice Department as well as Supreme Court cases involving Muhammad Ali, Marion Barry, John Hinckley, Jimmy Hoffa, Oliver North, and—as discussed in Chapter 1—Patricia Hearst, as well as the Watergate case. In 1984, covering a story about FBI surveillance, Stern sued the FBI to obtain the names of three FBI employees investigated in connection with a possible cover-up of illegal surveillance, and after an appeal, he was given the name of the agent in charge. After leaving NBC in 1991, Stern went to work as director of the Public Affairs Office of the U.S. Justice Department in 1993, where he was involved with coverage of the *McVeigh* case (discussed in Chapter 1). He has received Emmy, ABA, and Peabody awards, as well as honorary JD degrees. In 1996, he became a professor of media and public affairs at George Washington University.

Nina Totenberg (1944–)

One of the most recognizable voices in broadcast news, Nina Totenberg is the only radio correspondent who has spent nearly three decades as a legal affairs correspondent in Washington, D.C.

Born in 1944 in New York City, Totenberg—the daughter of famed violinist Roman Totenberg—spent ten summers in Aspen while her father played with the music festival. She dropped out of Boston University to take a newspaper job, a step that she told one reporter was a "hidden advantage": "After all, you're communicating with people who aren't lawyers. You have to speak their language, not lawyerese" (Wilner 1991, 1). In 1965, Totenberg went to work on the *Boston Record American,* followed by stints on the *Peabody Times,* the (now defunct) *National Observer,* and the *New Times.* She joined NPR in 1975.

Part of what has been referred to as a "troika" of women who came to fame via NPR (with Cokie Roberts and Linda Wertheimer), Totenberg was widely noticed in 1987 when she broke the story of Supreme Court nominee Douglas Ginsburg's use of marijuana. In 1991, she revealed Anita Hill's sexual harassment charges against Supreme Court nominee Clarence Thomas. The Hill revelations led to Senate Judiciary Committee hearings, and Totenberg won the SPJ, Polk, and Peabody awards for her coverage. In addition to NPR, she has appeared on ABC-TV's *Nightline* and as a panelist on PBS-TV's *Inside Washington.*

Totenberg's access to leaked information has led to some controversy about her work, including a public sparring match with Senator Alan Simpson (a Republican from Wyoming). Also arousing some comment is her status as one of the celebrity journalists charging high speaking fees. She has been awarded several honorary LLD and LHD degrees and was the first radio broadcaster to win *Broadcasting and Cable*'s Broadcaster of the Year Award. She has won the Dupont Award and eight ABA awards. In 1998, she was the first recipient of the American Judicature Society Toni House Journalism Award for coverage of the U.S. Supreme Court.

Totenberg was married to U.S. Senator Floyd Haskell (a Democrat from Colorado) for nearly twenty years until his death in 1998. In 2000, she married a Connecticut surgeon, with some controversy over the ceremony's being performed by Supreme Court Justice Ruth Bader Ginsburg, although Totenberg denied any conflict of interest. More recently, she has been outspoken in criticizing the new climate of government secrecy since the terrorist attacks of September 11, 2001.

Greta Van Susteren (1954–)

Lawyer Greta Van Susteren is one of the most talked-about media personalities involved in courtroom coverage today.

The daughter of a judge, Van Susteren was born in 1954 in Appleton, Wisconsin, where she attended Xavier High School. She earned a BA degree at the University of Wisconsin and a JD and then an LLM in trial advocacy at Georgetown University.

After working in private practice, Van Susteren began to serve as a legal commentator on the Marion Barry trial for the local CBS-TV affiliate in Washington, D.C., in 1991. She was also hired by Court TV and CNN to do commentary on the William Kennedy Smith trial (see Chapter 1).

From 1991 to 2001, Van Susteren was a legal analyst for CNN. She appeared on *Burden of Proof* with cohost Roger Cossack (the program included coverage of the Simpson trials and the 2000 election cases discussed in Chapter 1). In 2002, she moved to the Fox News Channel, where she is the host of *On the Record with Greta Van Susteren.* Controversies over her commitment to the Church of Scientology, her former work with her husband,

John Coale (an admitted "ambulance chasing" lawyer), her 2002 cosmetic surgery, and her appearance at the 2002 White House Correspondents' Association dinner with rocker Ozzy Osbourne as her guest received wide coverage. In 2003, she co-wrote her autobiography, *My Turn at the Bully Pulpit.*

Hiller Zobel (1932–)

The judge who presided over the 1997 "Nannygate" trial, Judge Hiller Zobel weathered a storm of controversy when he reduced the conviction of Louise Woodward—for the death of an infant in her care—from murder to manslaughter and her sentence from fifteen years to less than a year, jail time she had already served.

Judge Zobel was born in 1932 in New York City, an only child whose father died when Zobel was a year old. After attending private schools, he graduated cum laude from Harvard University in 1953, attended Oxford University in 1956, and earned the LLB at Harvard in 1959. While still in school, Judge Zobel, who had worked on the Harvard newspaper as an undergraduate, also worked as a copy boy on the *San Francisco Chronicle* and as a sports stringer on the *New York Herald Tribune.* He served in the Naval Reserve and after working in private practice, he became a professor of law at Boston College.

A noted historian, Judge Zobel wrote a 1970 book, *The Boston Massacre,* which won the American Historical Association Littleton-Griswold Prize. He also coedited *Legal Papers of John Adams,* cowrote a text on Massachusetts' rules of practice, and cowrote a book on medical malpractice, *Doctors and the Law: Defendants and Expert Witnesses.*

Judge Zobel served as an associate justice on the Massachusetts Superior Court from 1979 to 2002. He also wrote numerous scholarly articles and published columns and stories in the popular press. He was a hard-working judge who handled the state's asbestos claims and helped set up prison courts. Some of his decisions were overturned by higher courts, but he seemed to take it in stride. The bow-tie-wearing gingerbread-baking baseball-fan judge inspired a character in the Boston-based television show *The Practice:* Linda Hunt plays "Zoe Hiller."

Judge Zobel's most high-profile case was the aforementioned 1997 trial of Louise Woodward, a British babysitter, who was charged in the death of nine-month-old Matthew Eappen and was convicted of second-degree murder by the jury (*Com-

monwealth of Massachusetts v Louise Woodward). The conviction called for a mandatory fifteen-year sentence. The defense asked the judge either to dismiss the case, to order a retrial, or at least to reduce the sentence.

The judge announced he would release his decision in the case over the Internet (but a power outage to the server caused a slight delay so that traditional media obtained the information first). The judge then surprised many when, saying, "A judge is a public servant and must follow his conscience," he reduced the conviction to involuntary manslaughter and the sentence to the 279 days already served.

Judge Zobel generally supports the use of cameras in the court, but he is somewhat critical of media pundits (many of whom are lawyers). Regarding the Nannygate coverage, he says while watching commentators one night expounding upon what "Judge Zobel *has* to be thinking," he was talking back to his television: "Hey, I'm Judge Zobel, and I'm not thinking any of that" (Zobel 2001, 7).

Upon his retirement in 2002, Judge Zobel said he hoped to revise his civil procedure rulebook, write a book on Supreme Court Justice Oliver Wendell Holmes, and possibly write a historical novel.

References

Brill, Steven. 1998. "Reader's Welcome." *Brill's Content,* August.

———. 2003. *After: How America Confronted the September 12 Era.* New York: Simon and Schuster.

Bugliosi, Vincent. 1996. *Outrage: The Five Reasons Why O. J. Simpson Got Away with Murder.* New York: Norton.

Clark, Marcia, with Teresa Carpenter. 1997. *Without a Doubt.* New York: Viking Press.

Cochran, Johnnie, with Tim Rutten. 1996. *Journey to Justice.* New York: Ballantine Books.

Collins, Julia. 2000. "The Captain of the *U.S. v Microsoft.*" *Harvard Law Bulletin,* Fall, http://www.law.harvard.edu/alumni/bulletin (accessed 2002) (quoting Judge Jackson).

Darden, Chris, with Jess Walter. 1996. *In Contempt.* New York: Regan Books.

Denniston, Lyle. 1998. "From George Carlin to Matt Drudge: The Constitutional Implications of Bringing the Paparazzi to America." *American University Law Review,* 47:5 (June) 1255–1271.

Dershowitz, Alan. 1992. *Contrary to Popular Opinion.* New York: Pharos Books.

———. 1996. *Reasonable Doubts.* New York: Simon and Schuster.

Fox, Richard, and Robert Van Sickel. 2001. *Tabloid Justice.* Boulder, CO: Lynne Rienner Publishers.

Hamilton, Mike. 2000. "Jackson '58 Discusses New Fame." *The Dartmouth Online,* 3 October, http://www.thedartmouth.com (accessed 2002) (quoting Judge Jackson).

Mauro, Tony. 1995. "The Supreme Court and the Cult of Secrecy," in *A Year in the Life of the Supreme Court,* ed. Rodney Smolla. Durham, NC: Duke University Press.

Truitt, Rosalind. 1995. "Ordered from the Court? One Victim of the O. J. Simpson Trial Could Be the Presence of Cameras in the Courtroom." Newspaper Association of America, October, http://www.naa.org/presstime (accessed 2002) (quoting Judge Howard).

Wilner, John. 1991. "15 Who Made a Difference." *Current,* December 16 (quoting Nina Totenberg).

Zobel, Hiller. 2001. "Judicial Independence and the Need to Please." *The Judge's Journal,* Fall: 5–10.

5

Facts and Data

With the exception of the controversy over the use of courtroom cameras, there is not a vast body of empirical research regarding the issues involved in media coverage of the courts. However, several of the more recent studies are worth mentioning.

Moreover, since members of the press, the bar, the judiciary, and the government are interested in court coverage, descriptions of suggested guidelines and excerpts from codes and canons of ethics for those involved in press coverage of courts are included in the following discussion.

Research

There are scores of useful studies of individual high-profile cases already described in Chapter 1 (and the related portion of the bibliography in Chapter 7). One general work on the specific issue of media coverage of such cases is *The Press on Trial* (Chiasson 1997), in which academics discuss the details of press coverage of sixteen trials, including the Scopes, "Scottsboro Boys," Hauptmann, and Simpson cases discussed in Chapter 1.

The Simpson trial alone became the subject of approximately 100 books and studies. *The Spectacle* (Thaler 1997) gathered a great deal of data on press coverage of the case. And 6 weeks after the trial, a survey of all 50 states (Alexander 1996) found that the impact of the broadcasting of the sensationalistic trial on the developing use of courtroom cameras was minimal.

A First Amendment Center study of the controversies regarding press coverage of courts (Westfeldt and Wicker 1998) criticized news-media coverage of the criminal justice system. The authors concluded that the press generally overuses unidentified sources; presents "horse-race" coverage of trials; does not adequately explain the work of juries, lawyers, or judges; relies too much on leaks, mostly from prosecutors; makes errors in names, addresses, dates, and statistics, which are repeated once entered in a database; and describes constitutional rights as "technicalities."

In another journal study edited by Giles and Snyder of such controversies (reprinted as a book, *Covering the Courts*), journalists, lawyers, and judges involved in high-profile courtroom coverage discussed "free press, fair trials, and journalistic performance." Contributors included Linda Deutsch, Fred Graham, and Tony Mauro (see Chapter 4). The editors concluded that journalists now go beyond merely chronicling events in the courtroom; trial participants play to the press; and there is a strong case for courtroom cameras (Giles and Snyder 1999, x).

A study focusing on charges of sensationalistic media coverage—one aspect of the controversies discussed in Chapter 2—was conducted by two professors in 1999 (Fox and Van Sickell 2001). They conducted a poll, designed to judge the impact of the media culture on public attitudes toward the court system, with surveys of 1,000 people regarding cases including the *Smith,* King, *Menendez, Simpson,* and *Clinton* cases (discussed in Chapter 1) and Judge Zobel's handling of the *Woodward* case (discussed in Chapter 4). Fox and Van Sickell concluded that, in general, media coverage is sensationalistic, designed to entertain more than to educate, and misleading to the public. The authors say that media coverage (including talk shows and "tabloid" news magazines) leads to a lack of interest in legal issues and to a negative assessment of the courts. However, they said they were surprised to find no direct connection between the amount of news consumption and lack of confidence in the judicial system.

Several specific aspects of the controversies discussed in Chapter 2 were the subject of a participant-observation study of press coverage of the high-profile corruption trials of four-time Louisiana Governor Edwin Edwards. The "reality check" on courts and the media described the blanket sealing of documents, the use of anonymous jurors (whose names remained secret even after the trial was over), as well as restraining orders on all lawyers, witnesses, and even defendants—despite requests from the defendants for openness. As the author concluded, "despite years of effort to improve relations, two recent federal trials show just how far apart the judiciary and the media remain in areas such as access to records, jury anonymity, and 'gag' orders" (Alexander 2000, 146).

Cameras in the Courtroom

The use of courtroom cameras has been widely researched. Both the National Center for State Courts (NCSC) and the Radio-Television News Directors Association (RTNDA) (see Chapter 6) periodically publish statistics on the use of cameras. Table 5.1 shows the latest state-by-state data, including whether coverage of civil and/or criminal trials is allowed and whether coverage of trial and/or appellate courts is permitted.

The definitive social-science study of courtroom cameras (Barber 1987) gathered the results of dozens of surveys of journalists, judges, and lawyers—studies involving state experiments that led to the use of some form of cameras in all fifty states and in some federal courts today. The general consensus was that the benefits of camera coverage outweighed the drawbacks.

A seminal participant-observation study of coverage of murder trials during a year in one typical court (Alexander 1990, 1991) found no support for the speculation that press coverage interfered with the judicial process.

In 1993 and 1994, the federal courts published an evaluation of a three-year pilot program of camera coverage of civil cases in six trial courts and two appellate courts (Johnson, 1993–1994). Although the program was deemed a success by the majority of those surveyed, the Judicial Conference of the United States (the governing body of federal courts that commissioned the study) refused to extend the experiment or to establish permanent rules for camera coverage in all federal courts.

The two most recent comprehensive works, updating Barber's work in gathering results of studies and expanding the discussion, are *Cameras in the Courtroom* (Cohn and Dow 1998) and *TV or Not TV* (Goldfarb 1998). Both are excellent resources and are widely cited whenever the issue arises.

Table 5.1 Cameras in State Courts

State	Level	Division
States with Permanent Rules		
Alabama	Trial & Appellate	Civil & Criminal
Alaska	Trial & Appellate	Civil & Criminal
Arizona	Trial & Appellate	Civil & Criminal
Arkansas	Trial & Appellate	Civil & Criminal
California	Trial & Appellate	Civil & Criminal
Colorado	Trial & Appellate	Civil & Criminal
Connecticut	Trial & Appellate	Civil & Criminal
Florida	Trial & Appellate	Civil & Criminal
Georgia	Trial & Appellate	Civil & Criminal
Hawaii	Trial & Appellate	Civil & Criminal
Idaho	Supreme Court in Boise; Supreme Court on circuit	
Illinois	Appellate	
Iowa	Trial & Appellate	Civil & Criminal
Kansas	Trial & Appellate	Civil & Criminal
Kentucky	Trial & Appellate	Civil & Criminal
Louisiana	Appellate	
Maine	Trial	Civil
Maryland	Trial & Appellate	Civil
Massachusetts	Trial & Appellate	
Michigan	Trial & Appellate	Civil & Criminal
Minnesota	Appellate	
Mississippi	Supreme Court	Civil & Criminal
Missouri	Trial & Appellate	Civil & Criminal
Montana	Trial & Appellate	Civil & Criminal
Nebraska	Appellate	
Nevada	Trial & Appellate	Civil & Criminal
New Hampshire	Trial & Appellate	Civil & Criminal
New Jersey	Trial & Appellate	
New Mexico	Trial & Appellate	Civil & Criminal
New York	Appellate	
North Carolina	Trial & Appellate	Civil & Criminal
North Dakota	Trial & Supreme Court	Civil & Criminal
Ohio	Trial & Appellate	Civil & Criminal
Oklahoma	Trial & Appellate	Civil & Criminal
Oregon	Trial	Civil & Criminal
Rhode Island	Trial & Appellate	Civil & Criminal
South Carolina	Trial & Appellate	Civil & Criminal
South Dakota	Supreme Court	
Tennessee	Trial & Appellate	Civil & Criminal
Texas	Trial & Appellate	Civil & Criminal
Utah	Supreme Court	
Vermont	Trial & Appellate	Civil & Criminal
Virginia	Trial & Appellate	Civil & Criminal
Washington	Trial & Appellate	Civil & Criminal
West Virginia	Trial & Appellate	Civil & Criminal
Wyoming	Trial & Appellate	Civil & Criminal

(Continues)

Table 5.1 Cameras in State Courts (*continued*)

State	Level	Division
	States with Permanent Rules	
Delaware	Supreme Court	Civil
Idaho	Court of Appeals	Civil & Criminal
	Trial Courts	
Indiana	Appelate Courts	
New Jersey	Municipal Courts	Civil & Criminal
Pennsylvania	Trial, non-jury	Civil, Superior Court

Summary of State Rules

States with Permanent Rules*

Approved for Trial and Appellate Courts	36
Approved for Trial Courts Only	2
Approved for Appellate Courts Only	8

States with Permanent Rules*

Approved for Trial and Appellate Courts	1
Approved for Trial Courts Only	4
Approved for Appellate Courts Only	2
Total states allowing cameras in a courtroom	50
Total states allowing cameras in a criminal trial	37

Note: Some states fall into more than one category.

Source: National Center for State Courts, Knowledge and Information Services, Williamsburg, VA 23187, 2002. Reprinted with permission.

U.S. Supreme Court

Press coverage of the U.S. Supreme Court has also been the object of research. One major study (Davis 1994), based in part on interviews with leading journalists covering the High Court (including Lyle Denniston, Linda Greenhouse, Tony Mauro, and Tim O'Brien [see Chapter 4]), concluded that the Court manipulates the press to "promote institutional power" and that individual justices also possess separate objectives "pursued through a variety of interactions with the press."

Another study, by Slotnick and Segal (1998), researched the amount of time the television networks spent covering the High Court in addition to the content of the stories and was highly critical of the fact that each year fewer and fewer stories are covered, and there are often errors in the stories that do make the news.

Another commentator who studied press coverage of the Court said the Supreme Court reporters might be "Washington's most deferential press corps." He concluded that the press was "falling down in its role as a watchdog for an entire branch of government" (Schmidt 1999, 73).

Finally, there have been dozens of articles in legal journals delving into the complex constitutional aspects of media coverage of courts. Books by Matthew Bunker and Douglas Campbell (see resources for Chapter 3) include comprehensive discussions of such legal research in understandable language (unlike many of the original articles, which were written for scholars in "legalese").

Guidelines, Canons, and Codes

Free press/fair trial recommendations published by the media, the legal profession, and the courts are designed to enhance press coverage of the judicial process.

The Media

There are three valuable resources for journalists seeking guidance in covering courts. As mentioned in Chapter 4, Lyle Denniston, longtime Supreme Court reporter, in 1980 wrote the definitive book for print reporters, *The Reporter and the Law,* on the subject of press coverage (Denniston 1992). Denniston includes in-depth discussions of all aspects of the issue and specific suggestions for improved coverage.

Expanding on Denniston's approach, S. L. Alexander wrote *Covering the Courts,* a handbook for print reporters, photojournalists, and broadcast journalists, which is a useful tool in the courthouse or back in the newsroom (Alexander 1999, 2003). The last chapter of the handbook is a compendium of firsthand tips gathered from working journalists, lawyers, and judges (many of them already mentioned in earlier chapters).

Finally, Steve Weinberg of the Investigative Reporters and Editors organization (IRE) has written extensively on the subject, including "Investigating Government: The Judicial System" in the latest edition of *The Investigative Reporter's Handbook* (Weinberg 2002). Weinberg includes detailed suggestions for following the paper trail in a case and also descriptions of experienced courtroom reporters' discoveries of wrongdoing in the judicial system. The article includes examinations of the work of several authors discussed in Chapter 4.

There are also three major codes of ethics for journalists who are involved in courtroom coverage. The Society of Professional Journalists (SPJ) is one of the oldest and largest press organizations and includes journalists for print, broadcast, and cyberspace (see Chapter 6). The SPJ Code of Ethics (available at http://www.spj.org) is based on the premise that the journalist has a duty to serve the public with professional integrity. To that end, in addition to numerous general principles, the code includes three recommendations that specifically address courtroom coverage concerns:

- Be cautious about identifying juvenile suspects or victims of sex crimes.
- Be judicious about naming criminal suspects before the formal filing of charges.
- Balance a criminal suspect's fair trial rights with the public's right to be informed.

The RTNDA, originally open only to the heads of broadcast news operations, now welcomes all broadcast journalists (see Chapter 6). The RTNDA Code of Ethics and Professional Conduct (available at http://www.rtnda.org) is based on the premise that electronic journalists are trustees of the public. In addition to general principles, the code includes three recommendations, which address problems that have arisen for those involved with courtroom coverage:

- Professional journalists should not pay news sources who have a vested interest in a story.
- Professional journalists should treat all subjects of news coverage with respect and dignity, showing particular compassion to victims of crime or tragedy.
- Professional journalists should respect the right to a fair trial.

Finally, the National Press Photographers Association (NPPA) is an organization that welcomes all photojournalists (see Chapter 6). The NPPA Code of Ethics (available at http://www.nppa.org) is based on the premise that pictures enhance the public's ability to be truthfully informed. The code includes nine general principles of ethical conduct, most of which might be applied to the work of the courtroom photojournalist, based on the first principle: "The practice of photojournalism, both as a science and art, is worthy of the very best thought and effort of those who enter into it as a profession."

The Courts

Organizations of lawyers, judges, and court personnel all contribute guidance for those concerned with improvements in courtroom coverage.

The American Bar Association (ABA)—open to lawyers, law students, and interested associates (see Chapter 6)—is a key source of courtroom-coverage material. The ABA has produced guides to both criminal and civil courts, in print form as well as video. The most significant publication is *The Reporter's Key* (1994), produced in conjunction with the National Conference of Lawyers and Representatives of the Media (third edition [2002] at http://www.abanet.org). The *Key* includes discussion of rules and standards in criminal cases and looks at guidelines in civil cases as well.

The ABA codes of conduct, adopted by most jurisdictions, are generally treated as if they were laws. The Model Rule of Professional Conduct Rule 3.6 Trial Publicity (ABA 2002–2003b) is often cited when lawyers are asked to comment on a pending court case. Basically, Rule 3.6 says that a lawyer should not comment if the lawyer knows, or should know, that the information will have a "substantial likelihood of materially prejudicing an adjudicative proceeding in the matter." The rule adds a reminder about the traditional aspects of a case a lawyer may comment on, including "directory information" (names, addresses of clients), scheduling of legal proceedings, and—in a criminal case—information such as warnings when there is danger to the public.

The ABA *Standards for Criminal Justice, Fair Trial, and Free Press* (ABA 2002–2003a) includes rules for the conduct of attorneys in criminal cases as well as for the conduct of judicial proceedings in criminal cases. The standards call for limits on comments by attorneys outside of court; suggest judges avoid direct restraints on the media; and encourage public access to proceedings and court records while maintaining decorum via such techniques as assigned seating, jury sequestration, and admonitions to the jury regarding avoiding outside influences. The standards also suggest limiting broadcast coverage unless authorized by the supervising court or other authority, with all coverage subject to restrictions by the presiding judge.

The National Association of Criminal Defense Lawyers (NACDL) and the American College of Trial Lawyers (ACTL) (see Chapter 6) have called for a voluntary code of ethics for lawyers who serve as legal commentators for televised trials, such as that proposed by prominent lawyers Erwin Chemerinsky and Laurie Levenson (1996). For instance, Chemerinsky and Levenson suggest ethical provisions might say, "Commentators may be paid a reasonable fee for their work," and "[A] commentator must comply with all laws and refrain from conduct 'prejudicial to the administration of justice.'" Also, commentators "should not knowingly advise or assist another in a violation of the law" (1336–1338).

The American Board of Trial Advocates (ABOTA) (see Chapter 6), an organization of lawyers handling civil rather than criminal cases, has come up with a suggested "Accuracy in Legal Journalism Reporting Code" (available at http://www.abota.org). The code suggests journalists covering civil cases should state whether the defendant lacks assets or insurance so that even if the plaintiff wins, the award cannot be collected. And ABOTA also suggests journalists give the same coverage to verdicts that the defendant or respondent (often a large corporation) wins as to those won by the plaintiff (often in a class action suit), as well as follow up cases to the ultimate outcome.

Judges also receive guidance regarding the balancing of fair trial/free press concerns. As mentioned earlier, the NCSC (see Chapter 6) has published *Managing Notorious Trials* (Murphy, 1992, 1998), a bible for judges presiding over high-profile trials. An entire chapter is devoted to dealing with the media, including access to proceedings and records, protecting the jury from interference, and details on handling still and television cameras in the courtroom—information useful to state and federal judges.

The Judicial Conference of the United States (see Chapter 6), the governing body for federal judges, has developed a body of *canons,* or rules of conduct for judges, which are treated as if they were law. The *Code of Judicial Conduct for U.S. Judges* includes Canon 3A, "A Judge Should Perform the Duties of the Office Impartially and Diligently." Six suggestions are presented to help the judge adhere to the standards, including number six, which states:

A judge should avoid public comment on the merits of a pending or impending action, requiring similar restraint by court personnel subject to the judge's direction and control. This proscription does not extend to public statements made in the course of the judge's official duties, to the explanation of court procedures, or to a scholarly presentation made for purposes of legal education. (Judicial Conference of the United States 2002)

The Judicial Conference also developed *Guidelines for the Pilot Program in Photographing, Recording, and Broadcasting in the Courtroom*, used in the experiment in federal courts in the 1990s. The guidelines are also beneficial for use by various states as they adapt guidelines for camera coverage. Issues covered include general provisions (advance notice of requests for coverage, no use of public funds for coverage); limitations (no pickup of conferences between lawyers and clients); equipment and personnel (generally limited to one still camera and one video, with pooling arrangements—sharing cameras—the responsibility of the media); sound and light criteria (no modification of courtrooms, no distracting sound or light); location of equipment and personnel (designated by judge); and need for compliance (or subject to sanctions by the court).

The U.S. Justice Department and various courts have contributed recommendations of interest to those concerned with covering courts. The department's *U.S. Attorney's Manual* includes detailed guidelines for balancing the "right of the public to know; an individual's right to a fair trial; and the government's ability to effectively enforce the administration of justice" (1.700 Media Relations, available at http://www.usdoj.gov). The guidelines emphasize the need for both a free press and a fair trial and include numerous rules designed to contribute to attaining that goal: designating a media representative in every U.S. Attorney's Office; releasing information as long as it does not have a "substantial likelihood of materially prejudicing an adjudicative proceeding"; assisting the news media to photograph, tape, record, or televise a crime scene when appropriate; not providing advance information on search or arrest warrants; and requesting the news media to leave if their presence "puts the operation or the safety of individuals in jeopardy."

The U.S. Supreme Court Public Information Office (see Chapter 6; accessible at http://www.supremecourtus.gov) employs a full-time staff to help journalists assigned to cover the High Court. The website includes such helpful publications as *A Reporter's Guide to Applications Pending before the Supreme Court of the U.S.*, extremely useful for those attempting to understand the complex system of applications for stays of execution by condemned prisoners. Tips include how to contact public information officers, obtaining access to case filings, what television might be able to capture on camera, and how a reporter can find out what action takes place after hours.

Other federal and state courts have begun to hire media specialists as well. For example, Jerianne Hayslett of the Los Angeles County Courts is one of the more active court liaisons. Rebecca Fanning did such a fine job working with the Minnesota courts, she now heads the federal court community and educational outreach program.

A closer look at the work of such organizations, associations, and agencies concerned with courtroom coverage is the subject of Chapter 6.

References

Alexander, S. L. 1990. "Mischievous Potentialities." (PhD dissertation, University of Florida).

———. 1991. "Cameras in the Courtroom." *Judicature* 74, no. 6 (April–May): 307–313.

———. 1996. "The Impact of *California v Simpson* on Cameras in the Courtroom." *Judicature* 79, no. 4 (January–February): 169–172.

———. 1999, 2003. *Covering the Courts.* Lanham, MD: University Press of America, Rowman and Littlefield.

———. 2000. "A Reality Check on Court/Media Relations." *Judicature* 84, no. 3 (November–December): 146–149.

American Bar Association. 2002–2003 ed. *Model Rules of Professional Conduct*; also, *ABA Standards for Criminal Justice, Fair Trial and Free Press*, in *Professional Responsibility Standards, Rules, and Statutes.* Washington, DC: ABA.

American Bar Association, et al. 1994. *The Reporter's Key.* Chicago: ABA (3d edition [2002] at http://www.abanet.org).

Barber, Susanna. 1987. *News Cameras in the Courtroom.* Norwood, NJ: Albex.

Chemerinsky, Erwin, and Laurie Levenson. 1996. "The Ethics of Being a Commentator." *Southern California Law Review* 69: 1303–1339.

Chiasson, Lloyd, ed. 1997. *The Press on Trial.* Westport, CT: Greenwood.

Cohn, Marjorie, and David Dow. 1998. *Cameras in the Courtroom.* Jefferson, NC: McFarland.

Davis, Richard. 1994. *Decisions and Images.* Englewood Cliffs, NJ: Prentice-Hall.

Denniston, Lyle. 1992. Reprint. *The Reporter and the Law: Techniques of Covering the Courts,* rev ed. New York: Columbia University Press, 1980.

Fox, Richard, and Robert Van Sickel. 2001. *Tabloid Justice.* Boulder, CO: Lynne Rienner Publishers.

Giles, Robert, and Robert Snyder, eds. 1999. *Covering the Courts.* New Brunswick, NJ: Transaction Publishers.

Goldfarb, Ronald. 1998. *TV or Not TV.* New York: New York University Press.

Johnson, Molly Treadway. 1993–1994. *Electronic Media Coverage of Courtroom Proceedings.* Washington, DC: Federal Judicial Center.

Judicial Conference of the United States. 2002. *Code of Judicial Conduct for U.S. Judges.* Washington, DC: Judicial Conference of the United States. See also, *Guidelines for the Pilot Program in Photographing, Recording and Broadcasting in the Courtroom.* Washington, DC: Administrative Office of the U.S. Courts, reissued October 14, 1997.

Murphy, Timothy. 1998. *Managing Notorious Trials.* Williamsburg, VA: National Center for State Courts.

National Center for State Courts (NCSC). 2002. *Summary of Television in the State Courts.* Williamsburg: National Center for State Courts.

Schmidt, Robert. 1999. "May It Please the Court." *Brill's Content,* October, 73.

Slotnick, Eliot, and Jennifer Segal. 1998. *Television News and the Supreme Court.* New York: Cambridge University Press.

Thaler, Paul. 1997. *The Spectacle.* Westport, CT: Praeger.

Weinberg, Steve. 2002. "Investigating Government: The Judicial System," in *The Investigative Reporter's Handbook,* ed. Brant Houston et al. Boston: Bedford/St. Martin's, 249–308.

Westfeldt, Wallace, and Tom Wicker. 1998. *Indictment.* Executive Summary. Nashville, TN: First Amendment Center.

6

Organizations, Associations, and Government Agencies

Media

Court TV
600 Third Avenue
New York, NY 10016
(712) 973-2800; (800) COURT56 (Viewer Information Line)
http://www.courttv.com

Court TV was founded in 1991 by Steven Brill. Managing editor Fred Graham has been with the organization since the start (see Chapter 4).

The interactive website is extremely useful to anyone interested in coverage of courts, with its links to text and video clips from the live trial coverage of prominent court cases that dominates the daytime schedule. (Documentaries, courtroom dramas, and news shows are scheduled on evenings and weekends.)

Begun in 1997, a public service project, "Choices and Consequences," aims to help teenagers stay out of court. The Consumer Law and Small Business centers offer practical help, while the Constitutional Law Center and "Cases and Codes" provide useful links. The site also includes a legal dictionary with definitions of more than 1,000 terms.

Criminal Justice Journalists
Criminal Justice Journalists/Penn
720 Seventh Street NW, Third Floor

Washington, DC 20001
(202) 448-1717
http://www.reporters.net/cjj

Founded in 1997 by journalists Ted Gest and David Krajicek, the goal of the Criminal Justice Journalists (CJJ) is "to improve the quality and accuracy of news reporting on crime, law enforcement, and the judicial system." The nonprofit, member-supported organization is open to reporters, editors, news producers, and student journalists who cover the crime, court, and prison beats.

The organization compiles guides for journalists such as the recent *Understanding Crime Statistics* produced in cooperation with the Investigative Reporters and Editors (IRE) and *Covering Crime and Justice* (at http://www.justicejournalism.org/crimeguide). CJJ also organizes programs on topics such as access to court records; publishes periodic reports on criminal law topics such as "Behind the Beat: Guns"; and holds national conferences, sometimes in collaboration with the American Society of Criminology or the International Association of Chiefs of Police. CJJ also maintains a listserv and responds to requests from journalists.

Freedom Forum
1101 Wilson Boulevard
Arlington, VA 22209
(703) 528-0800; fax (703) 284-3519
First Amendment Center at Vanderbilt University
(Justice and Journalism)
1207 18th Avenue South
Nashville, TN 37212
(615) 727-1600; fax (615) 727-1319
http://www.freedomforum.org

Founded in 1991, the Freedom Forum is a nonprofit foundation "dedicated to free press, free speech, and free spirit for all people." The Forum sponsors the Newseum in Washington, D.C., and the First Amendment Center at Vanderbilt University.

The First Amendment Center serves by disseminating information and education about First Amendment issues. In partnership with the U.S. Courts Judicial Branch Committee, since 1999 the center has sponsored "Justice and Journalism," a series of forums bringing together members of the judiciary and the press to discuss such issues as access to courts and court records and press accountability. The goal of the program is "to encourage and assist in more accurate reporting to the public of what happens in federal courts, to help educate reporters about the courts' operations, and to help educate judges about the manner in which reporters and newspapers gather and present information about the justice system."

The Freedom Forum also publishes numerous reports and educational material on First Amendment topics including a collection of essays republished in book form as *Covering the Courts*, edited by Giles and Snyder (see Chapter 5).

Investigative Reporters and Editors
138 Neff Annex
Missouri School of Journalism
Columbia, MO 65211
(573) 882-2772
http://www.ire.org

The Investigative Reporters and Editors (IRE), founded in 1975, currently presents its mission as "to foster excellence in investigative journalism, which is essential to a free society . . . by providing training, resources and a community of support to investigative journalists, promoting high professional standards, and protecting the rights of investigative journalists."

In 1976, after investigative reporter Don Bolles was murdered while in the course of researching a story on organized crime in Arizona, IRE members volunteered to complete the award-winning story. IRE welcomes all investigative journalists, including professionals, academics, retirees, and student journalists.

The IRE website maintains a list of material including print and broadcast stories; tip sheets and guides on various topics such as coverage of courts; and a link with the IRE FoI Center, which monitors access issues.

National Press Photographers Association
3200 Croasdaile Drive, Suite 306
Durham, NC 27705-2588
(919) 383-7246; fax (919) 383-7261
http://www.nppa.org

The National Press Photographers Association (NPPA) is open to professional news photographers and those in related occupations, such as reporters, writers, editors, directors, copy editors, video editors, assignment editors, and designers, as well as student photojournalists.

In addition to publishing a code of ethics (see Chapter 5), NPPA services include the publication of a magazine, an audiovisual library, still photography and video critiquing, and information on competitions. The NPPA also works with attorneys to assist photojournalists with free press issues.

Radio-Television News Directors Association
1600 K Street NW, Suite 700
Washington, DC 20006-2838
(800) 80RTNDA; fax (202) 223-4007
http://www.rtnda.org

The Radio-Television News Directors Association (RTNDA), when founded in 1946, was open only to the heads of radio and television news organizations, but the organization now welcomes all broadcast journalists, including students. In addition to establishing a Code of Ethics and Professional Conduct (see Chapter 5), the RTNDA takes a leading role in promoting the responsible use of courtroom cameras and maintains a state-by-state guide of camera usage.

Also, the RTNDA maintains on its website comprehensive postings of the latest news on courtroom cameras as well as access to court proceedings and records. The RTNDA also supports journalists' attempts to obtain access to courts via filing *amicus curiae* ("friend of the court") briefs.

Reporters Committee for Freedom of the Press
1815 North Fort Myer Drive, Suite 900
Arlington, VA 22209
(800) 336-4243; (703) 807-2100
http://www.rcfp.org

Dedicated to "providing free legal assistance to journalists since 1970," the Reporters Committee for Freedom of the Press (RCFP) is extremely active regarding access to court proceedings and records. Useful publications include "Access to Juvenile Courts," "Access to Terrorism Proceedings," "Anonymous Juries," "Alternative Dispute Resolution," "Gag Orders," and "Judicial Records: A Guide to Access in State and Federal Courts." The RCFP publishes a quarterly journal, *The News Media and the Law,* and maintains a twenty-four-hour hotline for journalists. The RCFP also maintains a useful website, with a separate section "The Reporters' Privilege" (the statutes and case laws on shield laws and on subpoenas against the news media). Since 2003, the site includes a section "Behind the Homefront"—a "daily chronicle of news in homeland security and military operations affecting newsgathering, access to information, and the public's right to know."

Society of Professional Journalists
3909 North Meridian Street
Indianapolis, IN 46208
(317) 927-8000; fax (317) 920-4789
http://www.spj.org

Founded in 1909, the Society of Professional Journalists (SPJ) is dedicated to encouraging the free practice of journalism and stimulating high standards of ethical behavior.

The SPJ welcomes print, broadcast, and web journalists, as well as student journalists. In addition to publishing a Code of Ethics (see Chapter 5), the SPJ takes an active role in supporting journalists, including those seeking access to courts. To that end, the SPJ frequently files *amicus curiae* ("friend of the court") briefs supporting journalists denied access to court proceedings or court records or those challenging gag orders or use of anonymous juries.

Lawyers

American Bar Association
750 North Lake Shore Drive
Chicago, IL 60611
(312) 988-5000
http://www.abanet.org

The American Bar Association (ABA), which welcomes lawyers, law students, and interested associates, is a leading resource for anyone interested in the issue of press coverage of courts.

In addition to publishing rules and standards of conduct for lawyers and judges involved in judicial proceedings (see Chapter 5), the ABA has produced educational material to aid journalists in covering courts. These include *The Reporter's Key*, which explains the rules and standards of conduct, and both books and videos on civil procedure and federal criminal procedure (see resources for Chapter 5).

The Standing Committee on the Federal Judiciary evaluates the professional qualifications of federal judge nominees and thus has been a good source for information on judges. The organization has several other subdivisions of interest to those concerned with courtroom coverage, including the Standing Committee on Ethics and Professional Responsibility, the Forum on Communications Law, and the Public Education Division.

American Board of Trial Advocates
Bryan Tower, Suite 3000
2001 Bryan Street
Dallas, TX 75201
(214) 871-7523; (800) 779-5879; fax (214) 871-6025
http://www.abota.org

The American Board of Trial Advocates (ABOTA) was established in 1958 and is dedicated to "the preservation of the civil jury trial" as protected by the Seventh Amendment to the U.S. Constitution.

The ABOTA is open to lawyers concerned with civil trials. In addition to publishing the "Accuracy in Legal Journalism Reporting Code" (see Chapter 5), the ABOTA produces publications on the civil jury and a juror bill of rights. Educational materials include a video and an interactive CD-ROM game, "Justice by the People." Trial demonstrations are available, as are representatives of the speakers bureau.

National Association of Attorneys General
750 First Street NE, Suite 1100
Washington, DC 20002
(202) 326-6000; fax (202) 408-7014
http://www.naag.org

Founded in 1907, the National Association of Attorneys General (NAAG) states that its mission is "to facilitate interaction among Attorneys General as peers and to facilitate the enhanced performance of Attorneys General and their staffs." Goals include increasing citizen understanding of the law and law enforcement's role.

Useful material from the NAAG website includes the posting of documents from class-action suits, such as those in *U.S. v Microsoft* (discussed in Chapter 1).

National Association of Criminal Defense Lawyers
1150 18th Street NW, Suite 950
Washington, DC 20036
(202) 872-8600; fax (202) 872-8690
http://www.nacdl.org

Founded in 1958, the National Association of Criminal Defense Lawyers (NACDL) was organized to aid in ensuring "justice and due process for persons accused of crime or other misconduct." The NACDL is open to private lawyers, military defense counsel, law professors, and judges.

In addition to publishing the "Ethical Considerations for Criminal Defense Attorneys Serving as Legal Commentators" (see Chapter 5), the NACDL gathers information on cases and issues relating to criminal law.

National District Attorneys Association
99 Canal Center Plaza, Suite 510
Alexandria, VA 22314
(703) 549-9222; fax (703) 836-3195
http://www.ndaa.org

The National District Attorneys Association (NDAA) pledges "to be the voice of America's prosecutors and to support their efforts to protect the rights and safety of the people."

To this end, the NDAA offers research, training, and technical assistance and posts news regarding issues of the day on its website.

Courts

Administrative Office of the U.S. Courts
Washington, DC 20544
(202) 502-2600
http://www.uscourts.gov

Established in 1939, the Administrative Office of the U.S. Courts is devoted to serving the courts in fulfilling their critical mission of providing justice and resolving disputes.

The agency provides service to the federal courts in three essential areas: administrative support, program management, and policy development. It is also charged with implementing the policies of the Judicial Conference of the United States.

The Administrative Office maintains a website with links to all federal courts, including U.S. District Courts, U.S. Courts of Appeals, U.S. Bankruptcy Courts, and the U.S. Supreme Court. The office publishes information about the courts, maintains a library of publications, and posts updates on issues involving federal courts.

Conference of Court Public Information Officers
c/o Kimberly Swanson
National Center for State Courts
300 Newport Avenue
Williamsburg, VA 23185
(757) 259-1804; fax (757) 564-2025
http://www.flcourts.org/courtpio

Formed in 2000, the Conference of Court Public Information Officers states as its objective "to provide a focal point to improve the skill and knowledge required of those performing the duties of court public information officer." The organization holds conferences, seminars, and other educational programs.

The website of the conference includes a Document Exchange, which includes useful information on courts and media working together to enhance courtroom coverage.

Federal Judicial Center
One Columbus Circle NE
Washington, DC 20002-8003
(202) 502-4000
http://www.fjc.gov

The Federal Judicial Center is the educational and research agency for the federal courts. It was created in 1967 to "further the development and adoption of improved judicial administration" in U.S. courts. The website includes links to publications, information on federal judicial history (including biographies of federal judges and landmark legislation), and news on recent developments in the courts.

The current manager of the Federal Courts Educational Outreach Program, Rebecca Fanning, is a valuable contact for those interested in learning more about the federal courts.

National Center for State Courts
300 Newport Avenue
Williamsburg, VA 23185
(800) 616-6109; fax (757) 564-2022
http://www.ncsconline.org

The National Center for State Courts (NCSC) serves as a clearing-house on court issues. In addition to publishing data on cameras in courts and proposed guidelines for electronic access to court records (see Chapter 5), the NCSC answers queries on court-related topics. The website provides valuable links to state, federal, and international court websites and includes news on such issues as "technology and the law" and "public trust and confidence."

The NCSC also maintains a "Court Information Portal Search Engine" on its website. The portal provides links to NCSC's own material as well as to various court and court-related sites.

National Judicial College
Judicial College Building/358
Reno, NV 89557
(800) 25JUDGE; (775) 784-6747
http://www.judges.org

Formed in 1963, the National Judicial College (NJC) is dedicated to continuing education for judges. The purpose of the NJC is to "improve justice through national programs of education and training directed toward judicial proficiency, competency, skills, and productivity."

In 1996 and again in 2000, the NJC presented national conferences on courts and the media, bringing together judges, lawyers, and journalists who cover courts. The Reynolds Center for the Courts and Media of the National Judicial College was dedicated at the campus of the University of Nevada in Reno in 2000. The purpose of the center is "to foster discussion about the inherent tensions between the right to a fair trial, as guaranteed in the Sixth Amendment of the U.S. Constitution, and the First Amendment right of the free press to conduct its work largely unfettered by governmental restrictions." The center coordinates research projects and presents programs to enhance press coverage of courts.

U.S. Department of Justice: Bureau of Justice Statistics
810 Seventh Street NW
Washington, DC 20531
(202) 307-0765
http://www.ojp.usdoj.gov

The U.S. Department of Justice (DOJ) issues Guidelines for Media Relations (see Chapter 5). The DOJ's Bureau of Justice Statistics is the government's primary source of data on crimes and courts. Publications on crime, victims, and the justice system (including law enforcement, courts, and corrections) are available.

U.S. Sentencing Commission
One Columbus Circle, NE
Washington, DC 20002-8002
(202) 502-4500
http://www.ussc.gov

The U.S. Sentencing Commission was created by the 1984 Sentencing Reform Act. The commission is an independent judicial agency with duties including "developing guidelines for sentencing in federal courts; collecting data about crime and sentencing; and serving as a resource to Congress, the Executive Branch, and the Judiciary on crime and sentencing policy."

The agency website includes access to Sentencing Commission rules and procedures, biographies of Sentencing Commissioners since the agency's inception, and documents such as reports on identity theft and juvenile offenders.

U.S. Supreme Court
Public Information Office
Washington, DC 20543
(202) 479-3211
http://www.supremecourtus.gov

The Public Information Office of the U.S. Supreme Court (currently headed by Kathy Arberg) provides information on the Court and the justices, the docket of upcoming cases, and links to opinions. In addition to information such as *A Reporter's Guide to Applications Pending before the Supreme Court of the U.S.* (see Chapter 5), the website includes links to the U.S. Constitution, descriptions of the history of the Court, and biographies of all the justices from 1789 to the present.

7

Selected Print and Nonprint Resources

Chapter 1 Free Press/Fair Trial: A Historical Overview

Print Resources

General

Bergman, Paul, and Michael Asimow. *Reel Justice: The Courtroom Goes to the Movies.* Kansas City: Andrews and McMeel/ Universal Press Syndicate, 1996, 338 pp.

Two UCLA law professors present informative, witty reviews of films, including those inspired by the *Frank, Leopold and Loeb,* and *Scopes* cases.

Dunne, Dominick. *Justice: Crimes, Trials and Punishments.* New York: Crown, 2001, 337 pp.

The author (discussed in Chapter 4) reprints articles on celebrity trials, many from the magazine *Vanity Fair,* including *Menendez* and *Simpson.*

Geis, Gilbert, and Leigh Bienen. *Crimes of the Century: From Leopold and Loeb to O. J. Simpson.* Boston: Northeastern University, 1998, 230 pp.

The authors present an in-depth look at *Leopold and Loeb,* "Scottsboro," *Hauptmann, Hiss,* and *Simpson.*

Grant, Robert, and Joseph Katz. *The Great Trials of the Twenties: The Watershed Decade in America's Courtrooms.* Rockville Center, NY: Sarpedon, 1998, 282 pp.

The authors discuss cases including *Sacco and Vanzetti, Scopes,* and *Leopold and Loeb.*

Knappman, Edward, ed. *American Trials of the 20th Century: From the Scopes Monkey Trial to O. J. Simpson.* Detroit: Visible Ink Press, 1994, 1995, 627 pp.

The author gives summaries of 130-plus trials (including most of those discussed in Chapter 1), based on historic and legal significance, degree of public controversy, attention, legal ingenuity, and literary fame.

Kraft, Betsy. *Sensational Trials of the 20th Century.* New York: Scholastic Press, 1998, 216 pp.

This excellent young adult book includes discussion (and graphics) of six trials discussed in Chapter 1, including *Sacco and Vanzetti* (protest poster), *Scopes, Hauptmann* (ransom note), Rosenbergs (sketch of facsimile of A-bomb), Watergate (Nixon resignation letter) and *Simpson* cases.

London, Ephraim, ed. *The Law as Literature: A Treasury of Great Writing About and in the Law—From Plato to the Present.* New York: Simon and Schuster, 1960, 780 pp.

Reprints include newspaper and magazine commentaries on *Borden,* H. L. Mencken coverage of *Scopes,* and Felix Frankfurter on *Sacco and Vanzetti.*

Snyder, Louis, and Richard Morris, eds. *A Treasury of Great Reporting: "Literature Under Pressure" from the Sixteenth Century to Our Own Time.* New York: Simon and Schuster, (1949) 1962, 795 pp.

The authors provide brief introductions to reprints of the original coverage of cases including *Thaw, Scopes, Snyder-Gray,* and *Sacco and Vanzetti.*

Wilson, Theo. *Headline Justice: Inside the Courtroom—The Country's Most Controversial Trials.* New York: Thunder's Mouth Press, 1996, 238 pp.

A trial reporter's take on coverage of cases including *Sheppard,* "Pentagon Papers," *Manson, Hearst,* and *Simpson.*

Cases
Bush v Gore

Dionne, E. J., and William Kristol, eds. *Bush v Gore: The Court Cases and the Commentary.* Washington, DC: Brookings Institution, 2001, 344 pp.

The authors, representing a conservative viewpoint, discuss the case; their book includes useful reprints of relevant documents.

Greenfield, Jeff. *"Oh, Waiter! One Order of Crow!" Inside the Strangest Presidential Election Finish in American History.* New York: GP Putnam's Sons, 2001, 313 pp.

The journalist and commentator emphasizes press coverage of the election in his discussion of the case.

Kellner, Douglas. *Grand Theft 2000: Media Spectacle and a Stolen Election.* Lanham, MD: Rowman and Littlefield, 2001, 242 pp.

The author, a critical theorist, relying on alternative sources, concludes "[M]ainstream media failed democracy during the battle for the White House."

Merzer, Martin, et al. *The Miami Herald Report: Democracy Held Hostage.* New York: St. Martin's Press, 2001, 302 pp.

Based on an in-depth analysis of the events surrounding the case, the newspaper writers conclude Bush may have won the 2000 election anyway.

The New York Times. *36 Days: The Complete Chronicle of the 2000 Presidential Election Crisis.* Introduction by Douglas Brinkley. New York: Times Books, 2001, 380 pp.

The compendium of newspaper articles covering *Bush v Gore* also includes the Supreme Court case itself.

Posner, Richard. *Breaking the Deadlock: The 2000 Election, the Constitution and the Courts.* Princeton, NJ: Princeton University Press, 2001, 266 pp.

A discussion of the case by the respected jurist (understandably) takes a legalistic approach.

The Washington Post. *Deadlock: The Inside Story of America's Closest Election.* New York: Public Affairs, 2001, 271 pp.

The book is based on the eight-part election series by writers for the capital's foremost newspaper.

California v Manson

Bugliosi, Vincent, with Curt Gentry. *Helter Skelter: The True Story of the Manson Murders.* New York: Norton, 1974, rev 1994, 528 pp.

The Manson prosecutor's Edgar Award–winning best-seller on the case, the book was the basis for the movie of the same name. (See also Chapter 4, Bugliosi.)

King, Greg. *Sharon Tate and the Manson Murders.* New York: Barricade Books, 2000, 343 pp.

The updated information on the particulars in the case focuses on one of the victims, actress Sharon Tate.

Manson, Charles (as told to) Nuell Emmons. *Manson: In His Own Words.* New York: Grove Press, 1986, 232 pp.

The book presents the delusional ravings of the murderous monster who was convicted of masterminding the murders.

California v Menendez

Menendez, Lyle (as told to) Norma Novelli, with M Walker. *The Private Diary of Lyle Menendez.* Beverly Hills: Dove, 1995, 263 pp.

The book is based on self-serving, taped conversations with one of the two imprisoned brothers who were convicted of murdering their parents.

California v Simpson

Petrocelli, Daniel, with Peter Knobler. *Triumph of Justice: The Final Judgment on the O. J. Simpson Saga.* New York: Crown, 1998, 644 pp.

The lawyer for the families of the victims in the civil case explains why Simpson was correctly held liable for the deaths of his wife, Nicole, and her friend Ron Goldman.

Schiller, Lawrence, and James Willwerth. *American Tragedy: The Uncensored Story of the Simpson Defense.* New York: Random House, 1996, 702 pp.

An overwritten but complete look at the criminal case, written with the benefit of insider defense information. The book implies Simpson's guilt and was the basis for the 1996 TV miniseries of the same name.

Florida v Smith

Matoesian, Gregory. "Overview of the William Kennedy Smith Rape Trial," 9–34, 24 pp, in *Law and the Language of Identity: Discourse in the William Kennedy Smith Rape Trial.* New York: Oxford University Press, 2000, 267 pp.

This linguistic study is incomprehensible to laymen, but the first chapter provides, in ordinary English, an excellent presentation of the details of the trial and of press coverage of the case.

Georgia v Frank

Dinnerstein, Leonard. *The Leo Frank Case.* (University of Georgia, 1987); reprint including *The Tennessean,* "An Innocent Man Was Lynched, with Statement by Alonzo Mann, 3/7/82," Birmingham: Notable Trials Library, 1972, 267 pp.

The widely quoted academic work includes useful graphics.

Frey, Robert, and Nancy Thompson-Frey. *The Silent and the Damned: The Murder of Mary Phagan and the Lynching of Leo Frank.* New York: Madison Books, 1988, 248 pp.

This book, a popular version of the story, includes an epilogue on the pardon and numerous graphics.

Golden, Harry. *A Little Girl Is Dead.* Cleveland: World Publishing, 1965, 363 pp.

One of the foremost Jewish American journalists presents a comprehensive look at the case in the context of its time.

Oney, Steve. *And the Dead Shall Rise.* New York: Pantheon, 2003, 742 pp.

This exhaustive study includes discussion of all aspects of the case as well as numerous photographs.

Phagan, Mary. *The Murder of Little Mary Phagan.* Far Hills, NJ: New Horizon Press, 1987, 316 pp.

The interesting memoir-style account by the grandniece of Mary Phagan describes the family's opposition to the posthumous pardon of Leo Frank.

Hauptmann

Alexander, S. L. "Curious History: The ABA Code of Judicial Ethics Canon 35." 18:3 *Mass Comm Review,* 1991, 31–37+, 8 pp.

The author takes an in-depth look at how newsreel cameras became the scapegoat for the "circus" and the reasons for the resulting ban on courtroom cameras, including traditional press/ bar/bench politics and the newspaper radio war.

Kennedy, Ludovic. *Crime of the Century: The Lindbergh Kidnapping and the Framing of Richard Hauptmann* (originally *The Airman and the Carpenter,* Penguin Books, 1985), 2d ed, New York: Viking, 1996, 438 pp.

The writer's viewpoint is summed up by the new title: Hauptmann was framed.

Kielbowicz, Richard. "The Story Behind the Adoption of the Ban on Courtroom Cameras." *Judicature:* 63:1, June-July 1979, 14–23, 10 pp.

The revisionist writer was the first to show the scapegoating of the use of courtroom cameras in the case.

Whipple, Sidney. *The Trial of Bruno Richard Hauptmann.* (Doubleday, 1937); reprint Birmingham: Notable Trials Library, 1989, 565 pp.

Useful; includes numerous photos and excerpts from trial transcript.

"Hollywood 10"

Aronson, James. *The Press and the Cold War.* Indianapolis: Bobbs-Merrill, 1970, 308 pp.

The author presents comprehensive coverage of the issue.

Barson, Michael, and Steven Heller. *Red Scared! The Commie Menace in Propaganda and Popular Culture.* San Francisco: Chronicle Books, 2001, 160 pp.

The authors take a delightful, irreverent approach to the issues.

Bayley, Edwin. *Joe McCarthy and the Press.* Madison: University of Wisconsin Press, 1981, 270 pp.

The study of more than 100 newspapers and broadcasters shows the hesitation of the media (with few exceptions, such as

the *Washington Post* and CBS's Edward R. Murrow) to expose Mc-
Carthy.

Navasky, Victor. **Naming Names.** New York: Viking, 1980, 482 pp.
　The widely cited source presents a comprehensive study of
McCarthyism.

Illinois v Leopold and Loeb

Higdon, Hal. **Leopold and Loeb: The Crime of the Century.** (Putnam, 1975); rev Urbana: University of Illinois Press, 1999, 380 pp.
　The book presents objective descriptions and is widely cited.

Leopold, Nathan. **Life Plus Ninety-Nine Years.** Garden City, NY:
Doubleday, 1958, 381 pp.
　Introduction by Erle Stanley Gardner. The autobiography
includes everything you want to know about Nathan Leopold
except the facts of his early life and the details of the murder
itself.

Levin, Meyer. **Compulsion.** New York: Simon and Schuster, 1956,
495 pp.
　The popular book served as the basis for the movie of the
same name and also as the basis for Leopold's unsuccessful privacy suit against the author.

McKernan, Maureen. **The Amazing Crime and Trial of Leopold
and Loeb.** (Plymouth Court Press, 1924); reprint Birmingham:
Notable Trials Library, 1989, 380 pp.
　The useful work includes the arguments of the prosecutor
and the famous plea of Clarence Darrow for the defense.

"King"

Cannon, Lou. **Official Negligence: How Rodney King and the Riots Changed Los Angeles and the LAPD.** New York: Times Books,
1997, 698 pp.
　A comprehensive look at the case by the *Washington Post*
journalist who covered it.

Koon, Stacey, with Robert Deitz. **Presumed Guilty: The Tragedy of
the Rodney King Affair.** Washington, DC: Regnery Gateway,
1992, 269 pp.

The cops' version includes their defense that the public did not see King charging them on the edited version of the video, which aired extensively at the time.

Louisiana v Shaw

Brener, Milton. *The Garrison Case: A Study in the Abuse of Power.* New York: Crown, 1969, 278 pp.

The former New Orleans assistant district attorney's early book includes a description of local judges' unsuccessful libel case against Garrison, which contributed to his arrogance in the prosecution of Clay Shaw.

DiEugenio, James. *Destiny Betrayed: JFK, Cuba, and the Garrison Case.* New York: Sheridan Square Press, 1992, 423 pp.

The author blames media coverage for somehow damaging the prosecution of Shaw, but he offers little support for this speculation.

Epstein, Edward J. *Counterplot.* New York: Viking, 1969, 182 pp.

A contemporaneous critic of the Warren Report shows the vulnerability of the press to manipulation.

Final Report of the Assassination Records Review Board. Washington, DC: Government Printing Office, 1999, 208 pp.

The report includes the results of a hearing held in New Orleans which led to the release of long-hidden material on the *Shaw* case. (See also Alexander, S. L. "The Cases of Richard Angelico," *IRE Journal,* July-August 1996, 10–13, 4 pp.)

Garrison, James. *On the Trail of the Assassins: My Investigation and Prosecution of the Murder of President Kennedy.* New York: Sheridan Square Press, 1988, 342 pp.

The colorful New Orleans district attorney describes his prosecution of Shaw.

Kirkwood, James. *American Grotesque: An Account of the Clay Shaw/Jim Garrison Affair in the City of New Orleans.* New York: Simon and Schuster, 1970, 669 pp.

The colorful, nonscholarly account of the story was written by a writer who had hoped to sell the story to *Playboy.*

Lambert, Patricia. *False Witness: The Real Story of Jim Garrison's Investigation and Oliver Stone's Film* **JFK**. New York: M. Evans, 1998, 352 pp.

Following up on the work of others, Lambert says the case was based on manufactured evidence and perjured testimony, but the writing is marred by the *distracting* use of *italics.*

Posner, Gerald. "Black Is White and White Is Black," in *Case Closed: Lee Harvey Oswald and the Assassination of JFK.* New York: Random House, 1993, 423–452, 30 pp.

A chapter of his very persuasive book debunking conspiracy theorists is devoted to discrediting Garrison.

Massachusetts v Sacco and Vanzetti

Frankel, Osmond. *The Sacco-Vanzetti Case.* (Knopf, 1931); reprint Birmingham: Notable Trials Library, 1990, 550 pp.

The book includes testimony from the trial and the opinion of the trial judge.

Frankfurter, Felix. *The Case of Sacco and Vanzetti: A Critical Analysis for Lawyers and Laymen.* (Little Brown, 1927), 2nd ed, New York: Universal Library, 1962, 118 pp.

This work is a widely cited defense of the defendants by the Harvard law professor, later U.S. Supreme Court justice.

Russell, Francis. *Sacco and Vanzetti: The Case Resolved.* New York: Harper and Row, 1986, 245 pp.

Based on his research, the author concludes Sacco was likely guilty, but Vanzetti maybe not.

Stark, L. "Doubts That Will Not Down," *The New York Times*, 23 August 1927 reprint in *A Treasury of Great Reporting,* eds Louis Snyder and Richard Morris. New York: Simon and Schuster (1949), 2nd ed 1962, 452–460, 9 pp.

The article is a reprint of the coverage of the case by the nation's paper of record.

Young, William, and David Kaiser. *Postmortem: New Evidence in the Case of Sacco and Vanzetti.* Amherst: University of Massachusetts, 1985, 188 pp.

Based on their research, the authors conclude both Sacco and Vanzetti were likely innocent.

New York v Snyder and Gray

Runyon, Damon. "Murder in the Worst Degree," International News Service, 19 April, 27 April, 28 April, 9 May 1927. Reprint in *A Treasury of Great Reporting*, eds. Louis Snyder and Richard Morris. New York: Simon and Schuster (1949), 2nd ed, 1962, 439–445, 7 pp.

Positively Runyonesque, the articles are reprints of coverage of the case by the most well-known *noir*-style journalist of all time.

New York v Thaw

Cobb, Irvin. "You have ruined my wife!" *Evening World* (New York), 7 February 1907; reprint in *A Treasury of Great Reporting*, eds. Louis Snyder and Richard Morris. New York: Simon and Schuster (1949), 2nd ed, 1962, 283–291, 9 pp.

The widely quoted coverage of the case by an outstanding journalist.

Doctorow, E. L. *Ragtime.* New York: Random House, 1975, 270 pp.

The fictionalized version of the story mingles real-life figures with fictional, calls Nesbit the "first sex goddess in American history," portrays Thaw as sadist, and was the basis for the movie by the same name.

Lessard, Suzannah. *The Architect of Desire: Beauty and Danger in the Stanford White Family.* New York: Dial Press, 1996, 334 pp.

The personal memoir includes interesting details but adds little new on the trial.

Longford, Gerald. *The Murder of Stanford White.* (Bobbs-Merrill, 1962); reprint New York: Notable Trials Library, 1996, 270 pp.

The author discusses the case and includes photos and excerpts from various decisions in the case.

Mooney, Michael. *Evelyn Nesbit and Stanford White: Love and Death in the Gilded Age.* New York: Morrow, 1976, 320 pp.

The author provides rich detail and the social history of the case.

New York Times v Sullivan

Hopkins, Wat. *Actual Malice: 25 Years After Times v Sullivan.* New York: Praeger, 1989, 215 pp.

The author discusses the impact of the landmark decision which made it more difficult for public officials to win a libel case on the grounds of the constitutional need for "robust debate" on issues of public concern.

Lewis, Anthony. *Make No Law: The Sullivan Case and the First Amendment.* New York: Random House, 1991, 354 pp.

The award-winning journalist (see Chapter 4) presents a very readable story of the case.

New York Times v U.S.
(Pentagon Papers)

Anatomy of an Undeclared War: Congressional Conference on the Pentagon Papers. Ed Patricia Krause. New York: International Universities Press, 1972, 217 pp.

The objective work includes the friend-of-court appeals on behalf of the public's right to know.

Ellsberg, Daniel. *Secrets: A Memoir of Vietnam and the Pentagon Papers.* New York: Viking, 2002, 498 pp.

The book presents the views of the war-hawk-turned-dove, whose actions in leaking the Pentagon Papers (tireless photocopying of documents, giving copies to *The New York Times'* Neil Sheehan, and after the injunction to the *Washington Post* and others) contributed to the end of the war—and of the presidency of Nixon, who was obsessed with destroying Ellsberg.

Herda, D. J. *New York Times v United States: National Security and Censorship.* Springfield, NJ: Enslow, 1994.

This is the young adult version of the Pentagon Papers case.

The Pentagon Papers, ed. Neil Sheehan et al. (Chicago: Quadrangle Books), New York: New York Times/Bantam Books, 1971, 677 pp.

The newspaper presents one of several edited versions of the original document that studies how the U.S. came to be involved in Vietnam.

Rudenstine, David. *The Day the Presses Stopped: A History of the Pentagon Papers Case.* Berkeley: University of California Press, 1996, 416 pp.

The author implies that President Nixon—who generally hated the press—did have some valid concerns regarding publication of some of the material, but that no serious harm resulted from publication of the documents.

Ungar, Sanford. *The Papers and the Papers: An Account of the Legal and Political Battle Over the Pentagon Papers* (Dutton, 1972; Columbia University, 1989); reprint Birmingham: Notable Trials Library, 1996, 340 pp.

The author presents a very thorough account of the case. Written at the time of the events, it supports the notion of good journalism as "instant history."

Scopes v Tennessee

Caudill, Edward. *The Scopes Trial: A Photographic History.* Knoxville: University of Tennessee Press, 2000, 88 pp.

The photographs are fascinating, especially seeing Bryan, Darrow, Scopes, and the trial scene itself.

Ginger, Ray. *Six Days or Forever? Tennessee v John Tomas Scopes.* Boston: Beacon Press, 1958, 258 pp.

The author takes an objective look at the case and the teaching of creationism.

Grebstein, Sheldon. *Monkey Trial: The State of Tennessee vs John Thomas Scopes.* Boston: Houghton Mifflin, 1960, 221 pp.

The student casebook includes the trial transcript.

Larson, Edward. *Summer for the Gods: The Scopes Trial and America's Continuing Debate Over Science and Religion.* New York: Basic Books, 1997, 318 pp.

The work includes updates, with a discussion of U.S. Supreme Court cases dealing with the teaching of creationism, which arose during the 1960s in Arkansas and Louisiana.

Mencken, H. L. "Deep in 'The Coca-Cola Belt,'" *The (Baltimore) Sun,* 13 July 1925; *The New York Times,* "Monkey Business in Tennessee," 21 July 1925. Excerpt in *The Law as Literature,* ed.

Ephraim London. New York: Simon and Schuster, 1960, 66–81, 16 pp (and elsewhere).

The coverage by one of the most popular journalists of the times is still being read today by students of journalism.

The Scopes Trial. (Union, NJ: Tri-National Books, 1925; The Lawbook Exchange, 1971); reprint Birmingham: Notable Trials Library, 1990, 339 pp.

The reference work includes transcripts of the famous arguments.

Tomkins, Jerry. *D-Days at Dayton: Reflections on the Scopes Trial.* Baton Rouge: Louisiana State University Press, 1965, 173 pp.

The book includes reprints of valuable original resources.

The "Scottsboro Boys"

Bauer, Barbara, and Robert Moss; ed Thomas Moore. *Judge Horton and the Scottsboro Boys.* New York: Ballantine Books, 1976, 182 pp.

The novelization is based on the Carter book, *Scottsboro: A Tragedy of the American South,* and the TV production of the same name, which became the subject of the unsuccessful privacy case.

Carter, Dan. *Scottsboro: A Tragedy of the American South.* (Louisiana State University, 1969, 1979); reprint Birmingham: Notable Trials Library, 2000, 431 pp.

This definitive work is the basis for *The Scottsboro Boys,* 1976 NBC docudrama; revisions include coverage of the unsuccessful privacy case by the accusers, Ruby Bates and Victoria Street-Price, against NBC over the docudrama.

Goodman, James. *Stories of Scottsboro.* New York: Pantheon Books, 1994, 465 pp.

The Harvard professor's work is a widely cited version of events.

Norris, Clarence, with Sybil Washington. *The Last of the Scottsboro Boys.* New York: Putnam, 1978, 283 pp.

One of the defendants tells his story.

Sheppard v Maxwell

Conners, Bernard. *Tailspin: The Strange Case of Major Call.* Latham, NY: British American Publishing, Ltd, 2002, 506 pp.

The book is the story of AWOL Air Force Major James Call, who Conners speculates could have killed Marilyn Sheppard. It includes one section on the case (Part VI, pp. 197–232) and a lengthy Addendum (361–480) with a Schematic Timeline; however, the evidence is not nearly so persuasive as that in James Neff's book.

Cooper, Cynthia, and Sam Reese Sheppard. *Mockery of Justice: The True Story of the Sheppard Murder Case* (Northeastern University, 1995, 404 pp); reprint New York: Penguin, 1997, 502 pp.

Dr. Sheppard's son fights to clear his father's name.

Neff, James. *The Wrong Man: The Final Verdict on the Dr. Sam Sheppard Murder Case.* New York: Random House (2001) 2002, 421 pp.

The journalist who fought subpoenas implicates the window-washer. The paperback version published in 2002 includes a brief "Readers' Guide."

Robertson, Ed. Introduction by Stephen King. *The Fugitive Recaptured: The 30th Anniversary Companion to a Television Classic.* Los Angeles: Pomegranate Press, 1993, 208 pp.

A fan presents a detailed look at the popular series (with 72 percent of TV households tuned to the final episode when Kimball finally catches up with the "one-armed man").

U.S. v Clinton

Brock, David. *Blinded by the Right: The Conscience of an Ex-Conservative.* New York: Crown, 2002, 336 pp.

The former right-winger repents and admits a "vast right-wing conspiracy" manipulated journalists.

Carville, James. *. . . And the Horse He Rode In On: The People v Kenneth Starr.* New York, Simon and Schuster, 1998, 176 pp.

Clinton's political strategist counterattacks Starr.

Clinton, Hillary. *Living History.* New York: Simon and Schuster, 2003, 562 pp.

She says/he says; incredible initial sales justified the incredible $8 million advance.

Conason, Joe, and Gene Lyons. *The Hunting of the President: The Ten-Year Campaign to Destroy Bill and Hillary Clinton.* New York: St. Martin's Press, 2000, 413 pp.
   Focusing on the press, the authors present a detailed look at the right-wing campaign to discredit the Clintons.

Isikoff, Michael. *Uncovering Clinton: A Reporter's Story.* New York: Crown, 1999, 402 pp.
   One of the reporters who covered it all shows how the press affected the Paula Jones and Monica Lewinsky events.

Kalb, Marvin. *One Scandalous Story: Clinton, Lewinsky, and 13 Days That Tarnished American Journalism.* New York: The Free Press, 2001, 306 pp.
   The respected newsman describes economic pressures, dubious sources, and the tabloidization of coverage.

Lyons, Gene, and the Editors of *Harper's Magazine*. *Fools for Scandal: How the Media Invented Whitewater.* New York: Franklin Square Press/Harpers, 1996, 224 pp.
   The authors describe the right-wing smear campaign sustained by the media, including even *The New York Times* and the *Washington Post*.

Posner, Richard. *An Affair of State: The Investigation, Impeachment, and Trial of President Clinton.* Cambridge, MA: Harvard University Press, 1999, 276 pp.
   The judge presents the legalistic viewpoint and says the "much-maligned media" performed pretty well.

The Starr Report: The Findings of Independent Counsel Kenneth W. Starr on President Clinton and the Lewinsky Affair, with Analysis by the Staff of the Washington Post. New York: Public Affairs, 1998, 421 pp.
   The newspaper publishes an edited version of the official document (see Chapter 7).

U.S. v Hearst

Alexander, Shana. *Anyone's Daughter: The Times and Trials of Patty Hearst.* New York: Viking Press, 1979, 562 pp.

The book presents fine trial coverage by an experienced journalist who is also a true-crime writer.

Hearst, Patricia Campbell, with Alvin Moscow. *Every Secret Thing.* Garden City, NY: Doubleday, 1982, 466 pp.
The kidnap victim tells how she went from Junior Leaguer to "Tania," a self-described "urban guerilla."

U.S. v Hiss

Chambers, Whittaker. *Witness.* New York: Random House, 1952, 808 pp.
Best-selling autobiography by one of the two men most directly involved in the famous case.

Hiss, Alger. *In the Court of Public Opinion.* New York: Knopf, 1957, 424 pp; and *Recollections of a Life.* New York: Seaver Books/Holt, 1988, 240 pp.
In the second of the two installments of his autobiography, Hiss makes a convincing case that despite his conviction, he was innocent.

Smith, John Chabot. *Alger Hiss: The True Story.* New York: Holt, Rinehart, Winston, 1976, 485 pp; and Weinstein, Allen. *Perjury: The Hiss-Chambers Case.* New York: Random House, 1978, rev 1997, 622 pp.
Both books are pro Hiss, with the latter revision, which is based on newly released documents, suggesting a frame-up.

Swan, Patrick, ed. *Alger Hiss, Whittaker Chambers, and the Schism in the American Soul.* Wilmington, DE: Intercollegiate Studies Institute, 2002, 350 pp.
On the fiftieth anniversary of Chambers's book *Witness* (see above), the editor gathers a collection of twenty-three essays written about the case over the years.

U.S. v McVeigh and Nichols

Final Report on the Bombing of the Alfred P. Murrah Federal Building, April 19, 1995. Oklahoma City: The Oklahoma Bombing Investigation Committee, 2001, 556 pp.
With an introduction by Charles Key, the report contends the federal government had advance knowledge of the attack and

that the evidence suggests that in addition to McVeigh and Nichols, "multiple John Doe's were involved."

Hamm, Mark. *Apocalypse in Oklahoma: Waco and Ruby Ridge Revenged.* Boston: Northeastern University Press, 1997, 283 pp.
 The book is well researched and presents good background on the case.

Jones, Stephen. *Others Unknown: Timothy McVeigh and the Oklahoma City Bombing Conspiracy.* New York: Perseus Books, (1998) 2001, 382 pp.
 McVeigh's defense lawyer insists there were other "John Doe's" involved.

Michel, Lou, and Dan Herbeck. *American Terrorist: Timothy McVeigh and the Oklahoma City Bombing.* New York: Regan Books/HarperCollins, 2001, 426 pp.
 The home state journalists who covered the case provide background details.

Serrano, Richard. *One of Ours: Timothy McVeigh and the Oklahoma City Bombing.* New York: Norton, 1998, 321 pp.
 A journalist who covered the case takes an objective look.

U.S. v Microsoft

Auletta, Ken. *World War 3.0: Microsoft and Its Enemies.* New York: Random House, 2001, 436 pp.
 Stories by Auletta and Brinkley (see below) led to the trial judge's disqualification from the proposed retrial.

Bank, David. *Breaking Windows: How Bill Gates Fumbled the Future of Microsoft.* New York: Free Press, 2001, 287 pp.
 The author covers the basics in the case.

Brinkley, Joel, and Steve Lohr. *U.S. v Microsoft.* New York: McGraw Hill, 2001, 349 pp (also an eBook).
 The book is based on their coverage of the case in *The New York Times,* which along with coverage by author Ken Auletta (see below) led to the trial judge's disqualification from hearing the retrial.

Heilemann, John. *Pride Before the Fall: The Trials of Bill Gates and the End of the Microsoft Era.* New York: Harper Collins/ Perennial, (2001) 2002, 246 pp.
The author presents a secret history of the software industry.

U.S. v Nixon (Watergate)

Bernstein, Carl, and Robert Woodward. *All the President's Men.* New York: Simon and Schuster, 1974, 349 pp.
The Pulitzer Prize–winning reporters who broke the story present the comprehensive version of events: their book became the basis for the successful movie of the same name.

Congressional Quarterly. *Watergate: Chronology of a Crisis,* ed William Dickinson. Washington, DC, 1973–1974 (3 vols.).
The work includes copies of original documents along with helpful commentary.

Friedman, Leon, ed. *U.S. v Nixon: The President Before the Supreme Court.* New York: Chelsea House, 1974, 619 pp.
The book presents day-by-day trial coverage including orders for President Nixon to turn over the subpoenaed tapes.

Garment, Leonard. *In Search of Deep Throat: The Greatest Political Mystery of Our Time.* New York: Basic Books, 2000, 280 pp.
Nixon's former lawyer examines "Woodstein" (the combined names of Woodward and Bernstein, *Washington Post* reporters who uncovered Watergate), and he concludes their secret source "Deep Throat" was former Nixon lawyer John Sears.

Graham, Katharine. *Personal History.* New York: Knopf, 1997, 642 pp.
The *Washington Post* publisher who fought to cover both the Pentagon Papers case and Watergate writes a Pulitzer Prize–winning autobiography.

Mankiewicz, Frank. *U.S. v Richard M. Nixon: The Final Crisis.* New York: New York Times/Quadrangle Books, 1975, 276 pp.
The author focuses on the role of the press in Watergate.

Sirica, John. *To Set the Record Straight: The Break-in, the Tapes, the Conspirators, the Pardon.* New York: Norton, 1979, 394 pp.

A first-hand account by the presiding judge in the Watergate case.

U.S. v Rosenberg

Meeropol, Michael, ed. *The Rosenberg Letters: A Complete Edition of the Prison Correspondence of Julius and Ethel Rosenberg.* New York: Garland, 1994, 722 pp; and (with Robert Meeropol) *We Are Your Sons: The Legacy of Ethel and Julius Rosenberg.* Boston: Houghton Mifflin (1975), 2d ed 1986, 470 pp; also (Robert) *An Execution in the Family: One Son's Journey.* New York: St. Martin's, 2003, 288 pp.

Good sons defend parents, although Robert Meeropol admits in the 2003 book that, based on evidence in Sam Roberts's book (see below), his father likely did pass some secrets, although his mother did not.

Radosh, Ronald, and Joyce Milton. *The Rosenberg File, With a New Introduction Containing Revelations from National Security Agency and Soviet Sources.* (Yale University Press, 1983, 1997); reprint Birmingham: Notable Trials Library, 1999, 608 pp.

Based on new evidence, the revisionist authors say there is a likelihood of some degree of guilt on the part of the Rosenbergs.

Roberts, Sam. *The Brother: The Untold Story of Atomic Spy David Greenglass and How He Sent His Sister Ethel Rosenberg to the Electric Chair.* New York: Random House, 2001, 543 pp.

The book is written by a journalist who obtained new documentary evidence and the first unrestricted interviews with Greenglass (living under a new identity), who admits that he did spy and that he did perjure himself regarding the participation of his sister Ethel.

Vanderbilt v Whitney

Goldsmith, Barbara. *Little Gloria, Happy at Last.* New York: Knopf, 1980, 650 pp.

The definitive biography of Gloria Vanderbilt that was the basis for the TV docudrama of the same name.

Vanderbilt, Gloria. *Once Upon a Time: A True Story.* New York: Knopf, 1985, 301 pp.

Vanderbilt recalls her first 27 years, including the sensational custody case.

Nonprint Resources

Websites

Court TV

www.courttv.com (2003)
This website includes valuable information on current cases such as that involving the accused September 11th terrorists. The Crime Library includes archival information on many of the cases discussed in Chapter 1; videos are available for purchase via the website including those on "King," Manson, Menendez, Simpson (five-tape set and one update), Smith, and Scopes.

Videos

California v Manson

Helter Skelter
Date: 1976; 1985
Media: VHS
Length: 194 minutes; 92 minutes
Source: Movielab; Hemdale/Lorimar

This made-for-TV docudrama, based on Vincent Bugliosi's book of the same name, is a dramatic, frightening, graphically violent version of the events.

California v Menendez

The Menendez Murder Trial
Date: 1994
Media: Audiotape
Length: 60 minutes
Source: Simon and Schuster

The tapes feature excerpts from the first trial.

Power, Privilege, Justice:
Dominick Dunne, The Menendez Brothers
Date: 2002
Media: VHS
Length: 60 minutes
Source: Court TV

All the sensational details of the murder case are in this presentation, including the brothers' estrangement after their convictions and their jailhouse marriages.

California v Simpson

American Tragedy
Date: 2000
Media: VHS
Length: 70 minutes
Source: Trimark Home Video

In this TV docudrama, based on his book, with screenplay by Norman Mailer, producer/director Lawrence Schiller focuses on the lawyers, including Robert Shapiro (Ron Silver), Johnnie Cochran (Ving Rhames), and F. Lee Bailey (Christopher Plummer).

California v Simpson
Date: 1994–1995
Media: VHS
Length: 240 minutes
Source: Court TV

The video features excerpts from the coverage of the 1995 case in which ex-professional football player O. J. Simpson was accused of murdering his wife, Nicole Simpson, and her friend Ron Goldman.

Covering the Big Story: The O. J. Simpson Verdict
Date: 1995
Media: VHS
Length: 28 minutes
Source: First Light Video

The documentary shows the news media in action on the big day.

O. J.: A Study in Black and White
Date: 2002
Media: VHS
Length: 57 minutes
Source: HBO Studio Productions

This documentary focuses on the racial aspects of case.

Georgia v Frank

They Won't Forget
Date: 1937
Media: Film, b&w
Length: 94 minutes
Source: Warner

Directed by Mervin Leroy, the film is based on Ward Greene's book *Death in the Deep South,* with Claude Rains and Lana Turner. A fictionalized version of a Northern teacher Robert Hall going on trial in the South for killing student Mary Clay; he is lynched.

"Hauptmann"

Crime of the Century
Date: 1996
Media: VHS
Length: 116 minutes
Source: Warner Home Video

This TV docudrama is directed by Mark Rydell.

Every Parent's Nightmare
Date: 1989
Media: VHS
Length: 57 minutes
Source: Ohlmeyer Communications

Part of the television series "Crime of the Century." Mike Conners narrates the story of the *Hauptmann* case.

Kidnapped: Re-Living the Lindbergh Case
Date: 1989
Media: VHS
Length: 57 minutes
Source: NJ Network

A documentary on Anna Hauptmann (widow of Bruno Richard Hauptmann, who was executed after being convicted of kidnapping Charles Lindbergh's baby) and her efforts to clear her husband's name.

State v Bruno Hauptmann: The Crime of the Century
Date: 1964
Media: VHS
Length: 28 minutes
Source: Wolper Productions

The melodramatic version is part of the television series *Men in Crisis*.

"Hollywood 10"

The Front
Date: 1976
Media: VHS
Length: 95 minutes
Source: Columbia TriStar

Woody Allen stars in this feature film, a docudrama that realistically portrays the effects of McCarthyism on Hollywood.

Point of Order
Date: 1998
Media: VHS
Length: 103 minutes
Source: Zenger

Paul Newman narrates this documentary video, with excerpts from the 1950s Army McCarthy hearings originally aired on television in black and white. The presentation is riveting, especially prosecuting attorney Joseph Welch to Joseph McCarthy asking the famous question: "At long last, have you no sense of decency, sir?"

"King"

The Rodney King Case:
What the Jury Saw in California v Powell
Date: 1992
Media: VHS

Length: 116 minutes
Source: Court TV

Fred Graham hosts the video that is based on Court TV's extensive coverage of the case.

Illinois v Leopold and Loeb

The following four films are fictional representations of the case.

Compulsion
Date: 1959
Media: VHS, b&w
Length: 103 minutes
Source: Twentieth Century Fox/Zanuck

Murder by Numbers
Date: 2002
Media: VHS
Length: 94 minutes
Source: Warner Brothers

Rope
Date: 1948
Media: VHS
Length: 80 minutes
Source: Transatlantic/Universal

Swoon
Date: 1992
Media: VHS, b&w
Length: 80 minutes
Source: Argus Films/Fine Line

Louisiana v Shaw

He Must Have Something: The Real Story of
Jim Garrison's Investigation of the Assassination of JFK
Date: 1993
Media: VHS
Length: 88 minutes
Source: LEH/NOVAC

A documentary by director Stephen Tyler describing events surrending the JFK assassination.

JFK
Date: 1991
Media: VHS
Length: 189 minutes
Source: Warner/Stone

This feature film had five Oscar nominations and won one. It revived conspiracy theories and led to renewed interest in the assassination, including a specific public records law opening case documents.

New York v Snyder and Gray

Body Heat
Date: 1981
Media: VHS
Length: 113 minutes
Source: Warner/Ladd

This feature film, a remake of *Double Indemnity* (1944), stars William Hurt and Kathleen Turner. A shabby West Palm Beach lawyer falls for a vixen Miami wife and then helps kill her husband (arson plot); he's convicted, while she gets away. The film has graphic sex scenes.

Double Indemnity
Date: 1944
Media: VHS, b&w
Length: 107 minutes
Source: Paramount

This fictionalized version of the case is based on James Cain's book of the same name. It was directed by Billy Wilder, was nominated for six Oscars, and starred Fred MacMurray and Barbara Stanwyck. A California insurance salesman falls for a vixen wife. He helps kill her husband (train plot) and is foiled by his colleague (Edward G. Robertson); both the salesman and the wife die. It is classic film noir, with snappy (Raymond Chandler co-authored) dialogue.

The Postman Always Rings Twice
Date: *1946*
Media: VHS, b&w
Length: 113 minutes
Source: MGM

This feature film stars Lana Turner and John Garfield. A drifter falls for a vixen Midwestern wife and helps kill her husband (car accident). She dies in an accident and he's convicted. The film has good trial scenes and a melodramatic ending. It is another classic.

The Postman Always Rings Twice
Date: 1981
Media: VHS
Length: 121 minutes
Source: Lorimar

This feature film, a remake of the 1946 original, stars Jack Nicholson and Jessica Lang. He falls for you-know-who and helps her do you- know-what to you-know-whom; both murderers die. Graphic sex scenes replace the trial scenes in the original.

New York v Thaw

Ragtime
Date: 1981
Media: VHS
Length: 156
Source: Paramount Pictures

This feature film is based on the novel of the same name by E. L Doctorow, was directed by Milos Forman, and stars James Cagney. It focuses on Nesbit (Elizabeth McGovern).

Scopes v Tennessee

The Great Tennessee Monkey Trial
Date: 1994
Media: audiocassette
Length: 124 minutes
Source: LA Theatre Works/BBC/KCRW

Adapted from the trial transcripts by Peter Goodchild, Ed Asner stars as Bryan, Charles Durning as Darrow, with Tyne Daly as the narrator. It has an excellent climactic court scene.

Inherit the Wind
Date: 1960, 1993
Media: VHS
Length: 128 minutes
Source: United Artists, MGM/UA

This classic feature film is a fictionalized drama directed by Stanley Kramer. It stars Spencer Tracy as a Darrow-like character, Fredric March as a Bryan-like orator, and Gene Kelly as a Mencken-like journalist. It was nominated for four Oscars.

The Monkeyville Case
Date: 1997
Media: audiocassette
Length: 60 minutes
Source: Ivan Berg Associates

The tapes are a well-done docudrama, narrated by Edgar Lustgarten.

Sheppard v Maxwell

The Fugitive
Date: *1993*
Media: VHS
Length: 102 minutes
Source: Warner

This feature film docudrama was nominated for seven Oscars, including Best Actor awarded to Tommy Lee Jones. It also stars Harrison Ford. It is well done and suspenseful.

The Killer's Trail: Murder Mystery of the Century
Date: 1999
Media: VHS
Length: 60 minutes
Source: Marz Associates

As part of the *Nova* series on WGBH TV in Boston, the video takes an excellent look at blood spatter and DNA evidence while showing that Sheppard likely was not guilty and window-washer Eberling likely was.

U.S. v Clinton

Monica in Black and White
Date: 2002
Media: VHS
Length: 90 minutes
Source: HBO

As part of the HBO television documentary series *America Uncovered*, it tells more about Monica Lewinsky than you really need to know.

U.S. v Hearst
Patty Hearst
Date: 1988
Media: VHS
Length: 104 minutes
Source: Entertainment/Atlantic/Zenith

This docudrama is based on the newspaper heiress's autobiography and the dramatic story of her kidnapping by the Symbionese Liberation Army.

U.S. v McVeigh and Nichols
Media on Trial: Story of the Storytellers
Date: 1999
Media: VHS
Length: 56 minutes
Source: Colorado State University/First Light Video/Insight Media

This documentary describes coverage of the Timothy McVeigh trial in Colorado.

U.S. v Microsoft
Antitrust
Date: 2000
Media: VHS
Length: 108 minutes
Source: MGM

The film presents a fictional evil Gates-like computer mogul.

U.S. v Nixon (Watergate)
All the President's Men
Date: 1976
Media: VHS
Length: 139 minutes
Source: Warner/Wildwood (Redford)

This feature film is based on the book about the Watergate scandal by *Washington Post* reporters Bob Woodward and Carl Bernstein. It earned five Oscar nominations, winning for Best Writer (William Goldman) and Best Actor (Jason Robards). It is an outstanding dramatization.

Nixon
Date: 1995
Media: VHS
Length: 191 minutes
Source: Entertainment Films/Illusion/Cinergi

This feature film stars Anthony Hopkins and Joan Allen. It was nominated for four Oscars and presents a good character study of a flawed president.

The Nixon Tapes
Date: 7 March 2002
Media: 500 audiotapes (first six months of 1972)
Length: 5 hours
Source: National Archives; available at *cspan.org/executive/president/nixon.asp* (2002). Also,

U.S. v Nixon: The Nixon Tapes: Power Corrupts
Date: 2000
Media: 4 audiotapes
Length: 5 hours
Source: DH Audio

Some tapes are poorly made, but John Dean's "Cancer on the Presidency" presentation is all too chillingly clear.

Vanderbilt v Whitney

Little Gloria, Happy at Last
Date: 1982
Media: VHS
Length: 76 minutes
Source: Twentieth Century Fox/Cine Gloria, with London Films, Ltd.

This TV docudrama (based on the Barbara Goldsmith book of the same name) is pretty good for a TV movie.

Chapter 2 Controversies, Problems, and Solutions

Print Resources

Berendt, John. *Midnight in the Garden of Good and Evil: A Savannah Story.* New York: Random House, 1994, 388 pp.

The novel, based on a true story (with artistic license), spent four years on *The New York Times* best-seller list. A writer comes to Savannah to write about a leading citizen who ends up as the defendant in a murder trial. Also the basis for the popular movie by the same name.

Bridges, Tyler. *Bad Bet on the Bayou: The Rise of Gambling in Louisiana and the Fall of Governor Edwin Edwards.* New York: Farrar, Strauss and Giroux, 2001, 422 pp.

A *Miami-Herald* journalist who worked for *The Times-Picayune* for many years presents a comprehensive look at the four-time governor of Louisiana: the subject of two dozen investigations. Edwards was finally convicted in 2000 of riverboat-casino license-granting corruption and sentenced to ten years in federal prison.

Caplan, Lincoln. "The Failure (and Promise) of Legal Journalism," 199–207, 9 pp, in *Postmortem: The O. J. Simpson Case: Justice Confronts Race, Domestic Violence, Lawyers, Money, and the Media,* ed Jeffrey Abramson. New York: Basic Books, 1996, 239 pp.

One of the best in a collection of essays on various topics brought out by the criminal trial of O. J. Simpson for the murders of his wife and her friend. Caplan concludes that press coverage of criminal cases needs improvement.

Eichenwald, Kurt. *The Informant: A True Story.* New York: Broadway Books, 2000, 606 pp.

The journalist has written a fascinating account of corporate greed and corruption at Archer Daniel Midlands and shows how ill equipped the U.S. justice system is to deal with such massive corporate crime. The book is well written and reads like a suspense novel.

Grossman, Lewis, and Robert Vaughn. *A Documentary Companion to A Civil Action: With Notes, Comments and Questions.* New York: Foundation Press, 1999, 812 pp.

A student guide to Jonathan Harr's book (see next entry) that includes comprehensive explanations of the setting; pretrial, trial, and posttrial proceedings; and copies of documents.

Harr, Jonathan. *A Civil Action.* New York: Random House, 1995, 500 pp.

The winner of the National Book Award, this book tells the true story of a personal injury lawyer who takes on two major companies whose toxic wastes polluted the water supply in Woburn, Massachusetts, leading to twelve deaths, eight of them children. The writing is outstanding. The book was the basis for the feature film of the same name.

Humes, Edward. *Mississippi Mud.* New York: Simon and Schuster, 1994, 365 pp.

The intriguing story of the Dixie mafia and corruption in Biloxi that led to the murders of a prominent judge and his mayoral-candidate wife (with the eventual conviction of the judge's law partner—who had become the mayor—in the murder case).

Lederer, Fredric. *The Road to the Virtual Courtroom? A Consideration of Today's—and Tomorrow's—High Technology Courtrooms.* Williamsburg: State Justice Institute/William and Mary Law School, 1999, 42 pp.

The author describes the brave new world of video testimony, digitalized documents, and other technological advances—aspects of the virtual courtroom that have already begun to develop.

Mello, Michael. *The Wrong Man: A True Story of Innocence on Death Row.* Introduction by Mike Farrell. Minneapolis: University of Minnesota Press, 2001, 586 pp.

A defense lawyer credits the *Miami Herald* journalists whose stories saved his client, convicted murderer "Crazy Joe" Spaziano, from the electric chair. The charts help, but the book needs editing, particularly for length.

Miller, Gene. *Invitation to a Lynching.* Garden City, NY: Doubleday, 1975, 324 pp.

This book is the award-winning investigation of the wrongful murder convictions of Willie Lee and Freddie Pitts; the series inspired other journalists to do similar investigative stories.

Moses, Jonathan. "Legal Spin Control: Ethics and Advocacy in the Court of Public Opinion," *Columbia Law Review* 95 (1995): 1811–1856, 46 pp.

National Center for State Courts and State Justice Institute. *Developing CCJ/COSCA Guidelines for Public Access to Court Records: A National Project to Assist State Courts*, by Martha Steketee and Alan Carlson, 18 October 2002 (*www.courtaccess.org/modelpolicy*, 2002).
   Per the title, these are the proposed guidelines for public access to court records.

Possley, Maurice, and Rick Kogan. *Everybody Pays: Two Men, One Murder, and the Price of Truth.* New York: Putnam's Sons, 2001, 276 pp.
   The book is fine writing by award-winning journalists that shows the human side of corruption in Chicago's courts by focusing on the effects on individuals involved in a criminal case.

Reporters Committee for Freedom of the Press. *Access to Electronic Records* (Spring 2003) 8 pp; *Access to Juvenile Courts: A Reporter's Guide to Proceedings and Documents,* Washington DC (periodic) 8 pp; *Electronic Access to Court Records: Ensuring Access in the Public Interest* (Fall 2002) 6 pp; *Judicial Records: A Guide to Access in State and Federal Courts* (periodic) 8 pp; *Secret Justice I: Anonymous Juries* (Fall 2000) 8 pp; *Secret Justice II: Gag Orders* (Spring 2001) 8 pp; *Secret Justice III: Alternative Dispute Resolution* (Fall 2001) 8 pp; *Secret Justice IV: Access to Terrorism Proceedings* (Winter 2002) 8 pp; *Secret Justice V: Secret Dockets* (Summer 2003) 8 pp, also available at *www.rcfp.org*, 2002.
   These are extremely useful guides for those interested in the specifics of media coverage of the U.S. justice system.

Roschwalb, Suzanne, and Richard Stack. *Litigation Public Relations: Courting Public Opinion.* Littleton, CO: Rothman and Co., 1995, 240 pp.

Shapiro, Robert. "Secrets of a Celebrity Lawyer," *Columbia Journalism Review* (September-October 1994): 25–29, 5 pp.

The lawyer who would become a key member of the O. J. Simpson Dream Team gives specifics on how to manipulate the press.

Stewart, James. *Blind Eye: How the Medical Establishment Let a Doctor Get Away With Murder.* New York: Simon and Schuster, 1999, 334 pp.
The Pulitzer-Prize-winning *Wall Street Journal* journalist describes how a flawed judicial system let a doctor get away with murder for too long.

Nonprint Resources
Websites
Cornell University Law School
supct.law.cornell.edu (2003)

Free information on U.S. Supreme Court cases, including full text of opinions.

Emory University School of Law
"Emory Law School Federal Courts Finder"
www.law.emory.edu/FEDCTS (2003)

Free information on federal appellate courts, including opinions.

Lexis One
www.lexisone.com (2003)

Database includes access to all levels of courts. Some available free, some for a fee.

National Center for State Courts
ncsconline.org (2003)

A clearinghouse of free information, including links to state and federal courts and other court websites.

Northwestern University Law School
"On the Docket"
medill.northwestern.edu/docket (2003)

Free information on U.S. Supreme Court cases, including opinions.

Online Legal Services, Big Class Action
www.bigclassaction.com (2003)

A free database on class actions that includes summaries of major developments and an invitation for wronged people to become plaintiffs in pending class-action lawsuits.

Public Access to Courts Electronic Records, PACER
pacer.psc.uscourts.gov (2003)

A government source of both free and fee access to some federal court records.

Stanford University Law School
"Security Class Action Clearinghouse"
securities.stanford.edu (2003)

A source of free information on class-action civil suits.

U.S. Supreme Court
supremecourtus.gov (2003)

A government source of free information on justices, dockets, transcripts, briefs, opinions, and media releases.

West Doc
www.westdoc.com (2003)

A fee database of cases and other legal material.

Videos

A Civil Action

Date: 1999
Media: VHS
Length: 115 minutes
Source: Touchstone/Paramount

Based on the Jonathan Harr book of the same, the film stars John Travolta, Robert Duvall, Bill Macy, James Gandolfini (Tony Soprano as a good guy), and Sydney Pollack. It's not as good as the book; Travolta seems miscast.

Midnight in the Garden of Good and Evil
Date: 1997
Media: VHS

Length: 155 minutes
Source: Warner Brothers

Based on John Berendt's book by the same name. Kevin Spacey, John Cusack, Jude Law, and Lady Chablis (as herself) star in this feature film. It captures both the scenic beauty and the southern decadence of Savannah, Georgia. Cusack's character sums up the story: "like *Gone With the Wind* on mescaline."

Chapter 3 Chronology

Print Resources

Bunker, Matthew. *Justice and the Media: Reconciling Fair Trials and a Free Press.* Mahwah, NJ: Lawrence Erlbaum Associates, 1997, 151 pp.

An erudite professor supports a novel theory: The U.S. Supreme Court should not balance the First Amendment and the Sixth Amendment, but a categorical rule should grant First Amendment protection to all speech about the criminal justice system. Cases covered include most of those described in Chapter 3 (up to 1997).

Campbell, Douglas. *Free Press v Fair Trial: Supreme Court Decisions Since 1807.* Westport, CT: Praeger, 1994, 253 pp.

Cambell presents the definitive study of First Amendment/ Sixth Amendment U.S. Supreme Court cases, including background, circumstances, the Court's analysis, ruling, and significance. Cases include most of those described in Chapter 3 (up to 1991).

Friendly, Fred. *Minnesota Rag: The Dramatic Story of the Landmark Supreme Court Case That Gave New Meaning to Freedom of the Press.* New York: Random House, 1981, 243 pp.

Friendly describes *Near v Minnesota*, the 1931 U.S. Supreme Court case that extended the First Amendment ban on prior restraint to all levels of government.

Irons, Peter, and Stephanie Guitton, eds. *May It Please the Court: The Most Significant Oral Arguments Made Before the Supreme Court Since 1955.* New York: The New Press, 1993, 375 pp.

Authors describe how cases reach the High Court, how arguments proceed, and how justices decide. Cases include *U.S. v Nixon* and *New York Times v U.S.* (see Chapter 1). Also available on audiocassette.

Kamisar, Yale, et al. "'Trial by Newspaper'—and Television," 1348–1380, 32 pp, in *Modern Criminal Procedure: Cases, Comments and Questions*, 10th ed, St Paul: West Group, (1965) 2002, 1667 pp.
This is very clear writing—for lawyers.

Kane, Peter. *Murder, Courts, and the Press: Issues in Free Press/Fair Trial.* Carbondale: Southern Illinois University, 1986 rev 1992, 121 pp.
Kane presents a brief look at representative cases, including *Branzburg, Estes, Gannett, Nebraska, Richmond,* and *Sheppard.*

Murphy, Paul. "The Case of the Miscreant Purveyor of Scandal [*Near v Minnesota*]," 209–232, 24 pp, in *Quarrels That Have Shaped the Constitution*, ed John Garraty, New York: Harper and Row, 1964, rev 1987, 391 pp.
Murphy tells the story of the landmark case that extended the First Amendment prohibition on prior restraints.

Nonprint Resources

May It Please the Court: 23 Live Recordings of Landmark Cases as Argued Before the Supreme Court
Date: 1993
Media: audiotapes
Length: six 90-minute cassettes
Source: The New Press

Edited by Peter Irons and Stephanie Guitton, the tapes include Pentagon Papers and Watergate cases discussed in Chapter 1.

Chapter 4 Biographical Sketches
Print Resources
F. Lee Bailey
Nonfiction

with Harry Rothblatt. *Crimes of Violence.* Rochester, NY: Lawyers Co-op, 1973, 2 vols, 902 pp + 1997 Supplement.
The volumes include material for those interested in homicide and assault/rape and other sex cases.

with Harry Rothblatt. *Cross Examination in Criminal Trials.* Rochester, NY: Lawyers Co-op, 1978, 561 pp.
This is a reference work for lawyers.

with Harry Rothblatt. *Defending Business and White Collar Crimes: Federal and State.* Rochester, NY: Lawyers Co-op, 1969, 740 pp; 2d ed San Francisco: Bancroft Whitney, 1984, 2 vols, 1082 pp.
The volumes include information on the federal Freedom of Information requirements to provide access to certain business information.

with Harry Rothblatt. *Fundamentals of Criminal Advocacy.* Rochester, NY: Lawyers Co-Op, 1974, 589 pp.
This is a reference work for lawyers.

with Harry Rothblatt. *Handling Juvenile Delinquency Cases.* Rochester, NY: Lawyers Co-op; 2d ed San Francisco: Bancroft Whitney, 1982, 527 pp.
This is a reference work for lawyers.

with Harry Rothblatt. *Handling Narcotic and Drug Cases.* Rochester, NY: Lawyers Co-op, 1972, 549 pp.
This is a reference work for lawyers.

with Harry Rothblatt. *Investigation and Preparation of Criminal Cases.* Rochester, NY: Lawyers Co-op, 1970, 552 pp; 2d ed San Francisco: Bancroft Whitney, 1985, 838 pp.
This is a reference work for lawyers.

Successful Techniques for Criminal Trials. New York: Lawyers Co-op, 1971, 604 pp; 2d ed 1985, 897 pp.
This is a reference work for lawyers.

To Be a Trial Lawyer. Marshfield, MA: Telshare Publishing, 1983, 1985, 215 pp; 1994, 239 pp.
Popular guide for lawyer wanna-bes and all who want to understand what lawyers do: dealing with judges, working with a jury, cross-examinations, summations, and appeals. Includes a discussion of computers from one who understood early on how they would enhance trial work. Pearls of wisdom from a lawyer who most agree was a master advocate.

with Harvey Aronson. *The Defense Never Rests.* New York: Stein and Day, 1971, 262 pp.
Bailey's best-selling autobiography includes the *Sheppard* case and the Boston Strangler.

with Kenneth Fishman. *Criminal Trial Techniques.* Deerfield, IL: Clark Boardman Callaghan, 1994, pp.
This is a reference work for lawyers.

with Kenneth Fishman. *Handling Misdemeanor Cases* (2nd ed, see below). Deerfield, IL: Clark Boardman Callaghan, 1992, 545 pp.
This is a reference work for lawyers.

with John Greeny. *For the Defense.* New York: Atheneum, 1975, 367 pp.
These further autobiographical adventures include Bailey's involvement with Captain Ernest Medina and also the Glenn Turner cases (discussed in text).

with Henry Rothblatt (Criminal Law Library Series). *Complete Manual of Criminal Forms, Federal and State.* Rochester, NY: Lawyers Co- op, 1968; 2d ed 1974, 2 vols, 1437 pp + 1991 Supplement.
This manual includes suggested motions that respond to media requests for access to pretrial proceedings.

Fiction

Secrets. New York: Stein and Day, 1978.

A fictional Boston lawyer is on trial for murder of a former client. The book includes numerous allusions to Bailey's own cases as well as illustrations of his take on press/lawyer relations, including allusions to real-life reporters such as Theo Wilson.

Steven Brill

After: How America Confronted the September 12 Era. New York: Simon and Schuster, 2003, 723 pp.

Brill writes a comprehensive work, based on 347 interviews. He is generally optimistic about the resilience of his countrymen.

The Teamsters. New York: Simon and Schuster, 1978, 414 pp.

An in-depth look at the union, this book speculates on the whereabouts of Jimmy Hoffa.

with editors and reporters of *The American Lawyer* staff, ***Trial by Jury.*** New York: Simon and Schuster, 1989, 512 pp.

Sixteen articles on civil jury trials are presented.

about: "Brill's Bully Pulpit," *Vanity Fair* (August 1999), 56–64, 6 pp.

The article gives further information about Brill.

Vincent Bugliosi

Nonfiction

The Betrayal of America: How the Supreme Court Undermined the Constitution and Chose Our President. New York: Thunder's Mouth Press, 2001, 166 pp.

Outraged again, Bugliosi accuses the majority on the Court of borderline treason in *Bush v Gore.* Very persuasive and very well received, the book led to some talk of calls of impeachment of the five justices who voted in the majority.

No Island of Sanity: Paula Jones vs President Bill Clinton: The Supreme Court on Trial. New York: Ballantine Group, 1998, 146 pp.

According to this book, the decision not to postpone the case until the end of the presidency was an "incomprehensible and terribly flawed decision."

"None Dare Call it Treason," *The Nation* (5 February 2001), 7 pp.
This article describes how wrong the *Bush v Gore* case was. It led to his book *The Betrayal of America.*

Outrage: The Five Reasons Why O. J. Simpson Got Away With Murder. New York: Norton, 1996, 356 pp.
The reasons are as follows: (1) the jury was biased, (2) the prosecution was poorly done: not all the evidence was presented, the defense testimony went unchallenged, the final summations were weak, (3) the judge's conduct was unacceptable: he abused the prosecution, (4) cameras were allowed, and (5) the defense was allowed to play the race card.

The Phoenix Solution: Getting Serious About Winning America's Drug War (originally *Drugs in America,* 1991). Beverly Hills: Dove Books, 1996, 278 pp.
Bugliosi suggests either the U.S. Army capture of Columbian drug kingpins and/or the means to money-launder drug profits; he calls this book his magnum opus.

with Curt Gentry. *Helter Skelter: The True Story of the Manson Murders.* New York: Norton (1974) rev 1994, 528 pp.
The Manson prosecutor's Edgar-Award-winning best-seller, also the basis for the TV movie of the same name.

with Bruce Henderson. *And the Sea Will Tell.* New York: Norton, 1991, 574 pp.
A best-seller that tells the true story of two couples on Palmyra Island in the South Pacific. One couple is murdered. Bugliosi defends the woman accused of murder and she's acquitted. The basis for the TV movie of the same name.

with Ken Hurwitz. *Till Death Us Do Part: A True Murder Mystery.* New York Norton, 1978, 384 pp.
An Edgar Award winner and the basis for the TV movie of the same name, the book tells the true story of a couple: her husband and his wife are both murdered. Bugliosi successfully prosecutes her.

Fiction

with Ken Hurwitz. *Shadow of Cain.* New York: Norton, 1981, 309 pp.

In this fictional courtroom thriller a paroled mass murderer kills again.

with William Stadiem. *Lullabye and Good Night: A Novel Inspired by the True Story of Vivian Gordon.* New York: New American Library, 1987, 405 pp.
During the Roaring Twenties, a New York woman seeking child custody faces a sensational murder trial.

Marcia Clark
with Teresa Carpenter. *Without a Doubt.* New York: Viking Press, 1997, 502 pp.
This is an interesting autobiography, but many questioned whether it was worth the reported $4 million advance.

Adams, Lorraine. "The Fight of Her Life: Marcia Clark—Working Mother and O. J. Simpson's Lead Prosecutor—Takes Her Place Among Other Maligned, Adored and Misunderstood Modern Women." *Washington Post*, 10 August 1995.
The author presents information about Marcia Clark.

Johnnie Cochran
with David Fisher. *A Lawyer's Life.* New York: St. Martin's Press, 2002, 311 pp.
The book describes Cochran's pre– and post–O. J. Simpson years, including his three years of Court TV shows, the recent emphasis on class-action and civil rights cases, and his wealthy position as head of an eight-state, 120-lawyer firm.

with Tim Rutten. *Journey to Justice.* New York: Ballantine Books. 1996, 383 pp.
This is the first self-serving, but fascinating, bio, in which he disses his Simpson co-counsel, Robert Shapiro, as well as prosecutor Darden.

about: Alexander, S. L. "Heeere's Johnnie," *The Times Picayune,* 24 November 1996, D6.
The author presents a review of Cochran's first autobiography, *Journey to Justice.*

about: Berry Cochran, Barbara, with Joanne Parrent. *Life After Johnnie Cochran: Why I Left the Sweetest-Talking, Most Successful Black Lawyer in LA.* New York: Basic Books, 1995, 207 pp.

The authors present every ex's dream opportunity: she claims he was abusive, with such evidence of emotional abuse as his having a child with his white mistress while still married to Barbara.

about: Jervey, Gay. "Michael and Reggie's Magician," *American Lawyer,* May 1994, 56.

As an in-depth pre-O. J. portrait of Cochran, the article shows he has not really changed much since O. J.

about: "Lessons from the O. J. Simpson Trial" (interview), pp. 47–51 (5 pp), in *Covering the Courts: Free Press, Fair Trials, and Journalistic Performance* (originally *Media Studies Journal,* 1998). New Brunswick, NJ: Transaction Publishers, 1999, 146 pp.

This is an interview with Johnnie Cochran.

about: Lommel, Cookie. *Johnnie Cochran (Black Americans of Achievement).* Philadelphia: Chelsea House, 2000, 117 pp.

This young-adult biography is useful for all ages.

Christopher Darden

Nonfiction

with Jess Walter. *In Contempt.* New York: Regan Books/Harper Collins, 1996, 387 pp.

Darden's autobiography includes a lengthy discussion of the O. J. Simpson case. He discusses the "Darden Dilemma"—blacks prosecuting blacks in a racist criminal justice system (see below).

about: Close, Ellis, ed. *The Darden Dilemma: Twelve Black Writers on Justice, Race, and Conflicting Loyalties.* New York: HarperPerennial, 261 pp.

In this discussion of racism in the U.S. justice system by a "jury" of twelve prominent Americans, some suggest blacks should not prosecute blacks since the system is unfair.

Fiction

The Last Defense. New York: New American Library, 2002, 360 pp.

Darden's third legal thriller has a new hero, Los Angeles defense lawyer Mercer Early. The plot is complex—drugs, sex, and violence—and includes a romance between Early and his boss's daughter.

The Trials of Nikki Hill. New York: Warner Books, 1999, 434 pp.
A black female assistant to the Los Angeles district attorney prosecutes a defendant charged with the murder of a popular TV host. The story, with a somewhat unbelievable surprise ending, makes you wonder about Darden's former boss, the real Los Angeles district attorney.

with Dick Loche. *LA Justice.* New York: Warner Books, 2000, 434 pp.
In this sequel to the book *The Trials of Nikki Hill,* the prosecutor goes after a wealthy man's son who is charged with murdering his girlfriend.

Lyle Denniston

"The Defining Moments of Jayne Bray . . . and Justice Blackmun," 61–97, 37 pp, in ***A Year in the Life of the Supreme Court,*** ed Rodney Smolla. Durham: Duke University Press, 1995, 300 pp.
One of ten writers in an anthology, Denniston covers an abortion case.

"Federalism, the 'Great Design,' and the Ends of Government," 263–274, 12 pp, in ***Reason and Passion: Justice Brennan's Enduring Influence,*** ed E. Joshua Rosenkranz and Bernard Schwartz. New York: Norton and Company, 1997, 329 pp.
Denniston claims that Brennan was a federalist, evident from his positions on reapportionment, "incorporation," and rights-based jurisprudence under state constitutions.

"From George Carlin to Matt Drudge: The Constitutional Implications of Bringing the Paparazzi to America," *American University Law Review* 47, no. 5 (June 1998): 1255–1271, 17 pp.
Denniston suggests "paparazzi style" (incivility of reporters, sensationalistic coverage) might influence First Amendment jurisprudence, causing Supreme Court justices to become wary of the press and more skeptical of claims to First Amendment protection.

The Reporter and the Law: Techniques of Covering the Courts. (American Bar Association and American Newspaper Publishers Association Foundation, 1980). New York: Columbia University Press, 1992, 289 pp.

The book, the early bible for print journalists, includes detailed information on everything from arrest to parole hearings.

about: Grieser, Lindsay. "Denniston's Fascination with the Law Takes Him on a 52-Year Adventure." *Nebraska University College of Journalism and Mass Communications Alumni News*, 11:1, Summer 2001 at *journalism.unl.edu* (2002).

Grieser presents a biography of the outstanding alumnus.

Alan Dershowitz

Nonfiction

The Abuse Excuse: And Other Cop-Outs, Sob Stories, and Evasions of Responsibility. Boston: Little, Brown, 1994, 341 pp.

Dershowitz criticizes claims of a "history of abuse as an excuse for violent retaliation" by defendants such as the Menendez brothers.

America Declares Independence. Hoboken, NJ: John Wiley and Sons, 2003, 196 pp.

In this study of the Declaration of Independence, Dershowitz says the founding fathers such as the document's author, Thomas Jefferson, were not Christians.

The Best Defense. New York: Random House, 1982, 425 pp.

The "lawyer of last resort" shows the "dark underside of the legal profession," including rules of what he calls the Justice Game, which he sums up: "Nobody really wants justice."

The Case for Israel. Hoboken, NJ: John Wiley and Sons, 2003, 264 pp.

Dershowitz defends the idea of the modern Jewish state.

Chutzpah. Boston: Little Brown and Company, 1991, 378 pp.

Dershowitz describes life as a Jewish American, New York–born, Harvard Law professor.

Contrary to Popular Opinion. New York: Pharos Books, 1992, 398 pp.

Columns written for syndication and use in newspapers around the country, with topics including the First Amendment and the Noriega case.

Genesis of Justice: Ten Stories of Biblical Injustice That Led to the Ten Commandments and Modern Law. New York: Warner Books, 2000, 273 pp.

Just what the title says, the book is based on his law courses on the subject.

Letters to a Young Lawyer. New York: Basic Books, 2001, 206 pp.

This is a nifty gift book for law school grads.

Reasonable Doubts: The O. J. Simpson Case and the Criminal Justice System. New York: Simon and Schuster, 1996, 238 pp.

Simpson's "God forbid" (appeal) lawyer explains why the acquittal in the criminal case was correct and discusses the media effect on the course of the proceedings.

Reversal of Fortune: Inside the von Bulow Case. New York: Random House, 1985 rev 1990, 276 pp.

This is the story of Claus von Bulow's successful appeal of charges that he had attempted to murder his wife. It is the basis for the popular movie of the same name.

Sexual McCarthyism: Clinton, Starr, and the Emerging Constitutional Crisis. New York: Basic Books, 1998, 275 pp.

The discussion of the *Clinton* case is somewhat dated by subsequent events.

Shouting Fire: Civil Liberties in a Turbulent Age. Boston: Little Brown, 2000, 550 pp.

Dershowitz explains that civil rights derive not from God, nature, logic, or law alone, but from human experience.

Supreme Injustice: How the High Court Hijacked Election 2000. Oxford: Oxford University Press, 2001, 275 pp.

As the title implies, this book takes a very extreme liberal viewpoint. It is persuasively presented, with a useful website providing access to primary documents in the case.

Taking Liberties: A Decade of Hard Cases, Bad Laws, and Bum Raps. Chicago: Contemporary Books, 1988, 332 pp.
This book is a selection of weekly syndicated columns on the justice system, with issues including press coverage of courts.

The Vanishing American Jew: In Search of Jewish Identity for the Next Century. Boston: Little, Brown, 1997, 395 pp.
Dershowitz, an outspoken critic of anti-Semitism in all forms, calls for a new Jewish identity to counter assimilation.

Why Terrorism Works: Understanding the Threat, Responding to the Challenge. New Haven: Yale University Press, 2002, 271 pp.
Somewhat suprisingly, Dershowitz supports the idea of national identity cards to fight terrorism and concludes that torture may even be necessary as a last resort.

with Joseph Goldstein and Richard Schwartz. *Criminal Law: Theory and Process.* New York: Free Press, 1974, 1287 pp.
This book is a law text.

with Jay Katz and Joseph Goldstein. *Psychoanalysis, Psychiatry, and Law.* New York: Free Press, 1967, 822 pp.
This book is a law text.

Fiction

The Advocate's Devil. New York: Warner Books, 1994, 342 pp.
Defense lawyer Abe Ringel wrestles with the issue of lawyer-client confidentiality, the basis for the film of the same name.

Just Revenge. New York: Warner Books, 1999, 322 pp.
A legal thriller with a twist ending: Abe Ringel's defendant takes revenge on a man who had killed his family in the Holocaust.

Linda Deutsch

"Flash and Trash," pp. 53–56 (4 pp), in *Covering the Courts: Free Press, Fair Trials and Journalistic Performance* (originally *Media Studies Journal*, 1998), ed Robert Giles and Robert Snyder. New Brunswick, NJ: Transaction Publishers, 1999, 146 pp.
Deutsch gives key advice: reporters must separate news from show biz.

Foreword, 5 pp. in Theo Wilson, *Headline Justice: Inside the Courtroom—The Country's Most Controversial Trials.* New York: Thunder's Mouth Press, 1996, 238 pp.

The foreword includes Theo Wilson's Cardinal Rules of Trial Coverage: for example, reporters should never leave the courtroom.

with Michael Fleeman. *Verdict: The Chronicle of the O. J. Simpson Trial.* Kansas City: Associated Press, 1995, 126 pp.

The book presents concise but complete coverage, including photographs.

Schwartz, Jerry. "Covering a Beat: The Courts," 75–87, 13 pp, in *Associated Press Reporting Handbook.* New York: Associated Press/Schaum, 2002, 219 pp.

This book includes a sample of Deutsch's articles on the killer of Bill Cosby's son Ennis.

Dominick Dunne

Nonfiction

Fatal Charms and Other Tales of Today. New York: Crown, 1987, 206 pp.

The book presents reprints of *Vanity Fair* articles, including coverage of the trial of his daughter's murderer and the *von Bulow* murder case.

Justice: Crime, Trials and Punishments. New York: Crown, 2001, 337 pp.

Reprints of *Vanity Fair* articles are presented, including coverage of the *Menendez* and *Simpson* cases (see Chapter 1).

The Mansions of Limbo. New York: Crown, 1991, 268 pp.

The book includes reprints of coverage of cases including *Menendez* (see Chapter 1).

The Way We Lived Then: Recollections of a Well-Known Name Dropper. New York: Crown, 1999, 218 pp.

Dunne gives an account of the trials and tribulations of his life among celebrities.

about: Kennedy, Robert F., Jr. "A Miscarriage of Justice," *The Atlantic Monthly* 291:1 (January/February 2003), 51–74 (24 pp).
Kennedy attacks Dunne for making "an industry of the Moxley murder" and Dunne's implication that Kennedy cousin Michael Skakel deserved the conviction in the case.

Fiction

Another City, Not My Own: A Novel in the Form of a Memoir. New York: Crown, 1997, 360 pp.
This novel, based on Dunne's coverage of the O. J. Simpson case, presents a thinly disguised reality.

An Inconvenient Woman. New York: Crown, 1990, 458 pp.
The murder of Vicki Morgan, Alfred Bloomingdale's mistress, is the inspiration for Dunne's fictional work involving a California billionaire, a murder, and a mistress.

People Like Us. New York: Crown, 1988, 403 pp.
This book gives a fictional account of the rise and fall of a New York family of socialites.

A Season in Purgatory. New York: Crown, 1993, 377 pp.
A Catholic scion kills a neighborhood girl, which is followed by a decades-long cover-up. The fictional account is based on Kennedy cousin Michael Skakel's murder of Martha Moxley. It inspired Fuhrman's true-crime book and helped lead to a 2002 conviction.

The Two Mrs. Grenvilles. New York: Crown, 1985, 374 pp.
Based on the 1955 murder of William Woodward by his wife, Ann, a wife kills her husband and her mother-in-law covers up.

The Winners: Part II of Joyce Haber's The Users. New York: Simon and Schuster, 1982, 378 pp.
This trashy roman á clef is based in part on the David Begelman embezzlement.

Thomas French

South of Heaven: Welcome to High School at the End of the 20th Century. New York: Doubleday, 1993, 365 pp.

French spends a year inside Largo High School in St. Petersburg, Florida.

Unanswered Cries: A True Story of Friends, Neighbors, and Murder in a Small Town. New York: St. Martin's Press, 1991, 402 pp.

Based on a series in the *St. Petersburg Times,* the book describes the trial of fireman George Lewis for the murder of Karen Gregory in Gulfport, Florida.

Fred Graham

The Alias Program. Boston: Little, Brown, 1977, 239 pp.

The first study of the U.S. Justice Department's witness relocation program follows the case of one of the first of 2,000 relocated witnesses and points out the bureaucratic arrogance and bungles of the program.

"Doing Justice With Cameras in the Courts," pp. 35–41 (6 pp) in *Covering the Courts: Free Press, Fair Trials and Journalistic Performance* (originally *Media Studies Journal,* 1998), eds Robert Giles and Robert Snyder. New Brunswick: NJ: Transaction Publishers, 1999, 146 pp.

As the Court TV managing editor and chief anchor, Graham gives an educated analysis of the courtroom camera situation.

Happy Talk: Confessions of a TV Newsman. New York: Norton, 1990, 352 pp.

Graham writes of his roles as first *The New York Times* and then CBS-TV legal correspondent to a stint in local TV news, just prior to the advent of Court TV, his true home.

Press Freedom Under Pressure. New York: Twentieth Century Fund, 1972, 193 pp.

A founding member of the Reporters Committee for Freedom of the Press as well as a lawyer, Graham discusses issues such as prior restraint and the "Pentagon Papers" case (see Chapter 1).

The Self-Inflicted Wound. New York: MacMillan, 1970, 377 pp.

This study describes the Supreme Court's criminal law decisions during the Warren years.

Linda Greenhouse

"Learning to Live with *Bush v Gore.*" *The Green Bag: An Entertaining Journal of Law,* 2d series, 4, no. 4 (Summer 2001): 365–273, 9 pp.

Greenhouse describes possible approaches and concludes that the bottom line is, in a test of democratic self-governance," [T]he Court has the last word, and the Court knows best."

"Telling the Court's Story: Justice and Journalism at the Supreme Court." *Yale Law Journal* 105 (April 1996): 1537–1561, 25 pp.

Difficulties covering the High Court include lack of access to justices as sources, deadlines, and time and space limitations.

"Why Bork Is Still a Verb in Politics, Ten Years Later," *The New York Times,* 5 October 1997, 176–179 (4 pp), in **Written into History: Pulitzer Prize Reporting of the Twentieth Century for the New York Times,** ed Anthony Lewis. New York: Holt 2001, 355 pp.

Greenhouse's fine writing on the Bork nomination to the High Court is part of her Pulitzer Prize entry. She describes how the debate on his nomination redefined the mainstream of political thought on the issue.

Anthony Lewis

"Freedom of the Press," 108–118 (11 pp) in **The Burger Court: Counter-Revolution or Confirmation?** ed Bernard Schwartz. New York: Oxford University Press, 1998, 316 pp.

Lewis mentions more than 20 significant cases in 17 Burger years, including many of those discussed earlier ("Pentagon Papers" and *New York Times v Sullivan,* covered in Chapter 1, and *Branzburg, Cox, Near, Nebraska Press, Gannett, Oklahoma Publishing, Landmark Communications,* and *Richmond* in Chapter 2).

Gideon's Trumpet. New York: Random House, 1964 rep 1989, 277 pp.

Portions of the book, which won the Mystery Writers of America Award as the best factual crime book of the year, were published originally in the *New Yorker.* The book became the basis for the TV movie of the same name and tells the story of the landmark Supreme Court case that said that the Sixth Amendment means every criminal defendant facing serious charges is entitled to a lawyer.

Make No Law: The Sullivan Case and the First Amendment. New York: Random House, 1991, 354 pp.

Lewis provides a well-done story of the landmark case, which constitutionalized libel law (see Chapter 1).

"The Press: Free but Not Exceptional," 53–63 (11 pp) in *Reason and Passion: Justice Brennan's Enduring Influence,* ed E. Joshua Rosenkranz and Bernard Schwartz. New York: Norton and Company, 1997, 329 pp.

The authors show that Justice Brennan was concerned with all freedom of expression, not just freedom of the press, which he emphasized first by forbidding prior restraints. His second concern was the press's structural role in a democracy.

"The Quiet of the Storm Center," *South Texas Law Review,* 40:4 (Fall 1999):933–941, 9 pp.

Lewis says the press should focus more on conservative attacks on the independence of judges.

The Supreme Court and How It Works: The Story of the Gideon Case. New York: Random House, 1966, 211 pp.

This is a young adult version of Gideon's case, the landmark Supreme Court holding that all defendants facing serious charges are entitled to a lawyer.

Edited by Lewis. *Portrait of a Decade: The Second American Revolution [by] Anthony Lewis and the New York Times.* New York: Random House (1964) rep 1984, 322 pp.

Edited by Lewis. *Written into History: Pulitzer-Prize Reporting of the Twentieth Century from the New York Times.* New York: Holt, 2001, 355 pp.

Lewis served as the editor of desegregation stories, including his own, done on his Pulitzer Prize–winning beat.

Tony Mauro

"The Camera-Shy Federal Courts," 63–69 (6 pp) in *Covering the Courts: Free Press, Fair Trials, and Journalistic Performance* (originally *Media Studies Journal,* 1998), eds. Robert Giles and Robert Snyder. New Brunswick, NJ: Transaction Publishers, 1999, 146 pp.

Mauro explains why judges generally do not like courtroom cameras.

"Fair Hearing: Legacy to the Poor," 233–242 (12 pp) in *Reason and Passion: Justice Brennan's Enduring Influence,* ed E. Joshua Rosenkranz and Bernard Schwartz. New York: Norton and Company, 1997, 329 pp.

Mauro focuses on the impact of some of Brennan's positions on poverty law, particularly a case that gave welfare recipients due process hearings before benefits are terminated.

Illustrated Great Decisions of the Supreme Court. Washington, DC: Congressional Quarterly, 2000, 350 pp.

Cases included are *Clinton, New York Times,* "Pentagon Papers," Rosenbergs, "Scottsboro Boys," and Watergate (see Chapter 1) and *Branzburg, Near, Richmond,* and *Chandler* (see Chapter 2). It is an extremely readable reference book, enriched with photographs, political cartoons, and drawings.

"A Journalist's Perspective," 216–221, 5 pp, in *The Burger Court: Counter-Revolution or Confirmation?,* ed Benard Schwartz. New York: Oxford University Press, 1998, 316 pp.

Mauro gives fascinating insider details on Chief Justice Warren Burger's press bashing, but he also points out that despite Burger's personal antagonism, the Court during the Burger years produced generally pro–First Amendment decisions, including most notably the landmark *Richmond News* case on access to criminal courtrooms (see Chapter 3).

"The Supreme Court and the Cult of Secrecy," 257–279, 23 pp, in *A Year in the Life of the Supreme Court,* ed Rodney Smolla. Durham: Duke University Press, 1995, 300 pp.

Mauro discusses the inappropriateness of the Court's negative responses to the release of the Thurgood Marshall papers and the audiotapes of oral arguments and to the proposals to televise oral arguments.

Kelli Sager

"First Amendment Issues in the O. J. Simpson Trial," *Communications Lawyer* (Winter 1995): 3–7, 5 pp.

Sager presents an in-depth discussion, based on firsthand experience, of issues such as access to proceedings and records, courtroom cameras, and gag orders.

"Televising the Judicial Branch: In Furtherance of the Public's First Amendment Rights," 69:4 *Southern California Law Review* (1996): 1519–1549, 30 pp.

Sager's article presents constitutional arguments for treating print and broadcast press equally.

Carl Stern

"The Right To Be Wrong—Heretical Thoughts of an Ex-Newscaster," *The Responsive Community* 8, no. 2 (Spring 1998): 24–31, 8 pp.

Stern says the *Times v Sullivan* decision, which extended libel protection to coverage of public officials (see Chapter 1), was too broad: the right should be more limited when the issues are not of real public importance. Stern says the decision also eliminated the incentive to acknowledge error or to print retractions, which could be rectified by limiting a prevailing party to out-of-pocket expenses and attorney's fees.

Nina Totenberg

"Capturing an Audience's Attention: Explaining the Law Through Radio, Television, and Print," 40:4 *South Texas Law Review* (Fall 1999): 957–969, 13 pp.

Based on Totenberg's presentation at the Symposium on Popular Understanding of Law, the broadcast journalist describes her techniques for Supreme Court coverage: "[K]eeping the audience's attention is the name of the game."

Preface (4 pp) to Miller, Anita. *Complete Transcripts of the Clarence Thomas–Anita Hill Hearings* (Oct 11–13, 1991). Chicago: Academy Chicago Publishers, 1994, 480 pp.

Totenberg writes a brief introduction to the hearings on the nomination of Clarence Thomas to serve as justice on the Supreme Court.

Greta Van Susteren

with Elaine Lafferty. *My Turn at the Bully Pulpit: Straight Talk About the Things That Drive Me Nuts*. New York: Crown, 2003, 240 pp.

Van Susteren's autobiography is lightweight, but she does defend the use of courtroom cameras.

Hiller Zobel

The Boston Massacre. New York: Norton, 1970 rep 1996, 372 pp.
Judge Zobel, a respected authority, presents his award-winning version of the story of the Boston Massacre.

"Judicial Independence and the Need to Please," *The Judge's Journal* (Fall 2001): 5–10, 6 pp.
Judge Zobel says the media should treat the judicial system with the seriousness it deserves.

with Stephen Rous, MD. *Doctors and the Law: Defendants and Expert Witnesses.* New York: Norton, 1993, 208 pp.
The authors discuss dealing with the malpractice crisis.

with L. Kinvin Wroth. *Legal Papers of John Adams.* Cambridge, MA: Harvard University Press: 3 vols., 1965.
Judge Zobel wrote the introduction and co-edited this useful tool for historians.

about: English, Bella. "There Goes the Judge: Hiller Zobel Is Retiring After 22 Years of Ruling in Middlesex Superior Court," *The Boston Globe,* 21 February 2002, 1+, 4 pp.
The article presents information about Judge Hiller Zobel.

Nonprint Resources
Alan Dershowitz

The Advocate's Devil
Date: 1997
Media: VHS
Length: 96 minutes

Based on the 1994 fictional book of the same name by Alan Dershowitz, this film presents an interesting ethical dilemma. It stars Ken Olin.

Reversal of Fortune
Date: 1990
Media: VHS
Length: 111 minutes
Source: Warner/Shochiku

Based on the Alan Dershowitz book *Reversal of Fortune: Inside the von Bulow Case,* the film stars Glenn Close, Jeremy Irons (Oscar winner), and Ron Silver as Dershowitz. It is well done and presents von Bulow's innocence as somewhat plausible.

Linda Deutsch

Courtroom Classics From Scopes to Simpson, Associated Press, 1999, 5 pp (available at *www.epals.com*, 2003).

Deutsch sketches various "trials of the century," including many of those discussed in Chapter 1: Thaw, Sacco and Vanzetti, "the Scottsboro Boys," the Lindbergh kidnapping, the Rosenbergs, the Manson trial, the Pentagon Papers case, and O. J. Simpson.

Theo Wilson: Headline Justice
Date: 1998
Media: VHS
Length: 12 minutes
Source: Columbia: University of Missouri

Deutsch is seen on camera and is cowriter of this tribute to her late predecessor, Theo Wilson, the nation's leading courtroom reporter.

Dominick Dunne

Dominick Dunne's Power, Privilege, Justice. Court TV schedule and background material available at *courttv.com* (2003). Interesting programs, including coverage of Menendez brothers (see Chapter 1).

Fred Graham

Ethics on Trial
Date: 1986
Media: VHS
Length: 60 minutes
Source: WETA-TV, Washington, D.C.

The lawyer/journalist discusses issues such as the lawyers' Model Rules of Professional Conduct, access to legal services, lawyer advertising, and regulating lawyers' conduct.

Justice for All
Date: 1986
Media: VHS
Length: 57 minutes
Source: PBS-TV

Graham describes Attorney General Edwin Meese and the Justice Department's need for impartial enforcement of laws (outdated).

The Rodney King Case:
What the Jury Saw in **California v Powell**
Date: 1992
Media: VHS
Length: 56 minutes
Source: Court TV

The film features coverage of the Rodney King police brutality case (see Chapter 1).

Linda Greenhouse

Award-winning Supreme Court coverage (including her question-and-answer column) available at *nytimes.com* (2003).

Anthony Lewis

Gideon's Trumpet
Date: 1979
Media: VHS
Length: 105 minutes
Source: Worldvision Home Video

This 1979 TV docudrama, based on Anthony Lewis's book of the same name, is an excellent drama. It stars Henry Fonda and John Houseman.

Nina Totenberg

She Says/Women in News
Date: 2001
Media: VHS
Length: 60 minutes
Source: PBS-TV

This documentary includes interviews with ten media personalities, including Totenberg, who describe their pioneering work as the first females in newsrooms.

Chapter 5 Facts and Data
Print Resources

Alexander, S. L. *Covering the Courts: A Handbook for Journalists.* (Lanham, MD: University Press of America, 1999); rev Rowman and Littlefield, 2003, 173 pp.

Author's guide includes specific tips from working journalists, lawyers, and judges (including many discussed in Chapter 4, such as Dershowitz, Deutsch, French, Graham, Greenhouse, Mauro, O'Brien, Sager, Totenberg, and Zobel); an extensive legal glossary defined in layman's terms; and texts of codes of ethics for journalists and canons for lawyers and judges, as well as chapters on criminal cases (pre-trial, trial, post-trial), civil cases, and cameras in courts.

————. "Cameras in the Courtroom: A Case Study," *Judicature* 74:6 (April-May 1991):307–313, 7 pp.

Based on participant-observation of first-degree murder trials in a Florida jurisdiction over the course of a year, supplemented with surveys of judges, lawyers, and jurors as well as analysis of the content of news stories by print and broadcast journalists, the author concludes there is no support for the wide speculation that cameras interfere with the judicial process.

————. "The Impact of *California v Simpson* on Cameras in the Courtroom," *Judicature* 79:4 (January–February 1996):169–172, 4 pp.

Based on a survey of fifty states, the author concludes that despite speculation to the contrary, the Simpson criminal case had minimal specific impact on camera usage in state courts.

————. *"Mischievous Potentialities": A Case Study of Courtroom Camera Guidelines, Eighth Judicial Circuit Florida, 1989.* PhD dissertation, University of Florida, 1990, 314 pp.

———. "A Reality Check on Court/Media Relations," *Judicature* 84:3 (November December 2000):146–149, 4 pp.
See description for "Their Day in Court."

———. "Their Day in Court," *Society of Professional Journalists Quill* (June 2000): 10–13, 4 pp; "Trials of the Century: *U.S. v Edwin Edwards* 2000" *Louisiana State Bar Association Journal* 48:4 (December 2000):290–294, cover and 4 pp.
Based on the observation of federal trials of an ex-governor, a sitting insurance commissioner, and others accused of corruption, the author concludes that despite some progress, problems remain regarding court use of sealed records, anonymous jurors, and gag orders.

American Bar Association, *A Journalist's Primer on Civil Procedure.* Chicago: ABA, 1993, 42 pp, and *A Journalist's Primer on Federal Criminal Procedure.* Chicago: ABA, 1988, 52 pp.
Both publications are excellent sources of information for this area of the law; a video is available.

———. *Model Rules of Professional Conduct* and *Code of Judicial Conduct* and *Standards for Criminal Justice, Fair Trial and Free Press,* in *Professional Responsibility Standards, Rules, and Statutes.* Washington, DC: ABA. Current edition available at *www.abanet. org* (2003).
Rules that have the force of law in states that have adopted them cover what lawyers can say outside of court and include suggestions for judges presiding over high-profile cases.

American Bar Association and the National Conference of Lawyers and Representatives of the Media. *The Reporter's Key: Rights of Fair Trial and Free Press.* Chicago: American Bar Association, (1994) 1999, 121 pp.
The current edition is available at *www.abanet.org* (2002). The key is an excellent source, explaining in layman's terms the lawyer's Rules and Standards.

American Board of Trial Advocates (ABOTA). "Accuracy in Legal Journalism Reporting Code," available at *www.abota.org* (2002).
Proposals are given for improved reporting of civil cases.

Barber, Susanna. *News Cameras in the Courtroom.* Norwood, NJ: Albex, 1987, 160 pp.

As the definitive early work, it gathers the results of dozens of social science studies and surveys in the states prior to 1987.

Chemerinsky, Erwin, and Laurie Levenson. "The Ethics of Being a Commentator," 69 *Southern California Law Review* (1996): 1303–1339, 37 pp.

Experienced commentators suggest a voluntary code to cover confidentiality, conflicts of interest, competency, and remuneration of lawyers acting as TV commentators on trials.

Chiasson, Lloyd, ed. *The Press on Trial: Crimes and Trials as Media Events.* Westport, CT: Greenwood, 1997, 227 pp.

Academics look at sixteen high-profile trials including Thaw, Scopes, "Scottsboro Boys," Hauptmann, Hiss, Rosenbergs, and Simpson (Chapter 1).

Cohn, Marjorie, and David Dow. *Cameras in the Courtroom: TV and the Pursuit of Justice.* Jefferson, NC: McFarland, 1998, 193 pp.

This excellent overview includes the comprehensive presentation of the results of numerous studies; it is widely cited.

Davis, Richard. *Decisions and Images: The Supreme Court and the Press.* Englewood Cliffs, NJ: Prentice-Hall, 1994, 193 pp.

Davis's research includes interviews with Supreme Court reporters (Denniston, Greenhouse, Mauro, O'Brien—see Chapter 4). He concludes that justices both individually and as a Court manipulate the press.

Denniston, Lyle. *The Reporter and the Law: Techniques of Covering the Courts.* (American Bar Association and American Newspaper Publishers Association Foundation, 1980) New York: Columbia University Press, 1992, 289 pp.

Denniston wrote the definitive work for print journalists through the date of publication. (See Chapter 4.)

Fox, Richard, and Robert Van Sickel. *Tabloid Justice: Criminal Justice in An Age of Media Frenzy.* Boulder: Lynne Rienner Publishers, 2001, 225 pp.

Based on a 1999 survey, the book describes the impact of media coverage with references to *Smith,* "King," *Menendez, Simpson,* and *Clinton* (see Chapter 1) and Judge Zobel (see Chapter 4).

Giles, Robert, and Robert Snyder, eds. *Covering the Courts: Free Press, Fair Trials, and Journalistic Performance* (originally *Media Studies Journal,* 1998). New Brunswick. NJ: Transaction Publishers, 1999, 146 pp.
    Journalists, judges, and lawyers weigh in.

Goldfarb, Ronald. *TV or Not TV: Television, Justice and the Courts.* New York: New York University Press, 1998, 238 pp.
    Excellent resource that includes comprehensive presentation of results of numerous studies; it is widely cited.

Johnson, Molly Treadway. *Electronic Media Coverage of Civil Proceedings: An Evaluation of the Pilot Program in Six District Courts and Two Courts of Appeals,* and *Electronic Media Coverage of Courtroom Proceedings: Effects on Witnesses and Jurors.* Washington, DC: Federal Judicial Center Report to Judicial Conference Committee on Court Administration and Case Management, 1993–1994, 35 pp.
    Johnson presents the results of a survey of participants in the federal experiment with cameras in civil courts. Although the results were generally positive, the federal courts did not adopt camera usage save in the appellate courts on a circuit-by-circuit basis.

Murphy, Timothy. *Managing Notorious Trials.* Williamsburg: National Center for State Courts, (1992) 1998, 227 pp.
    Murphy's book is the bible for judges dealing with the media in high-profile cases.

National Center for State Courts. *Summary of Television in the State Courts.* Williamsburg: NCSC, 2002, 4 pp.
    This periodic update gives the status of camera usage in courtrooms, including whether cameras are used in civil and/or criminal courts, and trial and/or appellate courts.

National Press Photographers Association (NPPA). "Code of Ethics," available at *www.nppa.org* (2002).
    General guidelines are given for press photographers including those covering courts.

Radio-Television News Directors Association (RTNDA). "Code of Ethics and Professional Conduct," available at *www.rtnda.org* (2002).

   Guidelines are given for journalists and videographers, with specific reference to coverage of courts.

Schmidt, Robert. "May It Please the Court." *Brill's Content* (October 1999): 72–75+, 5 pp.

   Schmidt studied the U.S. Supreme Court and concluded that press coverage is inadequate and the trend is toward decreased coverage.

Slotnick, Eliot, and Jennifer Segal. *Television News and the Supreme Court: All the News That's Fit to Air?* New York: Cambridge University Press, 1998, 264 pp.

   The authors decry the increasing inadequacy of both the quality and quantity of coverage of the Supreme Court.

Society of Professional Journalists (SPJ). "Code of Ethics," available at *www.spj.org* (2002).

   Guidelines are given for print and broadcast journalists, with specific reference to coverage of courts.

Thaler, Paul. *The Spectacle: Media and the Making of the O. J. Simpson Story.* Westport, CT: Praeger, 1997, 325 pp.

   Thayer takes an in-depth look at the media coverage of the criminal case, especially the use of courtroom cameras.

U.S. Department of Justice. 1.700 Media Relations, in *U.S. Attorney's Manual,* available at *www.usdoj.gov* (2002), 3 pp.

   The department gives rules for dealing with the press in criminal cases.

U.S. Judicial Conference. *Code of Judicial Conduct for U.S. Judges.* Washington, DC: Judicial Conference of the United States, 2002. See also, *Guidelines for the Pilot Program in Photographing, Recording and Broadcasting in the Courtroom.* (Washington, DC: Administrative Office of the U.S. Courts, re-issued October 14, 1997).

   Rules for federal judges are presented.

U.S. Supreme Court Public Information Office. *A Reporter's Guide to Applications Pending before the Supreme Court of the U.S.*, available at *www.supremecourtus.gov* (2002), 19 pp.

This guide describes the process by which condemned prisoners apply for stays of execution.

Weinberg, Steve. "Investigating Government: The Judicial System," 249–308, 58 pp in *The Investigative Reporter's Handbook*, ed. Brant Houston, Len Bruzzese, and Steve Weinberg. Boston: Bedford/St Martin's, 4th ed, 2002, 589 pp.

Weinberg gives excellent tips and descriptions of examples of outstanding court coverage.

Westfeldt, Wallace, and Tom Wicker. *Indictment: The News Media and the Criminal Justice System.* Nashville: First Amendment Center, 1998, 82 pp.

This book is a critique, by a highly respected source, of press coverage of criminal cases.

Nonprint Resources

American Bar Association
A Journalist's Guide to Civil Procedure
Date: 1993
Media: VHS
Length: 40 minutes
Source: American Bar Association, Chicago

This is an excellent source. It accompanies the primer of the same name.

A Journalist's Guide to Federal Criminal Procedure
Date: 1989
Media: VHS
Length: 58 minutes
Source: American Bar Association, Chicago

This is an excellent source. It accompanies the primer of the same name.

Table of Cases and Legal Citations

Chapter 1 Free Press/Fair Trial: A Historical Overview

Cases

Bush v Gore. *Bush v Gore*, 531 US 98, Dec 12, 2000 (recount halted); *Bush v Gore*, 531 US 1046, Dec 9, 2000 (recount stayed); *Gore v Harris*, 772 So 2d 1243 (Fla Sup Ct), Dec 8, 2000 (recount to continue); *Bush v Palm Beach Cty Canv'g Bd*, 531 US 70, Dec 4, 2000 (Fla Sup Ct Nov 21 decision vacated and remanded); *Palm Beach Cty Canv'g Bd v Harris*, 772 So 2d 1220 (Fla Sup Ct), Nov 21, 2000 (recount to continue).

Sigel v LePore, 29 Med L Rptr 1190 (US Dist Ct, SD Fla), Nov 13, 2000 (no video coverage of hearings).

California v Manson. *California v Manson*, LA Cty Ct Crim No 22239, March 29, 1971 (conviction in the "Helter Skelter" murders); No 24376, April 19, 1971 (sentence); *affm'd*, 61 Cal App 3d 102 (Ca 2d Dist Ct App) 1976 (free press/fair trial at 172-190, Nixon headline N 82 at 185); *cert den*, 430 US 986 (1977).

Farr v Supr Ct, 22 Cal App 3d 60 (CA 2d Ct App) 1971 (contempt order for reporter who refused to reveal his news source on grounds of reporter's privilege); *cert den*, 409 US 1011 (1972); *Farr v Pitchess*, 522 F 2d 464 (US 9th Cir Ct Appl) 1975; *cert den*, 427 US 912 (1976) (contempt order upheld).

California v Menendez. *California v Menendez,* Supr Ct LA Cty, SA 002727 (Lyle), SA002728 (Erik), Jan 13, 1994 (mistrials due to hung juries in cases of brothers charged with murdering parents); BA 06880, 1995 (cameras not allowed at retrial); SC 031947, March 20, 1996 (convictions); *habeas corpus den,* Ca Sup Ct, 1999 Cal LEXIS 1960 (Lyle), 1999 Cal LEXIS 5148 (Erik), 1960 (1999).

Menendez v Fox, 22 Med L Rptr 1702 (US Dist Ct, CD Cal, 1994) (documentary *Honor Thy Father and Mother* not halted since any prejudicial effects could be mitigated during jury selection and jury instructions).

California v Simpson. *California v Simpson,* Los Angeles, Ca Dist Ct No BAO 97211, 1995 WL 704381 (criminal case on charges of murdering his wife and her friend, media hearing, Nov 7, 1994); Oct 3, 1995 (acquittal).

Rufo v Simpson, Supr Ct LA Cty No SC 031947, 1997 (civil case, held liable for murders); *affm'd,* 86 Cal App 4th 573 (Ca 2d Ct App, 2001); (Order Affirming Prior Gag Order and Banning Cameras from Trial, 8/23/96; In Re Anonymous Jurors, 10/28/96).

Florida v Smith. *Florida v Smith,* Palm Beach County, Dec 11, 1991 (acquittal).

Georgia v Frank. *Georgia v Frank,* Atlanta, Fulton Supr Ct, 1913 (conviction); *affm'd,* 141 Ga 243 (Ga Sup Ct, 1914); *affm'd,* 142 Ga 617, 741 (Ga Sup Ct, 1914); *affm'd, Frank v Mangum,* 237 US 309, 1915 (murder conviction upheld, Holmes dissent at 345-349).

"Hauptmann." *Hauptmann v NJ,* 180 A 809 (NJ Sup Ct, 1935); *cert den,* 296 US 649 (1935) (kidnap/murder conviction).

Anna Hauptmann v Wilentz, 570 F Supp 351 (US Dist Ct NJ, 1983) (unsuccessful civil suit to clear husband's name).

Illinois v Leopold and Loeb. *Illinois v Leopold and Loeb,* Chicago, Sept 10, 1924 (murder conviction) (Higdon: trial transcript available at Northwestern University, Chicago).

Leopold v Levin, 45 Ill 2d 434 (Ill Sup Ct, 1970) (no invasion of privacy in fictionalized version of murders in *Compulsion* due to lack of privacy of convicted murderer).

"King." *In re California v Powell: Powell, et al, v Supr Ct of LA Cty,* Supr Ct LA Cty, No. B058842, 232 Cal App 3d 785 (1991) (change of venue granted); *Briseno v Supr Ct LA Cty,* 233 Cal App 3d 607 (1991) (challenge to judge); April 29, 1992 (acquittal in criminal case of police charged with beating Rodney King).

US v Koon and Powell, No. CR-92-00686, 1993; *affm'd*, 34 F 3d 1416 (US 9th Cir Ct Appl) 1994; 518 US 81 (1996) (civil case, two of police officers held liable for violating King's civil rights).

Gates et al v Supr Ct LA Cty, 32 Cal App 4th 481 (1995) (Denny et al. unsuccessful in their civil case against the LAPD in regard to injuries sustained in the riots after "King" acquittals).

Louisiana v Shaw. *Louisiana v Shaw*, Orleans Parish, March 1, 1969 (Shaw acquitted on conspiracy charges regarding the assassination of President John F Kennedy).

Shaw v Garrison, 328 F Supp 390 (US Dist Ct, ED La), 1971 (after Shaw acquittal, New Orleans District Attorney Jim Garrison was restrained from proceeding with perjury case against Shaw or from prosecuting additional criminal charges on grounds Garrison abused prosecutorial powers, including media grandstanding).

Garrison v Louisiana, 244 La 787 (La Sup Ct), 1960; *rev*, 379 US 64 (1964) (Garrison's pre-*Shaw* criminal defamation conviction for claiming judges' "racketeering influences" was overturned in light of *New York Times v Sullivan*).

Massachusetts v Sacco and Vanzetti. *Massachusetts v Sacco and Another*, Dedham, July 14, 1921 (convictions); *affm'd*, 255 Mass 369 (Mass Sup Jud Ct, 1926); *affm'd*, 259 Mass 128 (Mass Sup Jud Ct, 1927); *affm'd*, 261 Mass 12 (Mass Sup Ct, 1927); *cert den*, 275 US 574 (1927) (murder convictions upheld).

New York v Snyder and Gray. *New York v Snyder and Gray*, Queens, New York, May 13, 1927 (murder conviction); *affm'd*, 246 NY 491 (NY Ct App, 1927).

New York v Thaw. *New York v Thaw*, New York, April 1907 (mistrial); Feb 1908 (not guilty by reason of insanity, committed); *Drew v Thaw*, 235 US 432 (1914) (returned to institute after escape); 167 AD 104 (NY Sup Ct, 1915) (declared sane).

New York Times v Sullivan. *New York Times v Sullivan*, 273 Ala 656 (Ala Sup Ct, 1962); *rev*, 376 US 254 (1964) (landmark press case in which subject attempted to find libel in coverage of civil rights activities after the 1954 US Supreme Court desegregation case).

New York Times v US ("Pentagon Papers"). *NY Times v US*, 328 F Supp 324 (US Dist Ct, SD NY, 1971); *affm'd*, 444 F 2d 544 (US 2d Cir Ct Appl,

1971) with *US v Wash Post,* 446 F 2d 1327 (US DC Ct App, 1971); *affm'd,* 403 US 713 (1971) (no injunction granted, publication allowed).

Scopes v Tennessee. *Scopes v Tenn,* Trial Nos 5231, 5232, Cir Ct Rhea Cty, Tenn (convicted of violating creationism law; transcript available in Grebstein, *Monkey Trial,* 1960; and also in *The Scopes Trial,* 1990 reprint); *affm'd,* 152 Tenn 424 (Tenn Sup Ct, 1925); *nolle prosequi,* prosecution dropped despite conviction, 154 Tenn 105 (Tenn Sup Ct, 1927).

Epperson v Ark, 242 Ark 922 (Ark Sup Ct, 1967); *rev,* 393 US 97 (1968) (Arkansas creationism law struck as a violation of the First and Fourteenth Amendments).

Edwards v Aguillard, 765 F 2d 1251 (US 5th Cir Ct Appl, 1985); *affm'd,* 482 US 578 (1986) (Louisiana creationism law struck as a violation of the First Amendment establishment of religion clause).

"Scottsboro." *Powell v Ala,* 287 US 45 (1932) (*rev* rape convictions, based on ineffective counsel, defendant denied due process).

Norris v Ala, 294 US 587 (1935) (*rev* rape convictions, based on systematic exclusion of blacks from grand jury, a denial of due process). Also, *Street v NBC,* 512 F Supp 398, US Dist Ct, ED Tenn, (August 13, 1976; April 6, 1977); *affm'd,* 645 F 2d 1227 (US 6th Cir Ct Appl), 1981 (docudrama not false light privacy because the plaintiff was a public figure who played a prominent role in a public controversy, she communicated with the public and thrust herself into the forefront, and the defendant did not maliciously portray the plaintiff in a defamatory manner).

Sheppard v Maxwell. *Sheppard v Maxwell* (*Ohio v Sheppard*), Cleveland, Dec 21, 1954 (murder conviction); *affm'd,* 346 F 2d 707 (US 6th Cir Ct Appl), 1965; *rev,* 384 US 333 (1966) (Kilgallen quote N 11 at 358); retrial, Cleveland, Nov 16, 1966 (acquittal).

Sheppard v Scripps, 421 F 2d 555 (US 6th Cir Ct Appl, 1970); *affm'd,* 421 F 2d 559 (US 6th Cir Ct Appl), 1970 (no libel found).

Sheppard v Stevenson, 1 Ohio App 2d 6 (Ct App Ohio, 1964) (no libel).

The Estate of Sam Sheppard v Ohio, No. 312322, No. 421593 Cuyahoga Cty Ct Com Pleas, April 22, 2000; *affm'd,* 8th Ohio Dist Ct App, Feb 22, 2002 (civil trial, no wrongful imprisonment of Sam Sheppard). Also, *Ohio ex rel Cleveland Plain Dealer v Ct Cmn Pls,* 90 Ohio State 3d 272 (Ohio Sup Ct), 2000 (access to records in civil case denied as moot). Also, *Sweeney v New York Times* (US Dist Ct, Ohio, 2003, no libel in case of former prosecutor falsely reported to have participated in earlier Sheppard case due to lack of malice by newspaper).

US v Burr. *US v Burr,* (US Cir Ct, D Va), 25 Fed Cas 49 No. 14,692g, 1807 (Marshall at 50); *affm'd, In re Trial of Aaron Burr for Treason,* 8 US 470 (1807) (treason case, jurors with open minds acceptable).

US v Clinton. *Clinton v Jones,* 520 US 681 (1997) (sitting president can appear in sexual harassment case); *Jones v Clinton,* No LR-C-94-290 (US Dist Ct ED Ark), 1994 LEXIS 5739; *dismissed as settled,* 161 F 3d 528 (US 8th Cir Ct Appl), 1998; 138 F 3d 758 (US 8th Cir Ct Appl), 1998 (access to sealed records remanded, returned, to district court); 27 Med L Rptr 1156 (US Dist Ct ED Ark), 1998 (district court releases most records).

US v Hearst. *US v Hearst,* San Francisco, March 20, 1976 (conviction); *affm'd,* 424 F Supp. 307 (US Dist Ct, ND Ca, 1976*); affm'd,* 563 F 2d 1331 (US 9th Cir Ct Appl), 1977; *cert den,* 435 US 1000 (1978); *affm'd,* 466 F Supp 1068 (US Dist Ct, ND Ca, 1978) (conviction stands despite fact Hearst case was subject of "most extensive news coverage in recent history" at 1073); *affm'd,* 638 F 2d 1190 (US 9th Cir Ct Appl, 1980); *cert den,* 451 US 938 (1981).

US v Hiss. *US v Hiss,* US Dist Ct, SD NY, Jan 25, 1950 (conviction on charges of perjury); *affm'd,* 185 F 2d 822 (US 2d Cir Ct Appl, 1950); *cert den,* 340 US 948 (1951); 107 F Supp 128 (US Dist Ct, SD NY, 1952); *affm'd, In re Hiss,* 542 F Supp 973 (US Dist Ct, SD NY, 1982).

Hiss v Hampton, 338 F Supp 1141 (US Dist Ct, DC, 1972) (re-instated retirement benefits); *In Matter of Hiss,* 368 Mass 447 (Supr Jud Ct Mass, 1975) (re-instated to bar).

Hiss v Chambers, 8 FRD 480 (US Dist Ct, MD, 1948) (libel).

In re Amer Hist Assoc, 49 F Supp 2d 274 (US Dist Ct, SD NY, 1999); 62 F Supp 2d 1100,1999 (access to Hiss grand jury records granted except for that of two witnesses).

US v McVeigh and Nichols. *US v McVeigh and Nichols,* 918 F Supp 1467 (US Dist Ct, WD OK, 1996) (change of venue granted); 931 F Supp 753, 756 (US Dist Ct, CO, 1996) (no audio access, "gag" upheld); 964 F Supp 313 (US Dist Ct, CO, 1997) ("gag" upheld); 955 F Supp 1281 (US Dist Ct, CO, 1997) (fair trial possible despite publicity); 119 F 3d 806 (US 10th Cir Ct Appl, 1997) (sealed documents upheld); 169 F 3d 1255 (US Dist Ct 10th Cir Ct Appl, 1997), Nichols conviction *affm'd,* 153 F 3d 1166 (US 10th Cir Ct Appl, 1998) (prejudicial publicity in McVeigh case does not warrant new trial); *cert den, Nichols v US,* 528 US 934, 1999; *Nichols v Jackson,* 30 Med L Rptr 1202, OK Ct Crim App, 2001 (Nichols records may not be closed wholesale), *Oklahoma v Nichols,* 2000 OK CR 12 (OK Ct

Crim App); June 2000 (camera coverage denied); May 2003 (access to documents denied). Also, *Entertain Net v Lappin*, 134 F Supp 2d 1002 (US Dist Ct SD Ind, 2001) (no netcast of McVeigh execution).

US v Microsoft. *US v Microsoft*, 334 US Ct Appl, DC 165, 1999 (Bill Gates depositions made public); US Dist Ct, DC 98-1232, 98-1233, 1998 US Dist Ct LEXIS 14231, 2000 (Finding of Fact memo and final judgment); *affm'd in part, reversed in part*, 253 F 3d 34 (US Ct Appl DC), 2001 ("Judicial Misconduct," judge banned from presiding at retrial, at 106-118); *New York v Microsoft*, Executive Summary (US Dist Ct, DC, Nov 1, 2002) Civ Act 98-1233 (CKK) (states' civil case, terms of settlement described in court memorandum opinion).

US v Nixon ("Watergate"). *In re subpoena of Nixon*, 360 F Supp 18 (US Dist Ct, DC), 1973 (Nixon ordered to comply); *affm'd, Nixon v Sirica*, 487 F 2d 700 (US DC Cir Ct Appl, 1973) (must comply); *Senate Select Comm v Nixon*, 370 F Supp 521 (US Dist Ct, DC, 1974, must comply); *affm'd, US v Nixon*, 418 US 683 (1974).

US v Rosenberg. *US v Ethel and Julius Rosenberg*, US Dist Ct, NY, March 29, 1951 (conviction); *affm'd*, 195 F 2d 583 (US 2nd Cir Ct Appl, 1952); *affm'd*, 344 US 838, 1952; 204 F 2d 688 (US 2nd Cir Ct Appl), 1953 (stay—halting—of execution denied); 346 US 273, 322, 324 (1953) (stay granted by Justice Douglas vacated, execution to proceed).

Vanderbilt v Whitney. *In the matter of Vanderbilt v Carew*, 242 AD 482 (Sup Ct NY Appl Div), 1934 (denial of *habeas corpus*, request for return of custody to mother); *affm'd*, 245 AD 211 (Sup Ct NY App Div, 1935); 246 AD 599 (Sup Ct NY App Div, 1935).

Legal Citations

"Hollywood 10." US 80th Cong, 1st Sess, Oct 1947, House Committee for the Investigation of Un-American Activities, *Hearings Regarding the Communist Infiltration of the Motion Picture Industry*, Washington, DC: US GPO, 1947 (HUAC sessions involving Hollywood, led to convictions of Hollywood 10).

Louisiana v Shaw. *President John F. Kennedy Assassination Records Collection Act*, 44 USCS Sect 2107, 1992 (Congress passed this law after Oliver Stone's film *JFK* revived public interest in the case. June 1995 hearings of Review Board covered by author for article including Garrison's dealings with WDSU-TV's Richard Angelico in this case. See Chapter 7, print resources for Chapter 1.)

US v Clinton. *US v Clinton, Proceedings of the US Senate in the impeachment trial of President William Jefferson Clinton.* Washington, DC: US GPO S doc/106th Cong, 1st Sess, 1999, Sen: 106-04. inc H Res 611, 105th Cong 2nd Sess 1998 (4 vols, 3121 pp) (president impeached, charged, but acquitted).

The Starr Report, Referral from Independent Counsel Kenneth W Starr, H Doc No 310, 105th Cong 2d Sess (9/11/98) and Append, H Doc No 316, 105th Cong 2d Sess (9/28/98); *Final Report of the Independent Counsel in re Madison Guaranty Savings and Loan Association,* Robert Ray, 3/6/02, 3/20/02, available at http://icreport.access.gpo.gov/final, 2003) (cost the taxpayers $60 million).

Chapter 2 Controversies, Problems, and Solutions

Cases

APBNews.com v Committee on Financial Disclosure, No 99-civ-1228 (JSR) (SDNY, 1999) (motion for access to judges' financial records, settled out of court).

Arkansas Democrat-Gazette v Zimmerman, 341 Ark 771 (Sup Ct Ark, 2000) (judge must modify a restraining order regarding photographs in juvenile case).

Ashcraft v Conoco, 218 F 3d 282, 288 (US 4th Cir Ct Appl) 2000 (appeal court modifies a gag order and overturns a contempt citation for reporters who received sealed records due to a clerk's error).

In re Beacon Journal Pub Co v Bond, 98 Ohio St 3d 146, 2002 (juror names, addresses, and questionnaires are not public record under FoI laws, but a First Amendment qualified right of access extends to juror names, addresses, and questionnaires, after crucial information such as Social Security numbers are redacted).

Broadman v Commission on Judicial Performance, 18 Cal 4th 1079 (Cal Supr Ct) 1998 (a judge is censured on grounds including talking to journalists about his unique sentences).

California v Jackson (Santa Barbara Cty Supr Ct DA No 03-12-098996 (2003) (media frenzy over charges of child molestation against pop singer).

California v Peterson (Stanislaus Cty Supr Ct No 1056770); *In re Contra Costa News*, 2003 Cal App Unpub LEXIS 7308; 31 Media L. Rep. 2048 (2003) (upholds June 12 gag order and sealed records, camera ban August 18).

Cape Publications v Braden, 39 SW 3d 823 (Ky Sup Ct) 2001 (a ban on access to jurors during a murder case was improper).

Center for National Security Studies et al v US Dept Justice, 215 F Supp 2d 94 (US Dist Ct, DC, 2002); *rev*, US Dist Ct Appl, DC Cir No 02-5254, 02-5300, 2003 (appellate court reversed lower court and said the government need not release information on those detained after 9/11/01).

Chicago Tribune v Bridgestone/Firestone, 263 F 3d 1304 (US 11th Cir Ct Appl) 2001 (many sealed records in a class action suit are unsealed).

Colorado v Bryant, Eagle Cty Dist Ct Case No 03CR204 (2003) (gag order, sealed records).

Connecticut v Skakel, Supr Court No FSTCR00135792T (2000) (successful press motion to obtain access to arraignment).

In re Copley Press (California v Westerfield), 98 Cal App 4th 145 (Ca 4th Dist Ct App, 2002) (most records must remain sealed until after the trial).

In re Court TV (New York v Boss), 182 NY Misc 2d 700 (NY Sup Ct, Albany Cty, 2000) (a judge grants a petition to broadcast despite a camera ban, declares the blanket camera ban is unconstitutional); *Court TV v NY*, 2003 NY Misc LEXIS 982 (Supr Ct NY, NY Cty) (appellate court says camera ban is constitutional).

In re Daily Journal v Police, 797 A 2d 186 (Supr Ct NJ) 2002 (a judge grants a media request for access to 911 audiotapes used as evidence in a police misconduct case).

Detroit Free Press v Ashcroft, 303 F 3d 681 (US 6th Cir Ct Appl) 2002 (found in favor of media access to hearings involving immigrants suspected of terrorist activity, but the decision conflicts with *North Jersey v Ashcroft* [below], and the US Supreme Court refused to hear an appeal).

In re Domestic Air Transportation Antitrust Litigation, 24 Fed R Serv 3d (Callaghan) 515 (US Dist Ct, MD Ga) 1994 (the records regarding airline payments to four million people were unsealed).

Earnhardt v Volusia Cty Office of Medical Examiner, 29 Med L Rptr 2173 (Fla Cir Ct Volusia Cty No 2001-3073-CICI) 2001 (denied access to autopsy photos in the death of racecar driver Dale Earnhardt and became a model for legislation in Florida and other states).

In re Enron Corp Securities Litigation (Newby v Enron), No H-01-3624 (SD TX, Oct 22, 2001) (Dow Jones leads a media challenge regarding which the judge first denies Enron's request for blanket secrecy of 19 million documents, then rules Enron must keep a log of documents and allow media interveners access to the log and the right to challenge documents classified as confidential).

Georgia v Marsh, 30 Med L Rptr 1507 (Ga Super Ct) 2002 (narrowed a gag order in a crematorium case).

Grutter v Bollinger; Gratz v Bollinger, 123 S Ct 2325, 2411, 2003 (case involved challenge to University of Michigan affirmative action rules; Court allowed audiotaping of oral arguments).

In re Houston Chronicle, 64 SW 3d 103 (Tex Ct Appl, 14th Dist) 2001 (a gag order was upheld in the Yates murder case).

Leggett v US, In re Grand Jury Subpoenas, US Ct Appl 5th Cir (unpublished) No 01-20745, 29 Med L Rptr 2301(2001); *cert den,* 122 S Ct 1593 (2002) (upheld a contempt citation for a freelance writer refusing to reveal a source in a murder case and resulted in a lengthy jail term for the writer).

Los Angeles Times v Superior Court, 2003 Cal App LEXIS 1853 (2003) (trial judge may not impose a blanket secrecy order on records of proceedings related to grand jury considering charges of sexual abuse by priests, but in this case, sealing was upheld).

McConnell v Federal Elections Commission (US Supreme Court) 2003 LEXIS 9195 (case found campaign finance reform constitutional; Court allowed audiotaping of oral arguments).

NBC (KNBC-TV) v Supr Ct LA, 20 Cal 4th 1178 (Cal Sup Ct) 1999 (the records in a civil case involving actor Clint Eastwood were ordered open and the court presented grounds for presumption of access to all civil cases in the state).

In re New Jersey v Mohammed El-Atriss, No 03-01-00095-A (NJ Super Ct, Feb 4, 2002) (a terrorist admits he aided 9/11/01 hijackers, and the plea bargain calls for him to testify in another case; some records opened in 2003).

North Jersey Media Group v Ashcroft, 205 F Supp 288 (US Dist Ct NJ) 2002; *rev*, 308 F 3d 198 (US 3rd Cir Ct Appl) 2002; *cert den*, 2003 US LEXIS 4082 (5/27/03) (2003) (denied access to hearings on immigrants suspected of terrorist activity, a decision which conflicts with *Detroit Free Press v Ashcroft* [above], and the US Supreme Court refused to hear an appeal).

Oklahoma v Nichols, 2000 OK CR 12 (OK Ct Crim App); June 2000 (camera coverage denied); May 2003 (access to documents denied).

Commonwealth of Pennsylvania v Gallman, 48 Pa D & C 4th 413 (Phil Ct Common Pleas) 2001 (a media request for posttrial access to a videotaped murder confession is granted).

In re Philadelphia Newspapers v New Jersey and Fred Neulander (NJ Supreme Ct) 801 A 2d 255 (NJ, 2002) (173 NJ 193, 2002); *cert den*, 123 S Ct 1281 (2003) (upheld contempt for journalists contacting jurors in the case of a rabbi accused of murder, although the press may use juror ID information included in the public record).

Phoenix News v US Dist Ct, 156 F 3d 940 (US 9th Cir Ct Appl) 1998 (the closed hearings during the Symington jury deliberation were an error).

Rosado v Bridgeport Roman Catholic Diocesan Corp, 60 Conn App 134 (CT Ct App, 2000) (due to failure to meet deadline for applying for openness, church files naming priests accused of sexual abuse remain sealed).

(Texas v Poe) in re Texas v Harrison, 2003 WL 291926 (Tex Crim Appl) (*Frontline* permission to tape is rescinded).

US v Brown, 218 F 3d 415 (US 5th Cir Ct Appl) 2000 (a gag order is upheld in a politician's fraud case which also involved anonymous jurors).

In re US v Cleveland, 128 F 3d 267 (US 5th Cir Ct Appl) 1997; *cert den, In Re Capital City Press*, 523 US 1075 (1998) (upheld juror secrecy in a case involving elected officials charged with corruption).

US v Edwards, US 5th Cir Ct Appl, MD La 98-165-13-M2, 2000; *affm'd* 303 F 3d 606 (US 5th Cir Ct Appl) 2002; *rehearing den*, 51 Fed Appx 485, 2002 (upheld fraud convictions despite sealed records, anonymous jurors, and extensive gag orders).

US v Lindh, 198 F Supp 2d 739 (ED VA, No 02-37-A, 2002) (a freelance writer is subpoenaed and records sealed in the case of the American Taliban fighter; the subpoena becomes moot after Lindh pleads guilty).

In re US v Moussaoui, No 03-4162 (US 4th Cir Ct App, 5/11/03) (holds that unclassified documents should be analyzed separately and disclosure granted when First Amendment concerns outweigh the need for secrecy); also, 205 FRD 183 (US Dist Ct, ED Va, 1/18/02) The Order Denying Court TV Access (unsuccessful challenge to Federal Rules of Criminal Procedure 53 banning courtroom camera).

In re Commonwealth of Virginia v Malvo [and Muhammed], (Fairfax Ct Cir Ct April 4, 2003) (motions to telecast proceedings and to allow still photography at pretrial and trial proceedings is denied); also, *In re Washington Post Motion to Open Juvenile Detention Hearing,* 2003 WL 721475 (D Md) (access to hearings of juvenile accused sniper Malvo in Baltimore are denied, although access to hearing transcript and other records in Virginia are granted; a gag order is also granted).

Legal Citations

Developing CCJ/COSCA Guidelines *for Public Access to Court Records: A National Project to Assist State Courts,* NCSC/SJMI, Oct 18, 2002, available at http://www.courtaccess.org/model policy (proposal).

"Domestic Security Enhancement Act," 2003 (proposed "USA Patriot Act II," also in response to 9/11/01).

Fla Stat Sect 405.135 Public Health, Medial Examiners: Autopsies; confidentiality of photographs and video and audio records, 2001 (autopsy access is denied by law in Florida after Dale Earnhardt's death).

Federal Juvenile Delinquency Act, 18 USCS, Sect 5038 Use of Juvenile Records, 2002 (denies access to most records involving juveniles in the federal court system).

Homeland Security Act of 2002, 107 Pub L No 296 (in response to 9/11/01, criminalized leaks of information and gave immunity to businesses that shared information with the government).

"Sunshine in the Courtroom Act," 105th Congress 1st Session HR 1280, 1997; 106th Congress 1st Session S 721, 1999; 106th Congress 2nd Session HR 1252, 2000; "A Bill to Allow Media Coverage of Court Proceedings," 107th Congress 1st Session S 986, 2001; 107th Congress 2nd Session, S 1858, 2002; 108th Congress 1st Session S 554, 2003 (proposal for cameras in federal courts introduced each year).

Terrorist Victims Courtroom Access Act, 107th Cong 2d Sess, HR 3611, 2002 (permits closed-circuit video feed for victims and families, similar to that allowed in the Oklahoma City bombing case).

The Uniting and Strengthening of America by Providing Appropriate Tools Required to Intercept and Obstruct Terrorism ("USA Patriot") Act of 2001, 107 Pub L No 56, 115 Stat 272 (in immediate response to terrorist attacks of 9/11/01, tightened access to government information and relaxed rights to individual privacy).

Uniform Mediation Act, National Conference of Commissioners on Uniform State Laws, available at http://www.nccusl.org, 2002 (proposal for civil cases to be settled out of court).

Chapter 3 Chronology
Cases

Branzburg v Hayes, 408 US 665 (1972) (landmark case, upheld contempt for reporters refusing to testify before grand juries when subpoenaed).

Bridges v California, 314 US 252 (1941) (overturned contempt for criticism of judge).

Butterworth v Smith, 494 US 624 (1990) (struck the Florida Bar Association rule forbidding grand jury witnesses from ever revealing their own testimony).

Chandler v Florida, 449 US 560 (1981) (landmark case, upheld states' rights to permit courtroom cameras and to design rules for their use).

Cox Broadcasting v Cohn, 420 US 469 (1975) (landmark case, held that the press cannot be punished for publishing truthful information lawfully obtained from open court records).

Craig v Harney, 331 US 367 (1947) (limited a court's power to find the press in contempt, widely quoted on public access to courts: "A trial is a public event . . .").

Estes v Texas, 381 US 532 (1965) (overturned a conviction for swindling on grounds which included the use of courtroom cameras, considered by many at the time as a blanket ban on camera use).

Florida Bar v Went For It, 515 US 618 (1995) (upheld the Florida Bar Association restrictions on lawyers' speech which required waiting to contact potential clients after a catastrophe).

Florida Star v BJF, 491 US 524 (1989) (narrowly tailored to facts in this case, held that the press cannot be punished for publishing truthful information lawfully obtained, and that such laws must apply to everyone, not just to the media).

Gannett v dePasquale, 443 US 368 (1979) (short-lived holding that the press/public has no right to attend pretrial hearings, superseded by *Press Enterprise I* and *II*).

Gentile v State Bar of Nevada, 501 US 1030 (1991) (landmark case, struck restrictions on lawyers' speech in this case as void for vagueness, but upheld the concept of restrictions since lawyers are officers of the court).

Globe Newspaper v Superior Court, 457 US 596 (1982) (struck the state ban on access to trials of those charged in sex crimes involving child victims).

Irvin v Dowd, 366 US 717 (1961) (overturned a murder conviction on grounds including prejudicial publicity).

Landmark Communications v Virginia, 435 US 829 (1978) (struck a contempt citation for merely publicizing the activity of a judicial commission that was investigating judicial misconduct).

Marshall v US, 360 US 310 (1959) (overturned a conviction on grounds including prejudicial publicity).

Mu' Min v Virginia, 501 US 1269 (1991) (upheld a murder conviction despite the failure to question jurors individually regarding exposure to possible prejudicial publicity).

Murphy v Florida, 421 US 794 (1975) (upheld a robbery conviction despite charges of prejudicial publicity regarding earlier convictions for theft and murder).

Near v Minnesota, 283 US 697 (1931) (landmark case "incorporating" the First Amendment via the 14th Amendment to apply to all levels of government—state and municipal as well as federal).

Nebraska Press Association v Stuart, 427 US 539 (1976) (landmark case, held that gag orders on the press are the "least tolerable infringement" on the First Amendment and a test must first be applied and a hearing must be held before applying such a gag).

Nixon v Warner Communications, 435 US 589 (1978) (unique case, denied access to audiotaped evidence on grounds including a federal law which provided for future release of presidential materials).

Oklahoma Publishing v District Court, 430 US 308 (1977) (upheld the right of access to juvenile proceedings).

Patton v Yount, 467 US 1025 (1984) (upheld a murder conviction despite charges of prejudicial publicity).

Pennekamp v Florida, 328 US 331 (1946) (overturned contempt merely for criticism of judge).

Press Enterprise v Riverside Superior Court I, 464 US 501 (1984) (upheld the right of access to jury selection).

Press Enterprise v Riverside Superior Court II, 478 US 1 (1986) (upheld the right of access to pretrial hearings).

In re Providence Journal, 820 F 2d 1342 (US 1st Cir Ct Appl, 1986); *mod*, 820 F 2d 1354 (US 1st Cir Ct Appl, 1987); *cert den*, 485 US 693 (1988) (the US Supreme Court refused to hear this lower court ruling granting journalists the right to disobey court orders while appealing their constitutionality, although the decision conflicts with *In re US v Dickinson*).

Republican Party of Minnesota v White, 536 US 765 (2002) (struck some aspects of restrictions on the speech of judges running for election but upheld others).

Richmond News v Virginia, 488 US 555 (1980) (landmark case, upheld the right of access to criminal trials).

Rideau v Louisiana, 373 US 723 (1963) (overturned a murder conviction on grounds including prejudicial publicity).

Seattle Times v Rhinehart, 467 US 20 (1984) (unique civil case, restricted information that was only obtained by the press in this case because the press itself was a litigant).

Sheppard v Maxwell, Warden, 384 US 333 (1966) (landmark case, overturned a murder conviction on grounds including the most extreme prejudicial publicity).

Smith v Daily Mail, 443 US 97 (1979) (struck a state statute banning the identification of juvenile criminal defendants).

In re US v Dickinson, 465 F 2d 496 (US 5th Cir Ct Appl, 1972); *affm'd,* 476 F 2d 373 (US 5th Cir Ct Appl, 1973); *cert den,* 414 US 979 (1973) (the US Supreme Court refused to hear this lower court ruling denying journalists the right to disobey court orders while appealing their constitutionality, although the decision conflicts with *In re Providence Journal).*

In re US v Noriega, 752 F Supp 1032 (US Dist Ct DC) 1990; 917 F 2d 1543 (US 11th Cir Ct Appl) 1990; *cert den, Cable News Network v Noriega and US,* 498 US 976 (1990) (the US Supreme Court refused to hear this unique case in which a contempt citation was upheld against CNN, which broadcast tapes of the defendant and his lawyer and then refused to turn the tapes over to the judge).

El Vocero de Puerto Rico v Puerto Rico, 508 US 147 (1993) (struck a rule in Puerto Rico which presumed pretrial hearings were closed, brought Puerto Rico into line with the US mainland).

Waller v Georgia, 467 US 39 (1984) (ordered a new trial in a case in which a suppression hearing had been closed).

Wood v Georgia, 370 US 375 (1962) (overturned a contempt citation merely for criticism of judge).

Legal Citations

Canon 3(A) 7, *ABA Lawyers Manual on Professional Conduct,* Chicago, 1984, 1992 (current restrictions on courtroom cameras).

Canon 35, *ABA Reports,* 1937, 1134-1135 (the original ban on courtroom cameras after the Hauptmann case).

Federal Rules of Criminal Procedure, Rule 53, 1946 (the ban on court-room cameras in federal courts).

Presidential Recording and Materials Preservation Act of 1978, 44 USC Sect 2202 *et seq*, 1978 (preserves audiotapes in the Watergate case, provides for their systematic release, which began in 2002).

Chapter 4 Biographical Sketches

Cases

Bailey. *In re F Lee Bailey*, No BC-2001-093; *affm'd*, Supreme Judicial Court of Massachusetts No SJC-08764, 2003 (Bailey disbarred in Massachusetts. Supreme Judicial Court says his outstanding career does not mitigate the damage he has done).

F Lee Bailey v US, 40 Fed Cl 449, 1998; 46 Fed Cl 187, 2000; *Judgment entered, dis*, 54 Fed Cl 459, 2002 (Bailey unsuccessfully sues the government, claims money they demanded re the Duboc case was his legal fee; the court finds there was no "meeting of minds" required for an implied contract).

Florida v Glenn Turner et al, 285 So 2d 623, 1973; 260 So 2d 274, 1972 (Turner, head of Dare to Be Great, was accused of mail fraud in a pyramid-sales case. Bailey said he had been included only because of what he had once written about the postal service. The jury deadlocked in May 1974, and after the mistrial, the government never retried the case).

The Florida Bar v F Lee Bailey, 803 So 2d 683 (Fla 2001), *cert den*, 122 S Ct 1916 (2002) (The Florida Supreme Court upholds disbarment after the Duboc case on grounds of commingling funds, misappropriating trust funds, being in contravention of two court orders, giving false testimony, self-dealing to the disadvantage of his client and ex parte communications with the judge. Held "egregious and cumulative misconduct . . . absence of any mitigating factors").

US v F Lee Bailey, 175 F 3d 966 (US 11th Cir Ct Appl) 1999; *reh'g* and *reh'g en banc den*, 192 F 3d 132 (1999) (Bailey claims Judge Maurice Paul should have recused himself in the contempt proceedings in the Duboc case, but the appellate court disagrees and upholds the order for Bailey to turn over funds).

US v McCorkle (US Dist Ct, MD Fla, 2000), No 6:98-CR-ORL-19C, Order at 25-26, 31 (Bailey found in civil contempt for failure to turn over funds in McCorkle case).

Stern.   *Stern v FBI,* 737 F 2d 84 (US DC Cir Ct Appl, 1984); *affm'd* in part, *rev* in part, 3 GDS S83, 202 (US Dist Ct. DC) 1983 (NBC Newsman Carl Stern sued to learn names of FBI agents disciplined for misconduct. Lower court ordered all three names disclosed, appellate court ordered two lower-level names kept secret since their actions were inadvertent, but the name of the special agent in charge was released since his actions were deliberate).

Zobel.   *Commonwealth of Massachusetts v Louise Woodward,* Supr Ct Crim No 97-0433 Memorandum and Order 1997; *affm'd,* 427 Mass 659 (Sup Jud Ct MA) 1998 (generally upheld decision of Judge Hiller Zobel in "Nannygate" trial to reduce conviction from murder to manslaughter and sentence to time served).

Chapter 5 Facts and Data

Legal Citations

American Bar Association, Rule 3.6 Trial Publicity, in *Model Rules of Professional Conduct* and *Code of Judicial Conduct* and *Standards for Criminal Justice, Fair Trial and Free Press,* in *Professional Responsibility Standards, Rules, and Statutes.* Washington, DC: ABA, 2002-2003 ed, 681 pp (although not actually laws, the rules have the power of law since states license lawyers to practice. These outline specific restrictions on lawyers' and judges' speech).

Judicial Conference of the United States. *Code of Judicial Conduct for US Judges.* Washington, DC, 2002 (restrictions on speech of federal judges).

Judicial Conference of the United States, *Guidelines for the Pilot Program in Photographing, Recording and Broadcasting in the Courtroom.* Washington, DC: Administrative Office of the US Courts, re-issued October 14, 1997 (used in the 1990s' federal experiment in federal courts as well as in the jurisdictions allow coverage, the guidelines are also the model for those in many state courts).

Glossary

acquitted   One of the possible verdicts in a criminal case: not guilty, the opposite of a guilty verdict or conviction. (The media sometime erroneously call an *acquittal* a finding of "innocent.")

alternative dispute resolution   Moving a civil case outside the jurisdiction of the government in favor of a private action. In *arbitration,* a neutral third party hears both sides and decides on the case (the decision is usually legally binding). In *mediation,* a neutral mediator counsels both sides in an attempt to find an amicable solution. Such processes are not usually open to the public.

arraignment   A preliminary hearing at which a criminal suspect is publicly charged with a crime and officially enters a plea: guilty, not guilty, or no contest.

canons   Rules of conduct for judges and lawyers, treated as if they were law.

"checkbook journalism"   The practice by tabloid journalists of paying news sources for stories. An example would be offers to witnesses for their stories prior to their testimony. Checkbook journalism is frowned on by mainstream news organizations.

civil action   A lawsuit in which one party sues another over conflicts in which one side claims injury due to actions of another—the parties involved may be individuals, corporations, or the government. Many parties to *civil actions* request closed proceedings and sealed records.

continue   To delay or postpone trial proceedings. Continuances are generally permitted by a judge after a request by one of the parties, often to allow prejudicial publicity to diminish.

criminal action   A legal action in which the government prosecutes a suspect (an individual or a corporation) on charges of violating a law. Most *criminal actions* are public.

deposition Sworn testimony of a witness outside of a court, usually prior to a trial, made in the presence of lawyers for both sides. Depositions are more common in civil cases than criminal, and they are not generally made public unless used at trial.

discovery The pretrial investigative process whereby lawyers for both sides gather evidence to be used in the trial. Evidence so gathered is not generally made public unless used at trial.

docket The chronological record of legal proceedings in a case. A case docket may be obtained from the court clerk.

due process Procedural safeguards that the system of justice under the U.S. Constitution requires, such as the Sixth Amendment right to a public trial. Sometimes due process rights conflict with the First Amendment rights of the free press.

felony A major crime (such as rape or murder) for which the penalty may be a prison sentence of at least a year or even the death penalty.

"gag" order A judge's restraining order before or during a trial limiting the public comments of trial participants. A gag order restricts the ability of the press to cover a court case.

grand jury A panel of citizens who hear prosecutor's charges and witnesses' testimony in secret in order to decide whether to charge a suspect with a crime. (A "petit jury" is the official name for the jury that hears the evidence at a trial.)

incorporation Complex legal reasoning by which in the 1931 *Near v. Minnesota* case the U.S. Supreme Court held that the First Amendment prohibition of Congress's making any laws restricting First Amendment rights also applies to all levels of government—including state, regional, and municipal.

indictment The decision to prosecute a suspect in a crime—usually a felony—generally issued by a *grand jury* after hearing in secret the testimony of the government and its witnesses. A suspect who is *indicted* is then called a "defendant."

injunction/"stay" Most commonly, a court order to delay or halt some action pending litigation, such as a stay of execution during the appeal process.

litigant Either of the parties in a legal case—the plaintiff or the defendant.

misdemeanor A minor crime (such as theft) for which the penalty may be a fine or a short jail term of a year or less. The press generally does not cover *misdemeanors* unless the defendant is a prominent citizen.

per curiam   A decision by an appellate court that is issued without any explanation by the judges of their decision.

peremptory challenge   To remove a prospective juror from the jury pool without having to give a reason. Each side in a criminal case has a limited number of such challenges but an unlimited number of challenges "for cause," for which the reason is obvious.

plea bargain   An agreement reached in a criminal case by lawyers for both sides and approved by the judge in which, in return for pleading guilty, a defendant receives a reduced sentence—the result in more than two-thirds of criminal cases in the United States today. All but the judge's hearing may be closed to the public.

plurality   A decision by an appellate court that is not a clear majority vote (such as 6 to 3) but rather an apparent tie broken by a "swing vote," which seems to agree in part with each side (4 to 1 to 4).

prior restraint   An attempt by the government, often in the form of a court order, to prevent information from being published. Such restraints generally violate the First Amendment mandate that the government shall "make no law" abridging freedom of speech or of the press.

remand   An order by an appellate court for a lower court to take some further action, such as a retrial, in a case.

respondent   The party against whom a complaint is filed—the defendant in a civil case. (In an appeal, whoever won at trial becomes the *respondent*.)

return   The notes regarding police actions such as those taken under a search warrant in a criminal case. Usually available to the public after an arrest.

sequester   To isolate the jury during a criminal case, generally in order to protect the jurors from possible prejudicial publicity.

subpoena   An official order to appear in court that may be issued to a journalist covering a case in order to question him about his knowledge of the case. However, most journalists invoke the First Amendment right to a free press and/or state shield laws protecting them from such forced testimony, although they may risk citations for contempt of court for doing so.

suppression hearing   A pretrial procedure by which a defense attorney in a criminal case asks the court to declare certain evidence inadmissible. The defense may attempt to keep such hearings closed to the public.

vacate   To cancel a previous court order.

venire   The jury pool, which may be selected from voter registration lists, tax rolls, and/or driver's license registrations.

venue   The place where a trial takes place. The defense in a criminal case may request the trial be moved to a different *venue*, one with less prejudicial publicity, within the court's jurisdiction.

"virtual trial"   A possible trial of the future—where all the proceedings would take place using digitized electronics, with no requirement that all participants actually appear in the same courtroom (rather than a trial taking place in a traditional courtroom).

voir dire   The pretrial process of jury selection during which members of the jury pool are questioned to determine suitability. The *voir dire* is generally open to the public.

writ (of *certiorari*)   A petition to a higher court, such as the U.S. Supreme Court, asking that the court consider hearing the appeal of a lower-court decision.

Index

*Page numbers in **bold type** indicate glossary definitions.*

215

About the Author

S. L. Alexander is an award-winning journalist who has worked in print, radio, and television.

She earned a B.A. at the University of Florida, an M.A. at the University of Miami, and a Ph.D. in Communications (Law School minor) at the University of Florida. While working on her Ph.D., Alexander was awarded the Fellowship in Freedom of Information and the Student Research Award.

A member of the Loyola University, New Orleans, communications department faculty since 1991, Alexander currently serves as the coordinator of communication law. Alexander has written extensively on press issues, with an emphasis on free press/fair trial concerns, including *Covering the Courts: A Handbook for Journalists* (1999, rev. ed 2003).

Alexander is an active member of the Society of Professional Journalists. With a grant awarded by the Knight/Ridder Foundation, she recently formed the Louisiana Coalition on Open Government (LaCOG), an organization of citizens, members of the press, and civic leaders dedicated to obtaining access to government activities.

A popular speaker, workshop leader, and consultant, Alexander has begun work on her next book, a collection of true, live tales of New Orleans courtrooms.